GETTING FREE

GETTING FREE

Women and Psychotherapy

BY
ANN PEARLMAN HINTON
LINDA B. SHERBY
LYNNE G. TENBUSCH

A FRED JORDAN BOOK
GROVE PRESS, INC./NEW YORK

ISBN: 0-394-17982-X
Library of Congress Catalog Card No.: 82-81101
Printed in the United States of America

A FRED JORDAN BOOK distributed by
Grove Press, Inc.
196 West Houston Street
New York, N.Y. 10014

Dedicated to the women

who have shared

their lives with us.

§

Contents

Introduction   11

1. *Opening Up*   19

2. *Separation From Mother:* The Fairy Godmother and the Wicked Witch   47

3. *Giving Up Daddy:* The Knight in Shining Armor and the Bad Guy   81

4. *The Struggle for Survival:* Omnipotence and Vulnerability   103

5. *Anger and Sadness:* The Chicken or the Egg   129

6. *Intimacy:* The Ability to Love   155

7. *Sexuality:* The Unveiling   197

8. *Sexuality:* Issues and Expression   219

9. *Autonomy:* Making Your Own Way   253

10. *Beyond Therapy*   293

ACKNOWLEDGMENTS

We want to thank the many people who have helped with this book. Gail Farley, Ph.D., our colleague, started this journey with us and then continued to help us crystallize our ideas and provide encouragement and support. We appreciated the patience and fortitude of Carole Bell, who typed this manuscript. We would also like to thank our agent, Patricia Berens, for all her efforts on our behalf. In addition, Shelley Aspaklaria's suggestions and support were invaluable. And, of course, the wisdom and insights gained from our therapists and supervisors are repeatedly reflected in these pages.

§

Introduction

Getting Free is about American women today, women of the eighties who have experienced the impact of contemporary feminism. We have written this book to help you look inside yourself—to help you understand the origin of your pains, conflicts, and joys. Our focus is on the universal issues we all share as we journey toward maturity.

From the birth of humanity, infants have suckled at their mothers' breasts and reached out to meet their fathers. They have journeyed from helplessness to competence, and from immediate, generalized reactions to complicated expressions of feelings. To satisfy their needs for intimacy and sexuality, human beings have reached outside the family, thereby assuring the continual evolvement of our species. But human beings have not only survived physically, they have grown culturally as well. And this cultural expansion has inspired the flowering of autonomy, which expresses humanity at its noblest.

The journey from infancy to adulthood is a universal one. Each culture and era prescribes the stages to be navigated and the tasks to be completed in our negotiation of life. Yet you, like every adult, have made your own individual journey— fraught with both excitement and difficulty as you were faced with the impetus to grow versus the retreat to safety and security. This tug and pull between the lust for new adventures and the desire for the security of the familiar creates conflict around each developmental stage. It is difficult to leave the familiar warmth of your mother's breast for independent feeding with a knife and fork. It is difficult to learn to control your childish bursts of rage and to move beyond daddy's warmth to brave the unknown arena of adult sexuality. It is the nature of growth to produce conflicts which peak at specific stages in your life. These conflicts arise for all of us and how they are resolved depends upon many interweaving factors: our biology, our individual life experiences, and our culture. Sometimes these conflicts are put to rest forever, but they always remain areas of sensitivity ready to impact on our life at periods of new development and concommitant stresses. It is these areas of sensitivity which we call universal issues. They are universal conditions with the potential for erupting into problems and concerns. An issue is always there; it may or may not materialize into a conflict. These universal issues are:

> Separation from mother
> Separation from father
> Omnipotence and vulnerability
> Anger and sadness
> Intimacy
> Sexuality
> Autonomy

All of us struggle with these universal issues and, during childhood, find solutions for them. We learn, for example, that eating with a knife and fork greatly increases our freedom and our temper tantrums can be channeled into prowess on the athletic field. In adulthood we may find that the solution we arrived at as a child no longer works for us. Or, events may occur in our life which rearouse a past conflict. For example, suppose you had little or no difficulty dealing with your growth into a sexual woman. Sex had always been fun and easy. Then, one day you are brutally raped. What was warm and loving before now feels brutal and violent. The issue of your sexuality has emerged as an area of conflict. Thus, these universal issues weave throughout your life like different threads in a multicolored fabric.

Life is a series of stages and all seven universal issues reappear in a different guise at each stage. For example, consider how the issue of separation from mother weaves throughout your life span. As an infant you move from total dependence on your mother to an increasing exploration of the world. You become a toddler and reach out to explore, daring to leave your mother a little behind, but always returning for love and reassurance. As a young child you go off to school, learning to leave your mother for longer periods of time to interact with others. You learn to exist on your own, apart from her; you learn self-sufficiency. This self-sufficiency continues to increase into and throughout adolescence. Here your relationship with your mother reaches its most stormy point. You push her away with a vengeance, struggling to find a sense of your own separate identity. Eventually you leave home, putting an actual physical distance between you and your mother and feeling that you are an adult. You are establishing your own personhood and your own life. Although creating physical distance does not in itself create autonomy, you no longer need to push your mother away as vehemently as before because physical space nurtures the conditions for development of your own identity. The issue of separation from mother is rearoused as you decide whether or not to become a mother yourself. Should you choose to have children, many of your own childhood feelings will be restimulated, particularly your feelings about your mother.

As you reach midlife, three factors impinge upon your life, each of which rearouses the issue of separation from mother. Your own children may be leaving home and you must let them go; you must let them separate from you, as you separated from your mother. Also, as your mother ages and becomes more dependent, the roles between you may be switched and you may become her caretaker. Thirdly, during this period many of you look to your career to give you more gratification. For many of you, being a career woman may make you feel more separate from your mother. Again, these three midlife events may all rearouse the issue of separation from mother. The final goodbye at your mother's death confronts you once more with this issue, for now all you have of your mother are your memories. As you yourself age and become infirm, you may find yourself dealing with your own death much as your mother dealt with hers. As you die, you are, of course, separating from everyone, and insofar as this is the final separation you are again separating from your mother, as well as from your image of her. Thus, the issue of separation from mother appears in different forms at different stages of life.

Each of the seven issues we discuss in *Getting Free* are universal issues. However, the way in which they are played out and resolved is very much determined by the culture in which you live, and your own personal psychological history. In recent years, the feminist movement has influenced that culture which, in turn, affects the way you can resolve these issues. The feminist movement allows each of you more options, more degrees of freedom in solving these universal dilemmas. Feminism has suddenly opened up new vistas to all of you, putting choices within your reach that were never available before. You can be doctors, bricklayers, lawyers, housewives, train engineers. Almost the entire spectrum of occupations is now available to you. True, you will find it harder than men to enter these occupations, but the possibilities are there and are continually increasing. Because of your greater economic opportunities, you are better able to care for yourself and your family without depending on a man. You are not as shackled to frustrating, dead-end marriages or to the role of homemaker. Without the pressure to marry or the fear of pregnancy, you can choose a number of sexual partners or lifestyles. You are not forced into the traditional female role. You can choose your own expression of your individuality. Additionally, your role as a sexual woman is now accepted by society. You are a sexual person, not simply a receptacle for men's pleasure. A woman's role can now include the enjoyment of sexual fulfillment. The woman's movement, with its impact on the various roles of men and women, has changed the nature of intimate relationships. Roles in the family are now open to negotiation rather than prescribed by tradition.

The women's movement has also affected the way you can express your anger and sadness. Women traditionally have buried their anger, translating it into sadness. Now women's anger has been accepted as natural and you may express it more freely. As sports arenas have opened up to women, this vehicle for channeling anger has also become available to you. The less you are defined as traditionally female (daughter, then wife), the more you define yourself as an individual power in the world. You move from feelings of vulnerability and dependence toward adult competence and realistic power. With each new advance in your growth toward womanhood your conflicts with your parents may sharpen. There is, after all, a generation between you. They may still expect you to be the soft, frilly housewife, while you seek to become the president of General Motors. In these rapidly changing times, you and your parents struggle to bridge the gap and find a new way for love and closeness despite separate identities.

In *Getting Free* we address the universal psychological issues with which all of you struggle as you move through your life. We try to understand the impact of contemporary feminism on the evolution and resolution of these issues. *Getting Free* combines traditional psychological theories and contemporary feminist ideas. We are three women psychotherapists who have listened to hundreds of women's life stories. Our listening has reaped an inheritance of women's strengths, wisdoms, agonies and joys. We have written this book in an attempt to share this inheritance with other women so that they may better understand themselves, and with men so that they may better understand women as well as themselves. Through our presentation of women's life stories we explore the problems with which women struggle and the issues which underlie these problems. Although you may see yourself or your best friend in one or the other of the women we present in *Getting Free*, all these women's stories are tailored to best exemplify the issues we present. They are composite portraits of women we have seen, and their psychological pictures are accurate presentations of how people function.

Getting Free is written from the viewpoint of women and women's psychology, in contrast to the majority of psychological theories which have been written from the perspective of men's history, development, and issues. The "you" we are addressing in these pages is the modern American woman. We do not intend to exclude men, but rather to address primarily women, even though many of the problems, issues, and theories we discuss apply to both sexes.

Getting Free also demonstrates how therapy helps you resolve issues which reemerge and stand in the way of further growth. We translate psychological jargon into everyday language and present therapy in action—how it works and what you can expect from it. You will learn about the special relationship between the therapist and the client, and how intellectual and emotional awareness continue to help you alter your behavior.

We believe that the self-fulfilled woman enjoys work, play, and love, and that this constitutes positive mental health. Each of you must find your own way to achieve self-fulfillment, your own unique way of relating to the world. Each of you must evolve a personal definition for work, play, and love. For example, you may find love within the framework of a marriage, while others may fulfill their needs for intimacy within a variety of relationships. Similarly, some may find satisfaction and peace in the role of a physician, while others may find it as homemakers or carpenters. You express your uniqueness in the special ways you choose to realize your potential.

Getting Free will help you to look at yourself and to understand the origin of your pains, conflicts, and joys. While reading this book you may experience a click of recognition as you see yourself in one of the women described in these pages and realize that both her problems and her reactions to them remind you of yours. In exploring her character you will begin to gain a greater understanding of your own inner workings, uncovering the sources of some of your own behavior and feelings. As you emphathize with the women in this book you will see aspects of yourself and develop a clearer picture of what makes you feel the way you do. You will learn that all your feelings are human feelings, and that all the issues you confront are human issues. You will learn that you are not alone. Reading about other women's lives may also stimulate you to reexperience the feelings that you confronted as you resolved your universal issues. This act of reexperiencing will allow you to combine your head and your heart in creating new resolutions to old problems. In this book you are embarking on a journey of reflection and self-discovery.

You are a unique, fascinating person. Your journey into yourself is an exciting one. We fervently hope that the reading of this book will launch you on that journey.

1

Opening Up

Three Women

The war was over. Leaves were decayed on the broken branches. Smoke hung like a cloud over the city, creating a perpetual twilight. Bricks lay scattered everywhere. Irene hunted through the rubble, looking, searching, although she knew not why. She simply felt compelled to search, picking up one brick after another. She felt all alone. The city seemed deserted. Then, among the bricks, lying like a discarded flower, she saw a piece of knitted green fabric. She tugged at it, revealing the sleeve of a sweater, a familiar sweater, which encased her son's arm. It had to be his because there, on one of the fingers, was his high school ring. Suddenly Irene knew what she was hunting for; she was hunting for the rest of his body. Searching through the rubble, she found a piece here and a piece there. She hugged them to her, trying to warm them. Now all she needed to find was his head and he would be whole again. He would be safe again. She would warm his parts and take care of him. But as she searched, she could not find the final part; his head was still missing. She became more and more desperate, more and more frantic. She began to fear that she searched in vain. Her terror mounted. She began screaming.

Irene's husband was shaking her, reassuring her that everything was all right. Irene realized it had happened again; she had had another nightmare. But again it had seemed so real. It was hard for her to believe it had been only a dream. She had so many nightmares these days that it was difficult for her to know what was reality and what was a dream. After all, her son's death had been a nightmare. It was now nine months since he had been killed by a tornado. The black tornado had destroyed a neighboring town and, in so doing, had pushed a wall on top of her son. A wall had fallen in on her son; the sky had fallen in on her life. One day her life was going smoothly. She was a 44-year-old married woman working as an executive secretary. Her son was away at college, her daughter in her third year of high school. Then the following day a tornado touched down in her son's college town and nine people died. The tornado flashed down for 30 seconds and then moved on to touch down some hundreds of miles away. Then the call came. Her son had been one of the nine—one of those nine people who happened to be in that particular place at that particular time; a coincidence that terminated their lives and forever altered hers; a chance occurrence that brought only tragedy. Irene's world was forever altered. It was no longer safe, no longer secure. Terrible things could strike from out of the sky at any time without warning.

Over the months Irene's sadness did not diminish; her tears were continual. The depth of her sorrow was fathomless. The reality of her son's death waxed and waned in her mind. Sometimes she felt as though her son would be coming home for Christmas, smiling and bringing presents for the family. At other times the reality of his death overwhelmed her. He was dead, he was gone; he would never be back. She felt despair. She sometimes even felt that the years of mothering him, worrying about him, sheltering him, were all wasted. Irene's fearfulness mounted, and she became increasingly reluctant to leave her home. She felt safe there, while venturing into the outside world filled her with panic. Stepping beyond her doorstep to work, shop, or visit friends seemed an impossible task fraught with terror and anxiety. Now, as the nightmares plagued her, she was afraid even to sleep. Every night she searched for her son's body, trying to put his broken limbs back together and bring him to life. Then her screams would awaken the entire family and they too would ache again. All of their lives had become a nightmare. Irene was glad she had an appointment with a psychotherapist. She did not know how it would help. She only knew that she was desperate.

Gail felt that she had been used, abused, and abandoned by men for all 25 years of her life. Now, here was a seemingly kind, stable man promising to be different. Could she believe his promises and did she really want what he had to offer?

Gail was a beautiful black woman who had spent the last four years of her life extricating herself from the street life of the ghetto. She had been raised by her mother and four older siblings, who had tried to keep the family afloat on their meager ADC payments. Her father, feeling as though another child was just too great a burden to bear, had abandoned the family at Gail's birth. At least on welfare the family could be assured of a regular monthly income. Gail grew up feeling her mother's anger at both "the man" and her own husband. Men were clearly untrustworthy, unreliable creatures who sweet-talked you, inpregnated you, and then left. Despite the chaos surrounding the family, Gail's mother was able to provide a sense of love and safety within their small apartment, a refuge from the bleakness of ghetto life. Gail loved her mother but knew that she did not want to be like her. She wanted more from life—more money, more freedom, more excitement. She did not want the harshness of her mother's life. Gail resolved that she would be different.

As a way out, Gail took to the streets and at a young age became street wise. She knew who was hustling for what. She knew where and from whom to find the best weed, coke, and heroin. She knew the pimps and the johns. Gail's mother tried to protect her, but Gail was just too ripe and too determined. Men always hit on her with ingenious schemes and con games. By the time she was 14, Gail had been indoctrinated into the adult street world of sex, clothes, cars, and drugs. Before her sixteenth birthday, the girl-woman Gail was a mother herself, having given birth to a daughter who seemed little more than a toy or, even worse, an encumbrance. Gail surrendered the infant to her mother, allowing the promise of money, drugs, and excitement to lure her back into the streets in earnest. She too went on ADC but depended on hustling for extra money. She had a regular pimp and relied on him to supply her with both johns and drugs.

Gail's mother was dismayed by the turn of events in Gail's life. She felt that Gail was not only beautiful but intelligent as well. She was young, gifted, and black and could achieve great things with her life. Her mother wanted the world for Gail, not the streets. By the time Gail was beyond her teens, she was beginning to wonder if this was all there was to life. The cars and clothes were beginning to wear thin. She had learned that being a prostitute was not all it was cracked up to be. It was hard work, dirty work. Then, when Gail was 21, her best friend died of an overdose, and Gail knew she had to get out—she had to change her life before the streets killed her too. Somehow, somewhere deep in her guts, Gail knew that she wanted a better life both for herself and for her daughter. She did not want to live in the streets any longer.

Fortuitously, Gail's aunt, who lived in another city, offered to provide Gail and her daughter a place to live, if Gail were interested in changing her life. Gail jumped at the chance, feeling that she was finally escaping the jail of her childhood. She transferred her ADC, passed her high school equivalency exam, and enrolled in a community college. Gail felt as though she could finally find some peace. But she was also terrified. This was a radical change for her. The straight world was an unknown; she was in uncharted territory, taking a huge risk. However, the risks on the streets seemed greater still.

To Gail's surprise and delight, her mother's prophecy was coming true. She was indeed bright and was able to maintain good grades in college. Her little girl was flourishing, and Gail finally felt that she had a good future. Unfortunately, her success with men did not improve with her new life style. They still conned her, sweeping her off her feet with meaningless promises, only to leave her again feeling used and abandoned. Now, here was a 35-year-old man again promising her that things would be different. How could she possibly know whether to trust him? And even if she could, did she want to give up her newly found freedom to become someone's wife?

Remembering the warmth and compassion of her social work teacher at school, Gail decided to call her, thinking that it might be helpful for her to talk with someone about her dilemma.

Mary Ann awoke with a vague, uneasy feeling. For hours the night before Tom had tried to bring her to orgasm but, as usual, nothing had worked. Sex was such a bother, but she cared so deeply for Tom and it seemed so important to him. He fretted, feeling inadequate because he could not bring Mary Ann to orgasm. He kept reading books on sexual techniques, trying new suggestions, but to no avail. The more he pushed her to have an orgasm, the farther she seemed from sexual responsiveness. Mary Ann loved Tom and wanted to please him but just could not get excited about sex. When Tom suggested that they see a sex therapist together, Mary Ann became terrified. As a less frightening option, she did agree to seek individual therapy for her sexual difficulty.

At 30, Mary Ann had obtained her Ph.D. in pharmacology and was involved in an interesting job doing cancer research. Her relationship with Tom was the first meaningful long-term relationship she had had with a man. In all of her previous relationships, Mary Ann had attributed her difficulty with orgasm to her uncertainty about her partner's love for her. Now, however, she did not have that excuse. She and Tom were very much in love and talking seriously about marriage. Her life seemed fulfilled in all aspects other than sex. In fact, Mary Ann could not remember ever having been happier.

All her life Mary Ann had felt as though a weight hung over her. Shortly after her birth, the discovery that her mother had cancer of the leg prompted an amputation. Mary Ann was, of course, too young to remember this time but was told that her mother had gained a daughter but lost a leg. Thus, the two incidences—Mary Ann's birth and the loss of her mother's leg—were always linked for her. When Mary Ann grew older she even wondered whether her birth had caused the cancer.

Mary Ann always felt that she was her mother's favorite. Her mother enjoyed cuddling her and keeping her as close as possible. During her infancy, Mary Ann's crib had stood by her mother's bed while her father was relegated to a separate bedroom. Then as Mary Ann grew older, she tried to do the things her mother could not do for herself. It was almost as if she had become her mother's leg. Most of the affection in the family seemed to occur between Mary Ann and her mother, with both her father and her older brother being excluded. Her father had not even been allowed back into his wife's bedroom, and Mary Ann had known that her parents had always maintained separate sleeping quarters.

Unlike her mother, Mary Ann enjoyed sleeping with a man. She liked the warmth and the closeness of Tom, although she felt no genital stirrings. She could not understand why it was so important to Tom. After all, he had orgasms and she enjoyed the touching. It seemed to her as though that should be enough, but it clearly was not enough for Tom. He was distressed about her inability to achieve orgasm. Because of her love for him, Mary Ann agreed to seek therapy.

Presenting Problems

Each of these women, Irene, Gail, and Mary Ann, chose to enter psychotherapy for very different reasons. For Irene, the sudden, unpredictable death of her 20-year-old son created for her a sense of overwhelming sadness and terror. She felt out of control; there was no way she could alter his death. Her whole life had become a nightmare. For Gail, the question was whether she could risk trusting another man and committing herself to him. Throughout her life men had been untrustworthy, and now she was being asked to risk trusting yet again. For Mary Ann, the issue was a sexual one. She was inorgasmic with a man whom she loved very much and wanted to have a full, rich sexual life.

You may choose to go into therapy for a multitude of reasons. Clearly, you are in pain if you are considering therapy, and your pain may stem from a wide variety of events. You, like Irene, may be having difficulty mourning the loss of a loved one or, like Gail, you may be concerned about embarking on a new venture. Like Mary Ann, you may realize that you have cut off a part of your psyche as its absence is thrown into sharp relief by a relationship with another person. You may be distressed about your child's entrance into school or her progressive separation from you. You may be concerned about your relationship with your spouse. You may find yourself spending large amounts of money and plunging your family into bankruptcy. You may be terrified of failure or undermine your success. You may become increasingly anxious about leaving your house or entering an elevator. Your doctor may encourage you to seek therapy because of a physical symptom for which she can find no organic base. You may find yourself unable to stop eating or unable to let yourself gain weight. You may feel increasingly numb or question whether life is really worth living. Any of these pains may be distressing enough to bring you into therapy in an attempt to understand the problem and undo the hurt or to stop the unsatisfying, destructive patterns in your life.

All of these problems create psychic pain. You hurt; you are in agony. Your pain is always with you; there seems to be no escape, no relief. The agony seems chronic. Even if you dull the pain with busy days, it is there to haunt you when you turn out your light at night. It has settled in your guts, a constant reminder that all is not right. Some psychic pain is an inevitable part of living. Feeling some sadness, anger, fear, or hurt cannot be avoided, for turmoil and sadness cannot be entirely eradicated. You cannot voyage through life without experiencing some of the pain of human existence.

Children often feel this psychic pain to be overwhelming. You may remember how, as a child, a painful event caused you to feel as though you would not survive, as though your world were coming to an end, as though you were going to be devoured or damned for all eternity. As a child you feel overwhelmed by your pain because your psyche is not yet sufficiently developed to handle trauma. You have not yet developed strategies for experiencing or resolving your pain. As a result, your psyche responds to pain with a variety of defenses. You may, for example, deny your pain, pretending that it does not exist. Or, to avoid feeling overwhelmed, you may change the emotional reality of your world into something you can handle more easily and, for example, translate your feelings into the opposite of what they really are. Or you may lock your feelings away in a corner of your brain, trying to disassociate yourself from them as much as possible. These defenses are necessary for you as a child because you are helpless and vulnerable and need these defenses to protect you against what otherwise would be overwhelming feelings. As a teenager, you loosen some of these defenses because you are strong enough to handle more of your feelings and manage more of your world. Yet, many of these old strategies continue to block feelings from emerging into your awareness. And there they lie, following you into adulthood, smouldering inside of you, and diminishing your potential for growth. These blocked feelings may surface unexpectedly in response to current events in your life, confusing you and increasing the difficulty of their resolution. For example, as an adult you may find that the death of your next-door neighbor restimulates the anguish and trauma you felt as a child when your father died. The intensity of pain surrounding your father's death was simply too overwhelming for you to experience fully at the time. So, to survive, you pushed your pain underground, only to find it surfacing later in response to the death of your neighbor.

One of the prerequisites for a full, rich life is realizing and accepting that you cannot avoid all psychic pain and that your experience of pain is not a condemnation of you or an accusation of those around you. In the process of your voyage through life you can learn to reduce psychic pain to manageable levels. First, as an adult you can work through your unresolved childhood pain, letting go of it once and for all, so that you no longer carry it with you into the present. For example, if, as an adult, you are able to reexperience and resolve your sadness about the death of your father and mourn his final loss, you will not be so traumatized by the death of your next-door neighbor.

Second, you can reduce the amount of psychic pain in your life by avoiding situations which automatically reopen old scars and restimulate the old, unresolvable pain. This does not mean that you would avoid all situations that might induce pain, but rather that you will not seek out situations in an attempt to remaster the old pain. For example, if you have not adequately mourned the death of your father, you may decide to become a funeral director, despite the fact that you always feel terribly distraught whenever you see a dead man of about the same age as your father. Although you are not aware of it, you have probably chosen your profession in an attempt to master your overwhelming sorrow for your father's death. Your occupation, however, intensifies rather than diminishes your pain.

You can also reduce the amount of psychic pain in your life by avoiding situations which restimulate old pain that you have worked on but have been unable to resolve. For example, vacationing in a certain place may restimulate the pain you carry with you about the death of your grandparents. This pain will always be there; it cannot be erased. But you may choose to avoid restimulating it by vacationing elsewhere. On the other hand, situations may arise where such avoidance would limit the richness of your life. Perhaps you have always felt that your mother preferred your younger brother to you. You are offered an exciting, high-paying job in which your colleague is a younger man and your supervisor is an older woman. You are aware of the similarities between this employment situation and your family. Yet you know that your colleague is not your brother and your supervisor is not your mother. You also know that you are not a helpless child any more, vulnerable and dependent upon your mother's love and approval. Certainly this new situation may bring some pain, but you feel that the excitement of the job is worth the risk. Besides, you know that you can survive the pain. You may avoid pain whenever possible, but you can survive it.

Psychic pain is an inevitable part of living, and coming to grips with it is testimony to your strength and creativity. How you deal with this psychic pain is a product of your personal history, your biology, and your culture. Each of you is a singular constellation of this age, this culture, this time, intermeshed with your biological and developmental history. You share biological and psychological issues with all women. You share your cultural dilemma with women in twentieth-century America. But only you experience your unique past, and only you attempt to order the pains and pleasures of that past. Some of your attempts to diminish old pains may not be working for you in your present adult life. If you are unable to resolve your psychic pain alone, this culture gives you permission to seek psychotherapy. Although some of you will still view psychotherapy as a stigma, it continues to become increasingly acceptable and choosing to enter it is a sign of your willingness to grow and change. Choosing psychotherapy as a way of resolving difficulties and conflicts is a product of the present cultural climate.

Cultural Issues

This is the first culture with technology sufficiently developed to allow you the time and energy to be concerned about happiness and fulfillment. In other cultures, the question has been, "Am I going to survive?" In the past, people spent literally all of their energy planting, harvesting, preparing food, building shelters, making clothes, and having babies. Today, survival requires less time and leaves people with the energy to ponder questions like, "Am I fulfilled? Am I content? Am I happy?" You can look at your life and say, "Is this what I want to be doing?" This society offers so many options that you can review your life and decide whether you are happy with your choices. If you are not, you can attempt to change, pursuing greater fulfillment and self-actualization. This is not meant to imply that changing your life is easy, for, indeed, such changes are usually fraught with much soul-searching and conflict. However, regardless of the difficulty, the fact remains that you have more options today than you would have had in the past.

The complexity of this culture itself breeds new confusions and difficulties. This is the era of "future shock," of living in a fast-moving, rapidly changing world. The traditional sense of family and community continuity no longer exists, often leaving you feeling isolated and alienated. More specifically, this rapidly changing society has brought with it a confusion about sex roles. On the one hand, it is clear that choosing one option means giving up other options. On the other hand, there is pressure on you to do it all—to run the gamut from a happy homemaker to a successful professional.

Biological Givens

Each of you is born with a unique biological constellation. You are the product of your parents and their parents before them, and so on back through the generations. Your genetic history creates a person that is uniquely you and provides the biological determinants of the person that you will become. Differences in temperament and activity are obvious from birth. Some of you were extremely active babies who reacted to the slightest noise by jerking and thrashing about. In contrast, some of you were placid infants who reacted to loud noises with a calm turning of your head and a quiet expression. These differences in temperament, of course, evoke different responses from different parents, depending upon their own personalities and activity levels. Some parents will ignore a placid infant; others will coddle it. Some parents will attend at once to an active infant; others will react with anger or frustration.

In addition to differences in activity level, biology also creates differences in appearances and may determine the genetic base for intelligence. Being born of Russian parentage will obviously result in a different physical appearance than African parentage. And, of course, your physical appearance is a strong factor in how you are treated by others. For example, you may have a teacher who is more partial to boys or one who is particularly biased against blacks.

Similarly, you are born with an intellectual potential. With regard to both appearance and intelligence, how you use your potential determines its ultimate expression. If you are of average intelligence but possess enormous perseverance and motivation, you are likely to achieve more than a person of superior intelligence who has no motivation for achievement.

Exactly how your biological givens affect your psychology is uncertain. It is not known whether a highly active nervous system which reacts to all pinches as assaults also reacts to all hurts as traumas. It seems clear that heredity creates the limits within which environment can make its mark, but how the two interact remains unknown. It is not clear, for example, to what extent your musical talent or your fine motor coordination is biological and to what extent it is learned. Biology and environment are inextricably interwoven to create a unique you.

Uniqueness

You are a unique human being, part of the evolutionary process, one dot in the continuum of time. You are unique and will never be repeated in all of infinity. Your biology, your culture, and your psychic history all interact to nurture your uniqueness as a human being. No one else has your biology, your particular parents, or your personal history. No one can feel exactly what you feel. No one experiences the world as you experience it; no one sees colors or smells aromas exactly as you do. The world as you experience it is yours alone. No one has felt your pain. No one has felt your joys. No one has lived your life as you have. All these things make you unique.

Your self-esteem is largely, though not totally, dependent upon how you view your uniqueness and your sameness. As you develop, you realize how you are different from and how you are the same as other people; you realize how you look different physically, how you view the world differently, how your unique capabilities and shortcomings contribute to defining you. These differences and similarities help create your self-image and are signposts by which you gauge yourself in relation to your peers. Learning to appreciate your differences is crucial. For example, your sensitivity on the playground which may have brought you much pain as a child will stand you in good stead as a therapist empathizing with the feelings of others. Similarly, your artistic ability that set you apart from your athletic family and caused problems for you as a child may bring you much joy as an adult. Thus learning to appreciate and build on your differences engenders self-esteem. Ideally, as you experience your own uniqueness and share it with the world, you will learn to appreciate yourself for the unique person that you are.

Of course, self-esteem is determined not only by your appreciation of your uniqueness but also by the comfort you take in the knowledge of your similarity to others. You appreciate and nurture your uniqueness and, at the same time, you enjoy your commonality with other human beings. As a fulfilled human being, you find security in both your uniqueness and your commonality. You know the ways in which you are different from others and the ways in which you are alike. Just as you must come to grips with your uniqueness, so too must you come to grips with the universal characteristics and issues that you share with all other human beings.

Universal Issues

All of you struggle with universal issues, and each of you finds your own solutions for them. The issues are internalized stances resulting from conflicts or problems. You find a solution which worked for you during a psychological conflict. Perhaps that solution does not work for you as an adult, or perhaps events conspire to rearouse the past conflict, necessitating a new stance on that issue. Thus issues may weave throughout your life like different threads in a multicolored fabric. As you learn to deal with each of them, you nurture the formation of your personality. For each issue, a motif develops which is unique to you. Although you are unique, you share much with other women in twentieth-century America and other women throughout all of human history. Your uniqueness and specialness exist side by side with a vast reservoir of shared experiences, developmental stages, and biological and psychological samenesses. Each of you, during the course of your life, must deal with the universal issues of separation from mother, separation from father, omnipotence and vulnerability, anger and sadness, intimacy, sexuality, and autonomy. These issues are inevitable and inextricable from the growing process. Issues that are resolved at one time in your life may reappear at a new crisis point. How you deal with these issues is determined partly by your psychological history and partly by the culture in which you live. One culture, for example, may provide a rite of passage as a way to assist in separation from mother. How you deal with these universal issues is simultaneously an expression and a development of the unique you.

Separation from Mother

Separation from mother is the first issue that you as an infant must deal with. Physical separation at birth begins the process, which progresses as you learn to walk and care for your body. As this physical progression continues, so does a psychological one. Your mother shows you the world through her eyes, and her view becomes your first view of the world. Her influence in this regard is never lost. You carry it with you in some form throughout your lifetime.

Mary Ann, who went into therapy because she was not orgasmic, is an example of a person still struggling with the universal issue of separating from mother. From birth, Mary Ann was brought up to feel very close to her mother, so close that she sometimes felt she was her mother's legs. Her mother kept her close, cuddling her, wanting her near to do those things which she herself could not do. Thus Mary Ann grew up feeling herself to be an extension of her mother, feeling extremely close to her mother both physically and psychologically. Their closeness was so intense that it did not allow the boundaries necessary for separateness. Thus, unknowingly, Mary Ann experienced herself to be like her mother and wanted to grow up to be even more like her.

Mary Ann's mother was asexual. She and her husband maintained separate bedrooms, and it was always clear to

Mary Ann that her mother discouraged physical contact with her husband. Thus in becoming a replica of her mother, Mary Ann also became asexual. It is not that Mary Ann knowingly decided to be like her mother, but rather that she was so close to her and so undifferentiated from her that she wanted to be with her forever. And, of course, the best way to have her forever was to become her. In order for Mary Ann to grow into a mature, sexual woman, she had to separate from her mother and become her own unique self. She had to discover who she was, separate from her mother, and develop her special traits, abilities, and characteristics. She had to be herself, not her mother.

Gail, who had been into "street life," went into therapy in an effort to decide whether she would again trust a man. She also was dealing with the issue of separating from her mother. Gail had rejected her mother's life style, wanting more money and excitement. She was determined not to be caught in the trap of poverty which controlled her mother. In an effort to be different from her mother, she rebelled against her mother's values and lived a life that her mother abhorred, that of a drug user and prostitute. Her behavior screamed to the world that she was different from her mother, that she was not like her in any way and therefore was separate from her.

Separation from mother is a universal issue with which all of you must deal at some time in your life. This separation is traumatic, frightening, and exhausting, but an absolute prerequisite to attaining your own adulthood.

Separation from Father

Just as you need to separate from your mother, so too must you separate from your father. You must find out who you are as a unique, separate person apart from your father and his characteristics. As with your mother, you follow in your father's footsteps. However, your relationship with him is thrown into sharpest relief in your choice of a love object. You may choose a man who is like your father or one who is very different from him. Either choice may reflect a lack of separation from him. Your freedom to choose a man who has some of your father's good points and as few as possible of his bad ones is the best indication of successful separation.

Gail had a history of relationships in which she was abandoned by her lovers. From her teenage years on, she was "screwed" and then left by lovers. Even the father of her baby abandoned her shortly after her pregnancy was confirmed. Later she was involved with men from the street, men who were totally incapable of a commitment. Gail's choice of men guaranteed short-lived relationships which terminated in abandonment. In this way she repeated over and over again her relationship with her father who had abandoned her shortly after her birth. The one thing that Gail knew about her father was that he had abandoned her; the one thing that she repeated in her relationships with men was that same abandonment of her. In a convoluted way, she was attempting to hold on to her father by involving herself with men who would relate to her in the same manner her father had.

In order to freely love a mate, you must be separate from your father and experience your lover as a unique person who is lovable in his own right and not as a substitute for your father.

Omnipotence and Vulnerability

You are born helpless. You have no power, no ability to determine your fate. You are at the mercy of your caretakers. It is this complete helplessness at birth which sets the stage for your need to both deny your vulnerability and feel as though you can master the world. As you grow into adulthood, your mastery of the world enables you to feel less vulnerable and more capable. However, being confronted by a situation over which you have no control can restimulate your earlier fears of vulnerability. Then, in an effort to deny your powerlessness, you may fall back on a defensive sense of omnipotence to avoid dealing with your fears of helplessness. On the continuum between omnipotence and vulnerability, reality falls somewhere in the middle. You are neither entirely helpless and vulnerable nor all-powerful and all-controlling.

You can take care of yourself, but you cannot completely control the factors that impinge upon you and your world.

The issue of omnipotence and vulnerability was restimulated for Irene by her son's sudden death in a tornado. His death devastated her. There was no way that Irene could have predicted either the tornado or her son's death. There was no way that she could have influenced the turn of events which culminated in his death. She could not redo it. Unlike the wish in her nightmare, finding all of his body parts would not bring him back to life. Her nightmares clearly indicated her struggle with this issue of omnipotence and vulnerability. Her dreams revealed her wish for greater control and power. However, Irene's increasing fear of leaving her home indicated her underlying sense of total vulnerability, of insignificance, her fear that the world was frightening, capricious, and capable of totally devastating her loved ones at any time. Thus her dreams of omnipotence were her attempts to compensate for her terror and vulnerability.

Omnipotence and vulnerability is another universal issue which all of you must confront and come to terms with. The final resolution is your mastery of that which you can realistically control and your surrender of that which you cannot.

Anger and Sadness

Anger and sadness are basic human emotions. A voyage through life without both of them is possible. Yet the difficulty of handling these emotions may seduce you into avoiding one or the other regardless of the psychic sacrifice. It may feel too painful to be sad. It may feel too frightening to be angry. But repressing the experience of either of these feelings occurs only at great psychological cost, as they are both inevitable and universal.

Irene was feeling both angry and sad about her son's death. Her sadness, however, was more available to her awareness. She knew she was sad. She cried all the time and felt a heavy weight of grief and mourning. Her anger was less prominent, because it was shrouded over by her depression and her feeling of emptiness. But if she could not give voice to her anger, she would not be able to get beyond numbness and become alive again.

Mary Ann also needed to deal with her anger. Understandably, she felt angry at always having to be her mother's errand girl—at having to stop what she was doing and fetch whatever it was her mother wanted. However, Mary Ann did not feel justified in her anger at her helpless, invalid mother, so she turned her anger into guilt. She felt guilty about her mother's infirmity. She told herself that it was her duty always to be the good daughter by being her mother's helper.

Feeling your feelings is necessary in order to be free, and this includes feeling your anger and your sadness regardless of how difficult or painful they may be.

Intimacy

Allowing yourself to be close with another human being is one of the great joys of being human. Expressing your thoughts and feelings and listening to the joys and agonies of another diminish your sense of aloneness and enhance the quality of your life. Intimacy, however, can also present difficulties for many of you. It can be frightening to allow the vulnerability necessary for such closeness and sharing. Determining how to satisfy your intimacy needs is one of the grand adventures of adulthood. Your sense of confidence as you embark on this adventure is significantly influenced by your relationship with your parents and their relationship with each other. They present you with the realm of possibilities for degrees of intimacy and predispose you to the probable outcome of your voyage.

Gail felt as though she were making this voyage alone on a stormy sea. She was terrified to allow anyone to guide her, afraid to trust that anyone could help her on her journey. The facts of her life reinforced this belief—all the men she had known had abused her feelings. She had not been able to trust them to be there for her. She was confused about the whole idea of intimacy with a man; it was new to her. Because she had not been exposed to an intimate male/female relationship as she was growing up, she felt that she was striking out on an unmarked trail. How to develop intimacy was a complete mystery to her. She was not really sure what it was or what it felt like, let alone how to get it.

Each of you must decide how intimate you are going to be with your fellow human beings. You must decide for yourself when and to what extent you will render yourself vulnerable by sharing your innermost thoughts and feelings. You must decide what degree of impact you will allow another person to have on your life. Determining the degree of intimacy that you need and want in your life is a universal concern.

Sexuality

Sexuality is a biological and psychological fact of your life, which is as basic as eating, sleeping, anger, and sadness. All of you must deal with yourselves as sexual beings.

Although she was not aware of it, Mary Ann had become like her mother in an effort to keep her mother with her at all times. In the process, she, like her mother, had become asexual. Mary Ann's primary problem was really one of separating from her mother. However, the manifestation of this problem for Mary Ann was her asexuality. She unknowingly felt that the only way to be a "good woman" was to be asexual like her mother, and she acted out this notion in her present romantic relationship. Those sexual difficulties made it difficult for Mary Ann and her lover to maintain their intimacy. It was essential for Mary Ann to work out her sexual problem in order to continue and maintain an intimate relationship. And it was necessary for her to separate her own identity from that of her mother in order to allow herself to be a fully sexual woman.

Unresolved sexual problems, for all of you, can bring great pain, whereas allowing yourself to be a fully functioning sexual woman can bring great joy.

Autonomy

Being autonomous involves the ability to enjoy work, love, and play, and to be free to choose from a variety of alternatives those which best suit your needs.

Gail was struggling with an autonomy issue. She had

worked against all odds to finance her college education and leave the street life behind. Now she was faced with a dilemma. Should she marry, and, if she did, would this jeopardize her autonomy? In contrast, Irene had already established her autonomy but found it eroded by the tragedy of her son's death. Prior to his death she had been a fully functioning worker, mother, and wife, but now she found herself paralyzed in almost all aspects of her life. She could not work, mother, or maintain the household. She had temporarily lost her autonomy.

All of you struggle with autonomy issues at various times in your life. You decide what to do about your job, your finances, your housing, your leisure time. You must choose what you want to do, when, and with whom. It is the ability to choose and execute that choice which confirms your autonomy.

Irene, Gail, and Mary Ann entered therapy with three different presenting problems. Their lives, their situations, and the way they expressed their problems were different for each. Their difficulties and their strengths were expressions of the unique women they were. But although each of them experienced her problem differently, all the problems contained elements of the same universal issues. Each woman at some time and in some way had struggled with and sought solutions to the issues of separation from mother, separation from father, omnipotence and vulnerability, anger and sadness, intimacy, sexuality, and autonomy. For Gail, Mary Ann, and Irene, most of these issues had been resolved in some way, but underlying each of their presenting problems was an unresolved aspect of a universal issue. Some of these they shared. For example, both Mary Ann and Gail were still struggling with separation from mother, though this issue was manifested differently in each woman's life. Issues that are resolved at one time may reappear during a crisis, demanding a new resolution. For example, Irene had been autonomous until her son's sudden and tragic death, at which time her autonomy was shattered and needed to be reworked. Like these three women, all of you have struggled with each of these issues at some point in your life. For many of you, some or most of these issues are now resolved. For some of you, the lack of resolution of one or more of these issues creates either little pinpricks of frustration or crushing pain.

These universal issues cause conflict and struggle at various times throughout your life. Some of you may feel you need help to better resolve these issues, to find a more satisfying solution to old problems and old patterns of behavior. Because the cultural climate in this society not only allows but even encourages psychotherapy as a way of improving your life, some of you will choose it as an instrument for growth.

The Therapeutic Process: A Way To Get Free

Everyone has some unresolved universal issues. It is impossible to navigate through life's morass without carrying along with you some personal quirks, some unresolved issues from the past. The way you resolve these issues to work within your life style is the manifestation of your unique personality. Past traumas contribute to your strengths and achievements as well as cause some of your pain. For example, Mary Ann's experiences with her mother and her mother's leg amputation played a major role in her life. The leg amputation made it inevitable that Mary Ann would have issues about her body image which would surface in one guise or another. They surfaced in her inability to be sexual; at the same time they may have contributed to Mary Ann's choice of a career as a pharmacist. That is, without realizing it, she may have chosen a career in the health sciences in an attempt to ward off or cure illness.

For most of you, most of the time, the conflicts arising from the unresolved aspects of these universal issues do not interfere with the enjoyment of your life. Occasionally the full thrust of a conflict will surface, putting you in the painful position of needing to re-resolve the issue. There are, of course, many ways to do this. You can use your own introspective ability to devise a new solution for this old problem. You can talk with a friend or lover about your difficulty in an attempt to gain insight or create a new solution to an old issue. Self-help books can also aid you in your exploration. And time contributes to the healing. If the pain and the problems created by the issue continue with you for some time, and your own efforts are to no avail, you may decide to seek the help of a psychotherapist, as Irene, Gail, and Mary Ann did. Irene was unable to keep her nightmares from plaguing her. Gail's ambivalence about men was so intense that she could not decide whether to trust again. And Mary Ann, despite her lover's efforts, was not able to be orgasmic. All three of these women decided to seek psychotherapy as a way out of the dilemma causing their pain.

What makes an experience with a therapist so different from simply talking to your friend or thinking about things yourself? First, the therapist is not a participant in your life. She is separate from you and, as such, is able to view with greater objectivity what is going on for you. She can see more easily the connections between your past and your present, and she is able to focus on your blocks, or blind spots. Her training aids her in this perceptiveness, for she has been taught to look for these connections, to listen with a "third ear," and to seek the hidden meanings behind your words and the messages in your body language. Her nonparticipation in your life outside her office also enables her to say things to you that other people probably would not say, to confront you about painful subjects, or to point out issues which might anger or distress you.

Feelings and intellectual insights are the core of therapy, the focus; your therapist helps you to draw them out and develop them. Your therapist is also an accepting listener, a person who is there exclusively for you, to attend to you and give you her undivided attention. The therapeutic session is a time for you to devote exclusively to thinking about yourself. It is a time for you to introspect out loud, to put feelings into words so that you may more easily know what you are feeling. Although you do not pay a therapist for her caring, you do pay her for her time. And it is the payment which enables you to take this time for yourself without holding back or feeling guilty. It allows you to look at yourself and, with her support and assistance, to journey into your past. It is this journey into the past which, in time, will elucidate the present and help minimize your pain. The therapeutic impact of your therapist's caring for you cannot be minimized. It is a prerequisite to effective psychotherapy. Last, therapy is a safe place because of the confidential nature of the contract between you and your therapist. Nothing that goes on inside those four walls can be revealed; it is between just the two of you. This is the sacred contract of psychotherapy.

Once you have decided to seek psychotherapy, your next question is with whom. How do you select a psychotherapist? There is a smorgasbord of different theories of therapy and a host of different strategies of psychotherapy within the same theoretical framework. Proponents of these may all present their way as the "true way" to self-fulfillment and happiness. Some examples are Gestalt therapy, polarity therapy, EST, Rolfing, primal scream therapy, Jungian therapy, Sullivanian therapy, co-counseling, psychoanalysis, transactional analysis, behavior modification, hypnosis, cognitive therapy, and encounter groups. All this may be confusing to you as a consumer. Whom do you seek out?

Most of you, in the end, select a therapist who has been recommended by word of mouth. You have a friend or a friend of a friend who is seeing a therapist and likes her. You attend a class and hear someone speak highly of a particular professional. In choosing your therapist this way rather than using the particular type of therapy as a basis of choice, you have inadvertently hit upon the best way to select a therapist; most research indicates that regardless of the type of therapy a person subscribes to, what makes for a good therapeutic experience is the relationship between you and your therapist. Regardless of a therapist's theoretical framework or the practical application within that framework, effective therapists frequently say and do similar things. The therapist's competence and humanness matter more than her theoretical orientation. Thus, when you go for your first appointment with a therapist, you need to come away feeling that you can talk with her, that you can respect her, and that you can develop a mutual bond between you. You need to feel a "click," a connection between the two of you that will reassure you about your decision. This is not to imply that you will not feel intense discomfort, for first therapy sessions are usually accompanied by anxiety. Anxiety and discomfort are inevitable given the fact that you are sharing your innermost self. Regardless of your anxiety, however, you must feel and believe that you can develop a sense of trust in your therapist.

In recent years, another consideration for many of you has been the sex of your therapist. With the advent of the women's movement, an increasing number of you have decided that you would feel more comfortable baring your soul to a woman, whom you see as more able to understand you and identify with your situation. You feel that because a woman can more easily understand the oppression, confusion, and pressures of the female role, you may be more able to be open with her and trust her comments and responses. Thus many of you seek women therapists. We do not mean to imply that male therapists cannot be equally warm, supportive, nurturing, and nonsexist. Competent therapists are not divided along sex lines. You need to choose your therapist on the basis of her or his reputation and your own feeling of trust. That "click" must be there, regardless of the therapist's sex.

Many of you may be unsure about what to expect in a therapeutic session. Usually you and your therapist are alone together in a quiet room. You talk about yourself. You are free to reveal whatever you wish, letting your mind wander and, in doing so, make important connections between the "whys" of your behavior and feelings. You talk about yourself, your present, your past, your feelings about people and events. Your therapist asks questions, makes comments, clarifies feelings, and draws connections between the present and the past. In effect, she holds up a mirror, revealing you to yourself as you have been, as others see you, and as you can be. Depending upon the therapist you have chosen, other strategies may also be used. Role-playing, in which you assume the role of another person in your life in an attempt to gain insight into the relationship between you and that person, is one such strategy. Or perhaps your therapist will use hypnosis to ask you to scream about a traumatic event in your life. But with most psychotherapists, most of the time, the vehicle through which therapy progresses is your talking about yourself, searching for the connections which will assist you in your voyage toward self-understanding.

Therapy inevitably progresses through various stages. In the beginning you are understandably timid and frightened. The first sessions are a time in which you and your therapist get to know one another. It is hard both to reveal yourself to someone you do not know and to trust the validity of a stranger's comments and interpretations. In time, though, your timidity decreases as your trust increases. You begin to feel closer to your therapist and thrilled about the new things you are discovering about yourself. This period of therapy is usually very exciting. You begin to have more insight into yourself, to understand yourself better, and to see greater connections between your past and your present. You start to recognize reasons for the undermining behaviors that you want to change. Aided by your therapist's view of you, you start to develop a new sense of yourself. You begin to like yourself more, to have greater confidence in yourself, and to be more enthusiastic about your potentialities. During this period you also try behaving in new ways and take new risks. You are testing your new-found knowledge in small ways. However, having these insights on an intellectual level is only the first step. At some point you must feel their validity. You must have the "ah-ha!" reaction, the gut-level understanding, the existential certainty. They must become part of the internal fabric of your being. Moving these insights from your head to your "guts" is the next phase of therapy and involves working with the unconscious.

What is the unconscious? Everything that has happened in your life is stored in your brain. Your brain retains the memory of your progress down the birth canal, the feeling of sucking on a nipple, the texture of your feces in your diaper, and the sight of your father naked. Some of these events are veiled simply because of their occurrence in the far distant past, but nevertheless they are there. For example, while performing surgery on the brain, Penfield found that stimulation of specific parts of the brain resulted in patients' recall of otherwise forgotten events. These memories were intact and included not only the factual memory, but all the feeling components as well. It was as if the person were reexperiencing the past in the present.

Some past events, however, are locked away in your brain because of the feelings associated with them. If as a young child you found an event too overwhelming for you—too sad, too frightening, too sexual—you may have dealt with this event by hiding it from your awareness. This process is called repression, and events such as these become lodged in your unconscious. Feelings that are too overwhelming to be experienced consciously are pushed underground into your unconsciousness. Yet in spite of your inability to remember these events, they are there, hidden in your brain cells, continuing to influence you. Suppose, for example, that you are four years old and calmly eating pineapple after a family meal. Suddenly your parents begin screaming at each other with what appears to be rage and hatred. You are terrified. The event is forgotten. However, you inadvertently link your eating of pineapple to the memory of the fight; the aroma, taste, and sight of pineapple are all interwoven as parts of the frightening disagreement between your parents. Thereafter, without realizing why, you dislike pineapple. This is an example of the unconscious at work.

The unconscious consists of all forgotten events that cannot readily be called to mind, some buried by time, others vehemently repressed as a defense against feeling their overwhelming impact. Of course, the memories stored in the unconscious are not necessarily accurate representations of the actual events. The unconscious may condense several events into one; it may omit important factors from a particular memory; it may combine the facts of one event with the feelings of another. Thus the events stored in the unconscious are distorted memories which influence your life. For example, your parents' screaming at each other may have been interpreted by your six-year-old mind as murderous rage, when in reality they were merely engaging in an excited political discussion. This event, along with some or all of the accompanying sights, sounds, feelings, and distortions, exists in your unconscious, influencing your behavior and your dreams.

Dreams reveal the workings of your unconscious. The wishes, fears, longings, and terrors of your daytime life are replayed, reexperienced, and sometimes resolved in your dreams. All of you dream, and many therapists utilize dream work to gain access to unconscious material. You, as the client, bring your dreams or fragments of dreams into your therapy session and talk about them. You discuss what they bring to mind and what feelings they invoke in you. Your dreams are a doorway to your unconscious; they provide a symbolic expression of your feelings and your past and present experiences. Your dreams are your past memories and your present life in code, and deciphering that code helps you to understand the whys and wherefores of your feelings and behaviors.

Much therapeutic work, then, is devoted to understanding your unconscious. Through understanding your unconscious, you can undo unfulfilling or undermining behaviors and feelings. When you know the reasons for your behavior, you can more easily change it if it troubles you. You can learn to forgive yourself and to appreciate and love yourself. Growing up inevitably involves numerous pains and traumas. Being a child is difficult. Being an adult is difficult. Understanding your unconscious means coming to grips with the knowledge that you have done the best that you can with what you have. Freeing yourself from monsters of the past increases your self-appreciation, which in turn frees you even more to try new behaviors. Little steps taken early in therapy lead to gigantic leaps. Old fears are gone and you are free to try your wings and explore uncharted territories.

The last hurdle in therapy is leaving your therapist. This step is both a termination and a graduation. You are saying goodbye to your therapist and at the same time experiencing yourself as an autonomous, free woman, able to handle future traumas. Leaving may be very difficult. Your therapist may represent to you people from your past, and by leaving her you may feel that you are again leaving them. Equally important is the fact that your therapist is someone that you have grown to care for very deeply, someone with whom you have shared so much of yourself. However, this relationship has played its role in your evolution. In order to be free you must give up this close, caring relationship with your therapist. But despite your fears and sadness about leaving your therapist, there is also a joy and excitement about going back into the world on your own. You are now free.

2

Separation From Mother:
THE FAIRY GODMOTHER AND THE WICKED WITCH

Charlotte put down the phone after another unsatisfying call to her mother. Well, what did she expect? Her mother was busy. Charlotte should have known better than to interrupt her mother during her favorite TV show. Well, maybe tomorrow or the day after would be better. Maybe she'd even have dinner with Charlotte over the weekend. In the meantime, Charlotte needed to respond to and refuse that job promotion. She realized that she was 45 years old and that she might not get a second chance, but Toledo was thousands of miles away from home and mother.

Charlotte went to her typewriter and sat there, perplexed. Her life had been so calm and peaceful. She had always been able to predict what the next day would bring. Now all these changes had suddenly occurred. First, her roommate of five years had left to remarry, and Charlotte's apartment seemed empty and strange. She did not look forward to still another in the string of roommates she had lived with over the past 20 years. Then, to make matters worse, Charlotte's menopause had begun. Charlotte had always known she would hate menopause. It brought home the reality that her only babies would be the babies at the hospital. That was yet another reason to turn down the job promotion she had been offered. After all, if she were an assistant hospital administrator, even at a pediatric hospital, she would not be able to cuddle and love the babies. Taking the job would mean giving up the babies as well as her mother, and she certainly did not want to do that. Charlotte knew what she had to do and slowly typed out the job refusal. Another chance lost.

Yet, even knowing that she had refused the job did not make Charlotte feel peaceful. In fact, she felt a wave of sadness, loneliness. She did not like this unsettled feeling. She wanted her calm life back again. Knowing that she needed someone to talk with, she dialed the number of a psychotherapist and made an appointment.

Charlotte was born in Pittsburgh when her mother was 34 years old. Her mother, at 31, had married a man ten years her senior, a middle-management counselor at the Employment Security Commission. He was a quiet, unassuming man who took his work very seriously. When at home, he was calm but removed from Charlotte, who was their only child. Her mother had worked in medical records at a hospital until she gave birth to Charlotte. After that she stayed at home, devoting herself to being a wife and mother.

When Charlotte was five years old, she contracted rheumatic fever and was bedridden for a year. Her only memories of this period were dim. She remembered that her mother cared for her but resented the time and attention that Charlotte demanded. When Charlotte got out of bed one year later, her mother felt it too soon for Charlotte to enter directly into the first grade. Instead Charlotte, at age six, entered kindergarten. This meant that Charlotte was not only a year older but also, paradoxically, a year less experienced than her peers. She was never quite on a level with her little friends. Even after recuperating from rheumatic fever she was not as strong physically as they were. She was not able to participate in rope-jumping, running, or playing with the other children. Charlotte felt different, set apart and left out.

The years after kindergarten were ordinary. Charlotte was a good student, but not exceptional. She did what was expected of her. She was very tied to her mother, wanting to please her, yet never feeling quite good enough. Her mother treated her with a mixture of protectiveness and resentment. She criticized most of Charlotte's behavior but at the same time dissuaded her from any growth away from home and mother. Consequently, Charlotte was afraid to take risks for fear that she might be hurt or criticized. So long as she took no risks, she could do nothing wrong. Charlotte never developed herself, she never did anything unique. She grew up bland and unexciting. She simply had no spark.

For Charlotte the transition into high school was uneventful. She was a thin and unexciting young woman. At 15 she began menstruating very irregularly. Her lateness on still another scene increased her feelings of alienation. She had girlfriends, but boys never seemed interested in her. During high school Charlotte realized that she liked taking care of people and decided to become a nurse. Her father seemed pleased by her career decision, but her mother remained unnoticing.

Charlotte went to college at the University of Pittsburgh and lived at home all four years. She graduated and took a job at a local hospital as a pediatric nurse, where she was to remain for 20 years. When she was 25, she moved into an apartment with a roommate who was also a nurse. She was promoted on her job, but always on the basis of seniority rather than inventiveness. Many of her colleagues and each of her roommates left to marry or have babies. Yet Charlotte's life remained unchanged. She was not disliked by people. She and her roommates often became good friends. Her colleagues at the hospital regarded her as a "nice" person, as amiable, as someone who did her job well and did not make waves. Nobody was particularly excited by her, but nobody hated her either.

Charlotte enjoyed the evenness and calmness in her life. She gave enormous amounts of love to the infants she cared for and was particularly drawn to abused children. She dreamed of someday having a family that would be warm and supportive, and a baby of her own. However, Charlotte was not overly concerned that men never seemed to notice her. Occasionally she felt that something was missing in her life but dealt with this void by spending an extra hour cuddling one of the infants on her ward, trying to fill herself up.

So here was Charlotte—45 years old, menopausal, having

lost still another roommate, and having refused a job so that she could stay in the same city as her mother and her infants.

The Importance of Mothers

Fusion. No closeness between two human beings ever duplicates the closeness between you and your mother prior to birth. Your first separation from your mother is at birth. Though at best delightful and exciting for your mother, your birth is very traumatic for you. You move from the warmth and safety of the womb into a world of many physical discomforts. You arrive, in the best of all possible worlds, as the focus of your mother's dreams, hopes, and yearnings. You leave the womb; your umbilical cord is cut. But you are still totally dependent upon your mother. Although you are now physically separate from your mother, you remain dependent upon her for your very existence. You need her for food, care, and love. You need to be fed, to be changed, to be moved from one place to another, to be kept warm, and to be clothed. Without these physical attentions you will obviously die. Never again are you so helpless. Never again is another human being so crucial to your survival.

The first six months of life are marked by a fusion, a unity, a oneness between you and your mother. During this time you are not aware of yourself as a being separate from your mother. You do not know where your boundaries stop and where hers begin. There is a molding, a fusing of your two beings, so that you have no awareness of yourself as separate. There is a uniqueness, a specialness, an intensity about this early relationship that is never again duplicated. You and your mother together create a harmony, an oceanic quality, a peaceful aura. This is the world you two share, the world that the two of you have created for each other—an all-encompassing, fused reality.

The way life begins sets the stage for how life is going to be. If you are born into a family where your mother is excited about sharing her life with you and helping you to grow and to explore the world, you are more likely to take a sense of uniqueness and specialness and love with you throughout your life. If you are born into a situation in which your parents are unable to devote emotional energy to you, you are more likely to take a sense of diminished self-worth with you throughout your life. Thus it is crucial to an infant that her mother communicate her excitement about and her love for her baby. She needs to be able to communicate, through her physical contact with the baby, her love, caring, and belief that her baby is unique and special. As an infant without love, you would die, even if all your physical needs were met. You cannot survive without love, care, and attention.

Separation. Between six months and three years you increasingly separate from your mother while at the same time developing a stronger sense of yourself. At 12 months of age you suddenly discover that you can walk, that you can propel yourself away from your mother. You are able to be more separate from her than ever before. A whole new world awaits you. You have an entire universe to conquer. You feel more grandiose, more powerful than you have ever felt before or will ever feel again. During this time you have a mistaken sense of your new-found power. This feeling of power stems from your feeling at one with both your mother and the world. You do not know yourself as a totally separate person and, hence, carry with you your mother's strength and power as well as your own. In addition, you feel your own power is limitless because of your ability to merge your upright body with the apparently infinite universe.

At 18 months you become increasingly aware of yourself as a separate entity, apart from both your mother and the world. As a result, you no longer feel as though your mother is with you always. You can no longer take her presence for granted. Additionally, as your thinking mind develops, you realize that you are not one with the world, that you cannot control the universe, but that rather you are a small, helpless, vulnerable creature.

At this time in your life there is a delicate relationship between you and your mother, one which proves crucial to your development of intimate relationships in later life. During this time your mother must be sensitive to your desire both to leave the nest and to return for reassurance. You want to test your wings, but you also need to come back to your mother and be a baby again in the safety of her arms. For example, imagine yourself at 18 months in the park with your mother. She takes you out of your stroller and you teeter away from her, looking around, feeling both excited and scared. You see a clump of dandelions in the grass and wander toward them. Just as you are about to reach them, you look back at your mother and run back to touch her. She smiles and gives you a pat, allowing you to go back and pick the flowers. This is an example of your mother's allowing you the safety and love necessary for your exploration and growing independence. She is allowing you to be both independent and dependent. When you go away, she stays there so that you can come back when you need to. Thus your mother must be sufficiently there for you to make you feel that the world is safe and secure, but she must not be too smothering or overprotective; she must maintain a delicate balance between allowing you freedom and giving you security.

As you continue to grow, this delicate balance must shift. Now imagine yourself again one year later, at two and a half years old. Walking, running, and climbing stairs are accomplished tasks that seem almost "old hat." You are again at the park with your mother. You walk over to a swing and pull yourself onto it. What is your mother's reaction to this? She can forbid you to swing, saying that it is too dangerous and that you might fall and hurt yourself. She can react with panic and rush over to you, pulling you away from the swing onto the greater safety of the grass. She can feel her panic but decide not to react to it and allow you to swing as you please. She can go over to you and offer to help you or allow you to swing by yourself. And finally, she can be totally indifferent to your attempt and sit there engrossed in her own thoughts.

How your mother responds to this situation is determined by both her feelings about the physical environment and her own feelings about separating from you. For example, does your mother feel secure in her own physical competence?

Does she feel comfortable with her body? Does she enjoy excercise and sports? If your mother feels physically competent herself, she is more likely to see you as physically capable as well. However, if your mother has been raised by an overprotective mother herself, she probably has not developed confidence in her own physical ability to deal with the world. Then she is more apt to see the world as physically dangerous and to see you as incapable of dealing with it unscathed. She will be overly protective of you, just as her mother was of her.

Another issue your mother must deal with in this situation is her own feelings about separation and letting you go. Many mothers enjoy a child during the first year of the child's life, reveling in the child's dependency. They like feeling needed and wanted and loved. They bask in the special body-molding closeness unique to mother and infant. Your mother probably devoted this entire year to you, often to the exclusion of other interests or people. Now you are ready to move on, to become more independent and grow beyond your mother. You do not need your mother quite as much, but your mother may not be ready to let you go. If your mother feels she would like to hold onto you, she will communicate this to you in any number of ways and may not even be aware that she is doing so. Thus, in the example above, if your mother rushes to protect you from the swing, she may be reflecting her desire to keep you close and prevent you from moving beyond her sphere.

On the other hand, your mother may be overly eager to let you go. She may feel tired of being tied down or may have a new infant to demand her attention. As a result, she may delight in the freedom that your first steps bring her and may be physically or psychologically unavailable to you when you need to return for reassurance. If this scenario should occur, you may become distrustful of your world, feeling fearful and always looking for the reassurance you did not get from your mother. You may also unknowingly defend against these feelings of fright and helplessness by pretending to be brave and indifferent, trying to convince yourself of your invulnerability.

Thus, by the time you are three years old, your mother has

given you a sense of what to expect of yourself, other people, and your environment. You feel either secure or frightened, either worthwhile or unlovable, either trusting or apprehensive. The fact that you and your mother are the same sex intensifies her influence on you.

Same-sex parent. The relationship between same-sex parent and child is a special one. It is unique. From the same-sex parent you learn how to see yourself, what kinds of roles you can play, how you can move about the world, and how to feel about yourself. The same-sex parent provides a kind of model that the opposite-sex parent does not. You as a little girl look to your mother to find out who you will be when you grow up. You learn your sense of yourself from how you view your mother and from how your mother views you. Your family is a microcosm for the world; your mother is the prototype of women. Your mother, by the way she lives her life, shows you one set of options. Your mother may allow and encourage you to be different from her, or she may insist that you be just like her. In addition, you often feel about yourself the way your mother feels about you. And the way your mother feels about you is often a reflection of how she feels about herself. If your mother loves both herself and you, you can more easily love yourself. If your mother dislikes herself, she will probably be critical of you, and you will be more likely to grow up disliking yourself as well. If your mother behaves toward you as though you are less than adequate, you will struggle against feelings of inadequacy. If your mother communicates to you that she sees you as irresponsible, you may feel irresponsible.

Your feelings about yourself are totally learned, and your mother is the first teacher. She is not your only teacher, but she is your first. If your mother is excited and joyful and feels that life is worth living, she communicates this to you and you more easily adopt these same feelings. If your mother enjoys new activities, excitement, and adventures, it is easier for you to enjoy your own adventures and explorations of the world. If your mother has close female friends, you will be more likely to grow up valuing women and will seek them out as friends. Your mother's view of herself and her world is the one she shows you. At first you see the world from her eyes. Later it becomes your world too.

Sexuality. Another arena in which your mother serves as a model concerns men and sexuality. If your mother does not trust her husband, you may learn that men are not very trustworthy. If your mother looks at her husband as a partner, you may view the union between men and women as a partnership. If your mother feels abused by her husband, then you may learn that men are cruel and abusive. If your mother feels that sex is fun and communicates this to you, you too may learn that sexual involvement can be fun.

Your sense of your sexuality is passed down from your mother. She does this by how she touches you, by how she kisses her husband, and by what she tells or does not tell you about sex. Nancy Friday's book, *My Mother, Myself,* discusses this issue in some detail. Many mothers believe, and our culture supports the contention, that mothers are not supposed to be sexual. In an attempt to present themselves to their daughters as asexual beings, they communicate that motherhood and sexuality are mutually exclusive. As a result, women often lose interest in sex after they become mothers, or even earlier, when they first marry. For example, you may have lived with your present husband several years before marrying him, enjoying an active and creative sexual life. After your marriage, however, you may have lost interest in sex, finding it a bothersome chore. For you, the status of "wife" was inconsistent with being a sexual woman; you became like your picture of your mother and were unable to enjoy sex.

Of course, there are other ways in which you behave like your mother. One of the most obvious is that you mother the way you were mothered. When taking care of your little daughter, you may fuss over her hair, remind her to keep her legs together when she is wearing a skirt, and make her feel guilty when she does something you do not like. You can remember how you felt when your mother did these same things to you. You felt hurt, unjustly criticized, and angry. Yet, though you swore you would not, you find yourself repeating these same patterns. As it was for your mother, so it is for you.

Rage at Mother. The love and concern that you feel for your mother are as inevitable as your feelings of dependency and desire for her. Also inevitable is your rage. No matter how loving a mother you have, no matter how conscientious, no matter how giving, there are times that you become enraged. How does this rage come about? It is a function of both the process of growing up and the culture in which you live. Your rage starts when you realize that you are not omnipotent. You cry lustily for your bottle and your mother does not come. You are enraged; you cannot make her do what you want. You are separate from her and cannot control her.

It is your mother you look to, for you live in a culture that has perpetuated the myth of the "perfect" mother, the myth that you as a child are happiest in the sole care of your mother. Your mother also subscribes to this myth, believing that she can be and should be a perfect mother to you. As you grow up, you experience your mother as less and less perfect. It is she who screams at you not to touch your grandmother's figurine. It is she who insists that you use the toilet, that you always be conscious of your bladder and bowels. Still later, it is your mother who teaches you to dress, to keep your room tidy. Slowly your mother molds you into a citizen of your culture. You, in return, give up some impulses, desires, and even talents. Of course you are enraged. You want to do what you want to do, but you love and need your mother so much that you give up a part of yourself in order to please her.

Despite your rage, you need your mother and collude with her in repressing this rage. She rewards you with praise. All the things you gave up were worth it because of the love you hope to receive from her. Thus the culture, you, and your mother are conspirators, conspiring to believe in her perspective on the world. You deny, ignore, or rationalize the ways in which she is not perfect. In the recesses of her mind, your mother knows that your rage is legitimate, an inevitable part of the evolution from total dependency to adulthood. But she feels that she must contain your rage, that she has to follow the role prescribed for her by the culture and raise you to be a citizen of your age. This conspiracy between you and your mother serves to heighten the intensity of your relationship. Both of you collude in repressing your rage so that you can live within her dictates and grow to be an "acceptable" citizen.

This collusion with your mother to repress your rage and to mold you into an acceptable citizen also sets the stage for the feelings of guilt you struggle with throughout your life. You adopt your mother's feelings and attitudes and feel "bad" if you ever feel or want or think something different. You regard yourself as a "bad" person and feel guilty if you become angry or struggle against her mandates. You must feel guilty if you are to be socialized a law-abiding adult in this culture. Basically, guilt keeps you in line; it keeps you from compulsively gratifying your every wish and ignoring the feelings or rights of others. Guilt is there helping you to navigate the world as a responsible, loving citizen. It is there to keep you from hurting others and to help you avoid dangerous situations. Unfortunately, if all the "no's" of childhood become prohibitions of adulthood, guilt may also become a great inhibitor, a great burden. Then it may crush you with self-dismay, preventing you from enjoying adult pleasures. You may hear your mother's voice inside you; you may remember her dictates and prohibitions and feel guilty.

The fairy godmother and the wicked witch. It is the combination of your mother's love, acceptance, and restrictions that leads you to view her with a combination of tremendous love and tremendous anger. These two conflicting feelings give rise to many of the myths of childhood. You long for the perfect mother, for the fairy godmother who is loving, calm, compassionate, and magically powerful. You are terrified of the wicked witch, the screaming, angry, critical, annoyed, exasperated mother who seems so powerful, malevolent, and terrifying. You have difficulty reconciling your playful and accepting mother with the grumpy and demanding woman she sometimes becomes. Many children split these two diverse feelings and insist upon seeing their mothers as either one or the other, either the wicked witch or the fairy godmother. This polarization, this insistence on extremity, allows the child to deal more easily with diverse events and differing adult moods. Successful maturation requires that the child finally accept the mother as a total human being, not perfect, neither a fairy godmother nor a wicked witch, but a human being with some of the qualities of each.

Your mother is both your primary caretaker and your model for womanhood. She nurtures and loves you from birth. With your father, she teaches you to walk and talk; she teaches you what and how to eat; she teaches you how to love and what to do with your feelings of anger, sadness, and joy. Not only has she given you all this, but also she is your model for being a woman in the world. Sorting out her models and her mandates and reaching a separate sense of yourself as a unique individual is a difficult process. You want to stay close to your mother; you want to continue to be protected, safe, and secure. Yet, in order to grow up and be an adult woman, you have to separate from your mother. You have to discriminate between those aspects of her that you want to emulate and the negative aspects you want to give up.

This, of course, is the difficult part of separation from mother. To be a separate woman, you need to appreciate the fine qualities of your mother and at the same time realize she is an imperfect human being. Giving up your mother is very painful; it is difficult to go from the safety and security of her protective world to the uncertainty of being on your own. The ability to separate from your mother is based on your knowing that you do not need her in the way you needed her when you were a child. Giving up your mother is facilitated by having had a healthy relationship with her. This enables you to go beyond that relationship and to feel competent and capable in your own right. If the relationship with your mother has been either overindulgent or rejecting, a healthy separation is more difficult.

Strategies of Dealing with Mother

Regardless of your relationship with your mother, she is crucial to your survival when you are a child. You need her for love, security, safety, warmth, and for your very existence. Your love for her fills you up, seeming almost too great for your small body to contain. As a result, you want to stay close to her and to take part of her with you as you proceed into womanhood. Holding onto your mother need not be unhealthy so long as you are able to find out who you are as a separate person. You must differentiate from her, maintain a sense of autonomy, and, at the same time, develop intimate relationships with other people. Growing up involves figuring out your own view of the world while taking aspects and images of your mother as you go.

Internalization. One of the ways of holding onto mother is by internalizing her, by becoming like her. Because your mother is the same-sex parent, you have a tendency to grow up mirroring your childhood experience of her. You grow up to be like your mother because that is what you have felt; that is what you have seen; that is what you have known. Because of your vulnerability and dependency, you internalize your mother, you take part of her inside of you. As an infant, you are obviously vulnerable to her. She chooses when to feed you, when to change you, when to play with you, when to love you, when to move you, when to punish you. She has the power over your survival, the power over your life. This renders you, as an infant, totally vulnerable and powerless. This vulnerability makes you want to hold onto your mother, to make sure she does not go away. One of the ways to insure she does not leave is to internalize her, to become like her. You internalize your mother in an effort to hold onto her, to attain those parts of her that have the power to satisfy your needs.

Internalization is a two-part process. You see your mother as a model and imitate her behavior, her attitudes, her ways of being. For example, if your mother enjoys cooking and teaches you to bake raspberry pies, you may learn to enjoy baking and other aspects of creative cookery. This shared experience with your mother may then lead you to enjoy cooking later in your life when your mother is no longer present. At this point, the behavior has been internalized. In other words, first you model your behavior after your mother, and later you grow to experience it as part of you, as your own, as a fact about yourself coming from your own needs and desires. The no's and yes's of your childhood and your mother's praises and condemnations become an integral part of you. This internalization occurs whether or not you are consciously aware that you are swallowing an aspect of your mother and using it in your own repertoire of behaviors. As an adult, in order to define yourself as a separate, unique person, you need to recognize those internalized aspects of your mother that are hurtful to you and let go of them.

Because of your dependency and powerlessness as a child, you tend to view your mother as a fairy godmother, as good and beneficent. You need to see her in this light in order to know that she will take good care of you. You may then internalize an image of your mother as the fairy godmother and try to become the fairy godmother yourself. Such a woman was Jane. At age 35, divorced, with a seven-year-old child, Jane had to admit that she had a drinking problem. She was not ready to label herself an alcoholic but knew that once she started drinking she did not stop. And, of course, she did start every day. She would come home from work and immediately reach for the bottle of vodka in her kitchen cabinet. When she first began this practice, she told herself she just wanted a drink to relax after work to help her prepare dinner and attend to her little girl. Now, however, she could not deceive herself. She knew it would be more than one drink. She knew that she would drink through the evening until finally she passed out in her bed.

Jane had always enjoyed drinking, but she had never drunk to excess, not until three years ago when her husband had suddenly left her. She had been crushed by his betrayal and desertion. Jane had believed they had a near perfect marriage; then he had told her he had been unhappy and unfaithful for years. That was when Jane started drinking to help her sleep and to blot out her pain and agony. It made her feel better to drink, warmer, not so alone, as if she were taking in something familiar and comforting. Now Jane felt that she had to isolate herself from people so that they would not condemn her for her drinking. She was also concerned about herself because she had begun to have blackouts. Increasingly there were periods when she did not remember what she had done, where she had been, or whom she had been with. This was very frightening to Jane, for she did not trust herself to care for or protect either herself or her child.

Jane had grown up in a home where drinking was fun and acceptable, but never carried to excess. In fact, Jane remembered her childhood as being happy and relaxed with few traumas or difficulties. Both her parents were warm, loving, and affectionate. Her mother was somewhat overprotective, but her father tempered his wife's protectiveness and encouraged Jane to take risks and try things on her own. Jane's most pleasurable memories were the times she and her mother played together. When Jane came home from school her mother would have a few drinks and the two of them would begin their fun-loving, creative, spontaneous play. Jane saw her mother as her best playmate. No girlfriend could be as funny or creative as her mother. Why, she and her mother would even play dress-up, pretending to be different characters exploring foreign lands. Jane felt that her relationship with her mother was perfect. No one had as good a mom as she did; no one could spend such wonderful, loving time with her as could her mother.

Now, although Jane lived hundreds of miles away from her mother, she still looked to her for support and comfort. She continued to see their relationship as the ideal mother-daughter relationship and her mother as a warm, loving, giving woman. Jane wished she could go home and let her mother take care of her again. But now she was a mother herself. She had to be a grownup, an adult, and care for her own daughter. She could not go back to those safe, joyful times of playing make-believe with her mother.

Why was it that Jane had developed a drinking problem? First, there was her divorce, a situational, stress-inducing crisis which left her adrift at sea without an anchor. At that point she had begun to use alcohol to numb her pain, to blot out her agony, and to help herself feel more relaxed. In addition, Jane had taken in, had internalized, a part of her mother, that is, her mother's drinking, which Jane then exaggerated as an adult. Jane felt close to her mother and remembered with joy the times they had spent together when she was a child. She remembered her mother's drinking during those close times; she even remembered helping her mother mix the cocktails, which signaled the beginning of their journey into fantasy-land. This was a precious memory for Jane and one she internalized and took with her into adulthood. Jane loved her mother and wanted to be with her always. By internalizing her "fairy godmother" mother, she unconsciously felt she would keep her mother with her forever. Although Jane was not aware of it, when she needed her mother most she acted like her; and in her present stressful situation, she exaggerated this particular aspect of her mother. When Jane felt empty and lonely, she turned to drinking as a way of feeling close to her mother by being like her.

Jane needed to realize that her mother was not and is not perfect, that she could be like her mother in some respects but without internalizing all of her. She could let go those aspects of her mother which reduced her own ability to enjoy her own life. She could be warm, affectionate, and creative like her mother, but she could discard the drinking which she carried to excess. Jane did not need her mother in the same way she needed her as a child. It is true that Jane was now lonely and sad because of the loss of her husband. But the drinking had exacerbated her problem and had even increased her social isolation. Jane had to learn that she need not turn to either the bottle or her mother for solace, but rather that she could remake a life for herself in a healthy and non-destructive manner.

It is not necessary that you see your mother only as a fairy godmother in order to internalize her. You may see her as frightening, as a wicked witch, and still internalize her. You may take in those aspects of her which you experience as most scary, as most powerful, so as to feel more powerful yourself. For example, suppose your mother was excessively neat and was always nagging at you to keep your room tidy. This annoyed you but you could do nothing about it. You had to be consistently neat, because your mother was both powerful and controlling. As a helpless child you yearned for the power and control your mother had. You wanted to become the victimizer as opposed to the victim. In order to obtain the power of your mother, you became like her; that is, you became as compulsive as she was in an attempt to gain the power you experienced her as having. Now, as an adult, you are as compulsive as your mother, but you are unaware of the connection between your childhood feelings of helplessness and your present behavior.

Nora, age 22, is an example of a woman who saw her mother as a wicked witch and became like her in the aspect she hated most. Nora hung over the sink in terror at the violent rage she had just felt toward her daughter Chris. She felt so out of control that she feared the spanking she had just administered could have killed her child. Chris, age three, had only spilled milk on the floor. Nora's terror brought back memories of the beatings she herself had received as a child. Nora's mother had had a very volatile temper and had abused Nora. As a child, she never knew when her mother would become enraged. Any small incident might set her off. Her rage seemed totally capricious and out of control. Nora could not believe she was repeating this pattern with her own daughter. Even when she was a child, Nora had been determined to be totally different from her mother, determined that she would never repeat with her own child the brutality she had experienced herself.

Now Nora was pleased about the ways in which she was

different from her mother. Unlike her mother, Nora loved her husband and enjoyed both working and maintaining a pleasant home. She had looked forward to having a child and in most ways was a good mother. She saw her daughter Chris as a beautiful and sweet child. Despite these differences, Nora was like her mother in the worst possible way. She could feel such intense rage at her baby. When the rage occurred, she could not stop herself from beating Chris. Nora, an abused child herself, knew the horror of such beatings. Yet she was repeating with her daughter her own nightmarish childhood. In an attempt to feel as powerful as her mother, Nora had unknowingly internalized that aspect of her mother which she hated and feared most. She had become like the wicked witch in order to gain power, but now hated herself for that very power, for being like her mother in the way she hated most. Becoming like the wicked witch is called identification with the aggressor.

Rebellion. Another way of holding onto mother is to rebel against her. This is an attempt to stay close to her by doing the opposite of what she says to do or being the opposite of what she is. It appears that you have let go of your mother, but actually, to quote Shakespeare, it is a case of "The lady doth protest too much, methinks." It is the excessive nature of the rebellion that indicates your continuing tie to your mother. Returning to the previous example, if your mother is compulsively neat, you may grow up to be very messy, keeping your home in disarray and refusing to devote much care and attention to orderliness. Old newspapers and dirty clothes may be strewn everywhere. This messiness is your rebellion against your mother's excessive neatness. On the surface it appears that you are free from your mother's influence. However, the extreme nature of your messiness reveals your continued connection to her. You are actively being not like her rather than simply being yourself.

Interpersonal relationships may also provide an arena for expressing rebellion. Suppose that your mother is a social butterfly. She has lots of friends and involves herself in numerous social activities and community affairs. As an adult you may prefer to spend most of your time alone or with a few carefully chosen friends. You may feel uncomfortable at parties and refuse to entertain in your home. As a child you resented your mother's social activities. She was always paying attention to her friends and never seemed to have enough time for you. As an adult you rebel against those aspects of your mother which were crucial to your childhood relationship with her and thereby limit your contact with other people.

Rachel, age 18, is an example of someone who rebelled against her "perfect" mother. She was brought into therapy by her mother, Roberta, who was extremely distressed about Rachel's continuing sexual promiscuity despite her abortion two months earlier. Roberta could not understand why Rachel was behaving so strangely. She had always been such a good girl. She had done well in school and had been a super-achiever. On the surface, Roberta was the perfect mother. She was always home; she felt that being a housewife and mother were the most important jobs in the world. She took care of the house and was always available for Rachel. Rachel experienced her mother as kind and loving. Compared to her friends, she felt as though she had the perfect mother. Her mother never screamed at her or told her she was bad. However, Roberta never wanted to let Rachel out of her sight. She objected to Rachel's riding a bike or ice skating, because she was afraid that Rachel would get hurt. She did not want anything to happen to her precious daughter. She even felt anxious when Rachel went away to camp. Camp seemed so very far away and so many things might happen to Rachel when she was away from home.

Rachel had always seen her mother's concern and involvement in all aspects of her life as evidence of her love. She had not even realized that her mother's overprotectiveness restricted her freedom. However, although she was not consciously aware of this connection, Rachel rebelled against her mother's restrictiveness by dating "unacceptable" boys and acting-out sexually. Although Rachel did not know it, her sexual acting-out was evidence of her need to separate from her mother for fear of otherwise being consumed by her. In therapy, Rachel learned that overprotectiveness does not equal love. Roberta's overprotectiveness expressed her need to experience her daughter as an extension of herself. She could display Rachel to the world as living proof of her own worth and ability as a mother. When Rachel was able to make this connection, she was able to feel her rage at her mother and then no longer needed to act out this rage by being sexually promiscuous. She no longer needed to rebel.

Another example of rebellion can be seen in the behavior of Barbara, age 23, who had experienced her mother to be more like the wicked witch than the fairy godmother. Now Barbara was everything her mother had not wanted her to be. She was married, had two children, and did not care at all about her appearance. Her mother had wanted her to be an attractive, self-sufficient career woman. Barbara had shown her mother how different she was from her, what a separate person she was. Or had she? Barbara's mother, Frances, was in retailing. Frances had worked herself into the position of buyer for a chain of department stores. She specialized in designer clothes and was always exquisitely groomed and stylishly dressed. When Barbara was a child, Frances had dressed her in the most expensive outfits. Barbara could not stay messy or dirty for more than two minutes without her mother swooping in to change her clothes and fuss over her. On the other hand, if Barbara felt sad and needed to talk or be held, she felt as though her mother was not there for her. She felt that her mother could buy her new clothes but could not give her love and attention in other more necessary ways.

Frances valued her career a great deal and always emphasized to Barbara the importance of having a career, how important it was for Barbara to become independent and self-sufficient. By the time Barbara was in high school, her mother was working more than 40 hours a week and Barbara was convinced that she did not want to be like her mother. Barbara was enraged at her mother for being so preoccupied with her job and so unavailable to Barbara. In high school, Barbara decided not to go to college and registered for a secretarial course. She fell in love with one of her classmates and they were married after graduation. Barbara's mother was distressed at the marriage but knew she could do nothing to prevent it. Frances warned her daughter that she was making a terrible mistake. Barbara thought she did not care what her mother felt. She did not recognize that some of her need to marry so young and to steadfastly avoid a career came from her excessive need to be different from her mother. Barbara was not free to make decisions on her own; she could only go against what her mother wanted.

Repetition of the relationship. Still another way to hold onto your mother is by repeating your relationship with her, by becoming involved with people who are like her.

Maggie, age 37, was never able to separate from her "perfect" mother. Maggie saw her mother as Supermom. Her mother was able to maintain a beautifully furnished home, hold a responsible job, and prepare gourmet meals. She was enthusiastic about her relationship with both her husband and her children. Maggie felt well loved by her mother, yet felt that she was unable to measure up. When she showed her mother something she had made, her mother responded with, "That's very nice, dear, but it would be a little bit better if you had done it this way." Maggie was always trying to do whatever would win her mother's unqualified praise and approval, trying to improve herself so that she could measure up to her own image of her mother and thereby win her mother's love.

In an effort to better herself and make herself more interesting, Maggie decided to take a course in creative writing. She felt an immediate bond to her teacher who seemed to resemble her mother in many ways. Maggie tried very hard to please her teacher, writing her stories over and over again. But she could never be creative enough. All her ideas seemed stiff and uninteresting. Her teacher was forever criticizing her—encouraging her, but criticizing her nevertheless. What was most painful was that Maggie felt devastated by the criticism. She felt as though she were a little girl again, unable to measure up to her loving mother's expectations.

Maggie was attempting to hold onto her "perfect" mother by putting her mother's "face" on her creative writing teacher and, again, being unsuccessful at measuring up. Maggie's anx-

iety about writing well enough to please her teacher no doubt
dampened her creativity and made it impossible for her ever
to succeed. Maggie kept trying to win her mother's love, either directly or through substitutes for her, and never succeeded in feeling worthwhile or valuable. Maggie did not
know that her relationship with her teacher was in any way
related to her relationship with her mother. She also did not
know that her relationship with her mother was not entirely
perfect.

Maggie needed to let go of her mother and to stop trying
to repeat their relationship in other adult relationships in her
life. She had to learn that her mother's inability to fulfill
some of her emotional needs interfered with the development
of her sense of worth. She had to learn she was not unlovable,
but rather that her mother could not give to her in a way that
nurtured her sense of worth. Once Maggie could realize this,
she could recognize her own ability and strength and not be
so dependent on her mother or her substitutes. She could
then let her mother go. This did not mean that she would
have to stop relating to her mother, but rather that she could
relate to her as a loving equal, not as a dependent child. Additionally, Maggie would not have to repeat the adoring relationship with her mother with other people in her adult life
and would thus be free to relate to them as peers.

Like Maggie, Adrian also repeated the relationship with
her mother by choosing to relate to people who were similar
to her. This was true even though Adrian's mother was cold
and distancing, more like a wicked witch. Adrian was now in
pain because another lover had left her. She came into therapy wondering why she continually chose women who could
not care for her as she cared for them. It had happened before
and now it had happened again. Here Adrian was, madly in
love with a woman whom she thought and dreamt about and
wanted to be with constantly. She had hoped they would
make a permanent life together and then, like a bolt of light-
ning, the woman had told her the relationship was over. Certainly Adrian could look over the history of the relationship
and see that her lover had never been particularly warm and

affectionate. In fact, Adrian had often viewed herself as a little puppy dog following her lover and begging for crumbs.

Adrian was a 28-year-old elementary school teacher. Her relationship with her students was very important to her. With them she was able to give and to receive warmth and attention. Adrian had no conflicts about being a lesbian. She became involved with a woman and "came out" as a lesbian during her first year in college. She felt as though this was where she belonged, with women. She valued them more, felt more comfortable with them, found them more exciting and more interesting. Unknowingly, however, from the beginning Adrian chose women who resembled her mother.

Through therapy Adrian learned that her lovers made her feel the same way her mother had made her feel. She realized that they resembled her mother in uncanny ways; they even seemed to look like her mother. All of them were slender, tall, and blonde, and had an icy perfectionistic quality about them. They were always women in positions of power. They were aloof, distancing, and seductive, and not able to be warm, close, and loving.

As a child, Adrian always found her mother preoccupied. She remembered her mother's spending hours reading and rereading Thomas Mann and Simone de Beauvoir, searching for an understanding of the meaning of life. Her mother even discussed Kierkegaard and existentialism with Adrian. Her mother's sense of despair was reflected in her reading which she then discussed with Adrian.

The house Adrian grew up in was always dark. The curtains were drawn, and she sometimes felt as if she lived in a haunted house, shut away from the world. Her mother's depressive preoccupation with the meaning of life hung in the air. Additionally, she seemed unable to attend to practical necessities. When Adrian became ill, even with a minor sore throat or stomachache, her mother found it impossible to give to her. She simply could not be loving or nurturing. She could not minister to Adrian's needs or empathize with her pain and discomfort. Furthermore, Adrian had to care for her two younger sisters. She was more able than her mother to see what they needed and to care for them. Of course, it meant that she had little time for herself or for a social life. It also meant that she was constantly giving to others rather than receiving the love and affection she needed as a child.

Adrian's adult life was a repetition of her childhood. Now she was teaching children instead of taking care of her younger sisters. Her lovers were cold and distant like her mother. She even lived in a basement. Why did Adrian repeat these aspects of her childhood which had been so painful to her? She needed to repeat her childhood because she still wanted to win her mother. She had not felt her mother's love as a child; she had not felt sufficiently cared for or loved. In an attempt to come to grips with her unhappiness, Adrian blamed herself rather than her mother. She thought there must be something she was doing wrong; there must be something she could do differently; she simply had not been lovable enough. If only she could find the magic formula. If only she could figure out what she had done wrong and do it differently, then she could win her mother's love and get what she had not received in the past.

Of course, Adrian was not aware of any of this. It was a pattern she repeated time and time again in an attempt to solve the same old problem of winning her mother's love. Adrian believed that she had given up her mother. She rarely saw her or even spoke to her, and she denied feeling that her mother was important to her any more. However, in time, she was able to see that she had in fact remained tied to her mother and had continued to want her mother's love as if she were still a little girl. She had merely substituted lovers for her mother in an attempt to win her mother's love.

Therapy helped Adrian to know that she no longer needed her mother as she had needed her as a child. Adrian had not had her mother in the past and could not have her now. In fact, she no longer needed her. It was not Adrian's fault that her mother had not loved her. She was, in fact, a very lovable person. Her mother had been unable to give to her because of her mother's own inadequacies. Her mother could not give to her what she had not received herself. In time Adrian was able to give up her childhood need for her mother and learn to love women who were able to love her in return.

Still Attached

A small percentage of you never separate. You are physically out of the womb, but psychologically you and your mother are still one. You are tied to her, a part of her, as if the umbilical cord remains uncut. There is no clear boundary between you; the two of you are still fused. Your psyches are linked and feed off each other. You feel as though the two of you make one complete human being. You feel as though without her you cannot navigate the world; without her you will surely evaporate.

Your continuing fusion with your mother comes about because of your mother's feelings about herself, her world, and you. Such a mother frequently sees the world as a frightening and dangerous place and has great doubts about her ability to operate in the world with confidence and success. She feels everything is too overwhelming. If she as an adult woman cannot cope with the world, how can you, as a helpless, dependent child? She must hold onto you to protect you, to keep you safe. She also desperately needs you to stay with her to protect her, to provide her with additional bolstering and support against the cold, cruel world. She wants you to stay cute and cuddly forever so that you can stay with her and be by her side.

In addition, she is enraged at you because you have made her life more difficult. She must take care of you, help you to grow, and protect you from the dangers of the world, adding additional stress and complication to her life. By seeing herself as so incompetent, this mother inevitably hates herself, for how can she love someone who is so ineffective and helpless? This self-hate, of course, is your inheritance. Since you came out of her body, since you are part of her, you too are hated. You too are helpless and incompetent. Thus she ties you to her, trying to protect both of you from the outside world. The dual umbilical cords of anger and fear tie the two of you together for life. Together you are a loving/hating dyad, going about the process of living, unaware that the intensity of the feelings between you will inevitably cause you both to fail. Your mother, of course, does not consciously know about the anger or the fear that binds the two of you together. She thinks only that she loves you, that she must protect you from the dangers of the world and keep you close to her always. She wraps you both in a bubble, a bubble labeled love, protection, and caring.

If your mother is like this, you will invariably have difficulties as you go through your life and struggle to attain your own identity. In the most extreme case, when the necessary biological preconditions are present, you may even become schizophrenic and lose contact with reality. Jennifer, age 20, was such a woman now hospitalized with a diagnosis of paranoid schizophrenia. Jennifer's serious difficulties began while she was away in college, struggling to make herself comfortable in what seemed to be an intimidating and hostile environment. She had, however, made a few friends and had even begun dating a man, Jim, for the first time in her life. By the close of the year their romance had intensified, and they began spending the night together, sleeping cuddled in his bed. He increasingly pressured her for sex and for further explorations of her body. Additionally, her academic success had soared beyond her wildest dreams. Toward the end of the year, her English professor read one of her themes to the class. She praised the theme highly, remarking that it was an example for other students to follow.

Jennifer found herself confused by both the praise received from the teacher and Jim's sexual demands. She became increasingly distraught and was unable to sleep. She spent nights tossing and turning in her bed, having thoughts she knew were strange. Maybe her teacher was singling her out because of her beautiful long hair and not because of the theme she had written. Maybe her teacher liked her looks and not her academic performance. She could not remove this thought from her mind and began to embroider it. Maybe it was the clothes she was wearing; maybe it was her legs. She became increasingly confused by her thoughts. Finally she imagined that her teacher was playing a trick on her, praising her work so as to win Jennifer's confidence and crush her all the more when she gave her a failing grade. When Jennifer walked on the streets she became increasingly convinced that people were staring at her and knew about her teacher's attempt to trick her. At night she still could not sleep and began to have the feeling that her body was floating around the room, slowly getting bigger and filling up all the spaces. Jennifer's sentences no longer made sense, and Jim became increasingly concerned about what was happening to her. Finally, in alarm and desperation, he drove her to a hospital and talked her into admitting herself for treatment.

Jennifer's parents had been divorced when she was an infant, and from that time on she lived with her mother, older brother, and grandparents. She and her mother, Carla, shared a bedroom, and Jennifer could always remember feeling safe in the knowledge that her mother was sleeping in the next bed. Carla devoted herself to her children, particularly Jennifer, holding onto her and protecting her from the world. She protected Jennifer just as her parents had protected her. The two of them were always together. Carla sat and watched Jennifer's swimming lessons and drove her back and forth from school. Jennifer gave meaning to her mother's life.

When Jennifer wanted to walk to the park by herself or go to a friend's house to play, her mother reacted with horror. There was too much danger in the world and she loved her daughter too much to allow her to take such risks. Besides, she did not want Jennifer to leave her; she had planned for Jennifer to come grocery shopping with her. After all, she had devoted so much of her life to caring for Jennifer that it was only fair that Jennifer be there when she needed her, when she wanted her. Every time Jennifer took a step toward independence she felt terrified. The world outside was dangerous. She needed her mother. She was dependent upon her mother. Maybe she and her mother could go out into the world together, but Jennifer certainly could not do it on her own. She was little and helpless, and without her mother she might die. Even thinking about steps toward independence was "wrong," for it upset her mother and made Jennifer feel guilty. Thus Jennifer learned to always stay close to her mother; in her mind she was her mother. It was not clear to her where she stopped and her mother started, and, as she grew older, it was not clear to her where she stopped and other people started. She could not always tell whether it was she who was feeling something or whether it was her mother. She could not always tell whether it was she who was thinking something or whether it was her mother. They simply seemed to be one.

Carla hated herself; she hated her life. Her husband's desertion was proof of her unlovability. She saw herself as a big ugly duckling and, unfortunately, her little daughter could not be very different from her. Because Carla hated herself, she could easily focus this self-hate on her little ugly duckling, and frequently gave Jennifer mixed messages that left Jennifer feeling unsure of who she was or what she could or could not do. Thus there were times that her mother wanted her with her and meant it. She wanted her to go to the store with her and be by her side. At other times, however, Carla would call Jennifer to come sit on her lap and then, almost immediately, shriek in horror as she noticed that Jennifer had wrinkled her dress or stained her blouse with the pencil she was holding. The message was simultaneously come here and go away, be here and don't be here, be with me always and be with me never. Nothing was clear for Jennifer. Her mother loved her and hated her. She could be sure of nothing. Reality was ambiguous, confusing, and constantly changing.

Why did Jennifer retreat into schizophrenia just when it looked as though she were about to succeed on her own and become an independent adult? It was exactly the move toward success and independence which precipitated Jennifer's terror and subsequent psychotic breakdown. If Jennifer were to succeed in her own right, both in school and in her involvement with Jim, it would mean that she had separated from her mother. It would mean that she was a separate, independent adult. This thought evoked all of Jennifer's terrifying fantasies about separation. She really could not live without her mother; she could not survive without her. For 20 years, Carla had instilled the belief that they needed each other, that the web of love, hate, and fear binding them to each other was all that allowed them to survive in the world. Jennifer could not simply cast off her mother's teachings. She and her mother were linked together, and leaving her mother felt worse to her than cutting off a limb would feel. In the final analysis, separating from her mother meant her death, and since success meant separating, success itself meant death. Her flight into schizophrenia was her way of avoiding death.

Thus Jennifer could not allow herself to be successful. One of the ways she kept herself from believing in her success was to define her teacher's praise as trickery rather than reality. Feeling that her teacher and .other people were tricking her made Jennifer feel more helpless and vulnerable. This feeling of helpless suspicion increased her sense of not being successful and simultaneously reinforced her mother's belief that the world was dangerous. Jennifer accepted her mother's analysis of the world so that she could stay close to her, become one with her, and negate her strides toward independence and separation. Over and over, Jennifer proved to herself that any separation from her mother was dangerous, whether through a love relationship or academic success. Her mother was right. The world was dangerous and Jennifer was helpless and incompetent. Jennifer needed her mother to feel whole.

Not all of you who are still attached to your mothers have such extreme difficulties as Jennifer. Charlotte, the 45-year-old nurse discussed at the beginning of the chapter, is another example of a woman who was still attached to her mother. Although her lack of separation diminished her capacity to function fully and freely in every sphere of her life, she was able to function within the normal bounds of this society.

Getting free: Charlotte

Charlotte had now been in therapy for 14 months. She had looked at the situations which had brought her into therapy, understanding that she was mourning the loss of both her roommate and her own fertility. She also understood that it was her need for her mother which had led her to reject a promising job in Toledo. Her mother had been rejecting of her as a child and this had created in her a tremendous amount of neediness which stemmed from her unmet infantile and childhood needs.

The following part of a therapy session occurred two years after the beginning of treatment:

CHARLOTTE: I saw these flowers on my way over here and brought them for you.

THERAPIST: Oh, thank you. They're just lovely. Is there a special occasion?

CHARLOTTE: Oh, I don't know, they just looked real pretty and, ah, it's such a pretty day . . . and I just thought I'd like to give you something.

THERAPIST: That's really kind of you. It's interesting that it's so close to Mother's Day.

CHARLOTTE: Yeah, I guess it is.

THERAPIST: Do you suppose there's a connection between these flowers and Mother's Day?

CHARLOTTE: Well, I suppose, yeah, probably. Yeah, you've really been like a mother to me. You've been, you know, supportive and caring. I mean, you've been, in fact, you've been a better mother to me than my mother.

THERAPIST: A better mother than your own mother?

CHARLOTTE: Well, I'm real glad that I had you. Ah, umm, I mean, I suppose I would have been happier if I had had my mother when I, you know, when I really needed her. And I would have thought, I don't know, I guess it makes me sad, you know, that I didn't have her, but . . . Is it okay that I brought you the flowers?

THERAPIST: Yes, I really like them, but I'm wondering what it means.

CHARLOTTE: Well, you know, I think I said what it means to me. You're so important to me. You've been more of a mother than my mother and, uh . . . I'm going to have to be

seeing her for Mother's Day and, I don't know, I guess I feel
. . . ah, for the first time in my life I'm not really sure that I
want to. I've always really gone out of my way and made it a
real special day for her and . . . I don't know, I really don't
know if I even feel like doing that this year.

THERAPIST: Do you have some fantasies about what it will
be like when you see her?

CHARLOTTE: Well . . . I'm pretty angry at her. It's hard for
me to see her now and not let that anger come out. I really
feel I was cheated and that it wasn't fair.

THERAPIST: Sounds as if you feel very hurt and angry.

CHARLOTTE: Yes, I am. When I was a kid I always used to
be . . . I always used to see how my friends' mothers were
different from my own mother. My friends' mothers used to
hug 'em and kiss 'em and bake 'em cookies, and generally
seemed much warmer. Well, and look, look at the difference
between what I get from you and what I get from my mother.
I mean, you listen to me and care about me and you, you're
concerned about me and you try . . . and you're good to me
without telling me what to do.

THERAPIST: What does all that mean to you?

CHARLOTTE: Well, it means that you're real important to
me, and I realize how much you've given to me. That's why,
that's why I wanted to give you the flowers. I guess I hadn't
thought about it in relation to Mother's Day, but I'm sure
that there's a connection.

THERAPIST: Um hmm. So in some ways I'm a substitute
mother for you.

CHARLOTTE: Um hmm . . . a substitute mother and a better mother.

THERAPIST: It sounds as if I've become the ideal mother
for you.

CHARLOTTE: Yeah, you are. You're just like what I would
have wanted my mother to be. I mean, you're just so different
from how my mother was. Even when I was sick with rheumatic fever, my mother just couldn't be there for me; she
never wanted to listen to me and she would never really take
care of me. It's not at all like you, like even when I have a

cold or something you really are more concerned about me and ask about me, and I really . . . that's really important to me.

THERAPIST: So I've become the fairy godmother and your mother is the wicked witch.

CHARLOTTE: Yeah, that's about how it feels to me by now. It hasn't always felt that way to me. I used to feel that my mother was the fairy godmother and that it was all my fault . . . that I had been . . . that I hadn't been good enough. But, yeah, now when I've seen that somebody can be warm and care for me, yeah, I feel you're my fairy godmother and my mother is the wicked witch.

Charlotte is now seeing her therapist the way she saw her mother when she was little. She sees the therapist as the perfect mother, as a fairy godmother, as a powerful woman who is able and willing to give her everything. And, in fact, Charlotte's therapist was able to provide warmth, understanding, and acceptance through which Charlotte was able to develop a new sense of herself. She learned that people can be giving rather than rejecting, loving rather than hostile. Of course, this is not the end point of therapy. Charlotte still needs to understand that her mother really is not the wicked witch but simply a human being with strengths and weaknesses, a mother with adequacies and inadequacies. Similarly, Charlotte's therapist is not a fairy godmother. She is also a human being, an imperfect being with strengths and weaknesses. She is not even a perfect therapist.

What has happened in these two years of therapy to lead Charlotte to feel so strongly about her therapist? Charlotte has grown to realize that her mother was not perfect, that, in fact, she was rejecting and unable to give of herself. Most importantly, Charlotte has learned that this rejection was not Charlotte's fault. She was and is lovable, despite the fact that her mother could not give to her. Charlotte had felt so unloved that she had become a pediatric nurse so that she could give babies and abused children the love she wished she herself had received.

Charlotte also began to understand that, in addition to being ungiving, her mother was unable to let her go. Charlotte's childhood illness had increased her dependency on her mother. Her mother had then unknowingly used Charlotte's illness to maintain her dependence, to keep Charlotte from growing up. She had enrolled six-year-old Charlotte into kindergarten rather than into the first grade. This began the pattern of trying to hold onto Charlotte. In therapy, Charlotte learned that her asexuality was her way of staying young and childlike, her way of remaining close to and tied to her mother. She had no other allegiances in her life. At age 45, Charlotte still called her mother daily and made decisions on the basis of her mother's feelings and attitudes. A woman who never really separated from her mother, Charlotte remained tied to her, fused with her, and therefore could not grow into a mature, separate adult.

In addition to making these intellectual connections, Charlotte had begun to be more aware of her feelings toward herself, her mother, and other people. Thus, as the therapy excerpt demonstrates, Charlotte has begun to talk about her anger at her mother, her anger at not receiving the love and caring that she deserved. She is now able to feel this anger because she knows she is, in fact, a lovable person who deserves the warmth and affection that her mother was unable to give her. Much of her awareness of her lovableness has come from her relationship with her therapist. Her therapist's warmth, kindness, and support have enabled Charlotte to know that people can be warm and loving, and, most importantly, that Charlotte deserves that kind of care and attention. A person learns that she is lovable by being treated as a lovable person, and that is what the therapist made possible for Charlotte.

Another aspect of Charlotte's therapy was the exploration of new behaviors. The therapist encouraged her to have successes outside of therapy which, in turn, bolstered Charlotte's self-esteem and her awareness of the world as a more positive place. For example, Charlotte, with the therapist's encouragement, risked taking a ceramics class and became more active in her church. She began to make friends outside of work and enjoyed dining out, bowling, and even ice skating with her new-found friends. This was all very frightening to Charlotte at first, but she took the risk and began to develop some solid friendships. Unfortunately, men still seemed a strange breed to Charlotte. She had spent so much of her life without them that she did not know if she could open up to them now. Charlotte may have waited too long before trying to separate from her mother and, as a result, may be unable to become totally free of her. It is possible that a part of her may always remain too childlike to open up freely to men. Charlotte was willing to try, but she did not know if she would be successful.

Charlotte's eventual leavetaking from her therapist might help her to gain greater freedom from her mother and offer her a greater possibility of exploring sexual relationships. Charlotte must realize that even her therapist is not perfect and that she can let go of her as well. Charlotte's increased involvement in new relationships may help her to see her therapist as a human being rather than as the perfect mother. She may come to realize that other people as well will love her and fulfill her needs for warmth, caring, and affection. In the therapy excerpt, Charlotte still believes in the myth of the perfect mother and continues striving to find this mother in the person of her therapist. Charlotte needs to learn that she no longer needs a mother, that she is an adult, that she can take care of her own needs. This knowledge, in conjunction with her increased relationships outside of therapy, will help her to let go of her therapist as the idealized mother figure.

Separating from mother involves the resolution of both your dependency and your rage. Your mother was not the fairy godmother and she was not the wicked witch. The vulnerability, the dependency, and the terror of your childhood are no more. You are an adult and you can take care of yourself.

3

Giving Up Daddy:
THE KNIGHT IN SHINING
ARMOR AND THE BAD GUY

Dorothy had always hated funerals. Now, her father, the person she loved most in the world, was dead. Seventy years old and dead of a heart attack. Standing by her father's grave, surrounded by her mother, four older brothers, and her father's other friends and relatives, she felt numb.

"What will happen to me without my father?" she thought. Shocked by the finality of her father's body going into his grave, she could feel her heart pounding, hear its echo in her ears, and feel her pulse beating in her temples. A wave of nausea swept over her. Her palms were sweaty, and she could feel sweat trickling under her coat. Her heart pounded louder and louder, the tempo increasing. She struggled for breath, gasping, "I'm having a heart attack too. This is what it feels like. This is what it felt like for him," she thought, her terror and panic rising even more sharply.

"Think about something else, anything," she thought, and focused on her next project at work. She managed to get herself under control but was terrified by her experience. After the funeral she tried to forget her father's death, threw herself back into her work, and tried to feel nothing. However, her dizzy spells, combined with fast, loud heartbeats, continued. Dorothy became convinced that something was wrong with her heart and consulted a cardiologist. The doctor's examination revealed no physical basis for her symptoms, and he referred her to a psychotherapist.

Dorothy was the only daughter of an upper-middle-class

family. The relationship between Dorothy's parents was polite but not loving. Her father was a successful corporate attorney; her mother devoted herself to being a perfect housewife—keeping a neat house and cooking gourmet meals and being president of the Junior League.

Dorothy was a good little girl. Her father doted on his infant daughter, rocking her on his leg and spending hours playing with her on the floor. He was always cuddling her and rubbing her back to help her go to sleep. When she was in elementary school, he loved showing her off to all his colleagues. As a teenager, Dorothy would often be mistaken for her father's girlfriend and would be treated with a mixture of curiosity and hidden sexuality. Dorothy reacted to this response with a mixture of pride at being considered so grown up and humiliation. When Dorothy was 19, she learned that her father was having an affair with a woman her own age.

As an adult, Dorothy became a successful businesswoman, rising high in her profession and receiving much esteem from others, especially from her father. She lived alone, and although she had many superficial friendships she had no close friends or intimate relationships. She had several affairs during college and her young adulthood, but these were fleeting and meaningless. Sex was not important to Dorothy, and she was never orgasmic except when masturbating.

Dorothy did not, however, enter therapy because she was unhappy or felt that anything was lacking in her life. She simply had to stop her "attacks," and she hoped therapy would provide the means.

The Importance of Fathers

Your father is important because you love him. When you are a child your father cares for you, feeds you, clothes you, holds you, and loves you. Your father helps you to discover who you are. He gives you joy; he shows you how to have fun. Your father is half of your entire world. The ideal situation is one in which you, the infant daughter, crawl around the floor exploring the world and, when you touch his shoe, he smiles down at you; he encourages your exploration and lets you know that you are doing fine. The importance of your father is that, together with your mother, he makes you feel safe and secure.

Men's image and role. Your father also provides you with the earliest image of what to expect of men in later life. If, for example, your parents are affectionate to each other and to you and your siblings, you learn that men and women can have fun together. On the other hand, if your father comes home and beats your mother, you learn that men can be dangerous. If your father vacillates between warmth and indifference, you learn that men cannot be trusted. By his relationship with both you and your mother, he shows you as a growing girl what you can expect from men in your adult life. Inevitably, when you are a little girl you feel that your house is a microcosm of the whole world. You assume that what is happening in your family, between your mother and father, is what happens between men and women everywhere.

You also learn each of your parent's role, both in the family and in the outside world. Traditionally, your father is the primary person who deals with the outside world and has the greatest degree of freedom. It is his job to protect the family and to be the connection between the nuclear family and society at large. He works outside the home and brings in money. His position defines the status of your family. The traditional picture consists of the man as the breadwinner for the family and the woman as the homemaker. The man makes the decisions outside the home, the woman makes them within the home.

If your father is excited about dealing with the world and is successful at it, you have the opportunity to feel more competent in the world, to experience the world as less frightening. This is possible so long as at least one of your parents gives you permission to follow in your father's footsteps. Thus, while your father provides a model for mastery in the outside world, you need your mother's permission to define yourself as a woman who can be successful. For example, suppose your father is a carpenter and your mother is excited about and respects his work. If your mother is able to share these feelings with you and give you permission to learn to be a carpenter, you may grow up enjoying cabinetmaking or carpentry. It is important to note that for successful mastery, the feeling of competence and satisfaction is the issue rather than the acquisition of prestige or status. In other words, to be successful is to feel good about one's work, whatever it is and aside from how much money it may bring in.

Thus your father is a potential model. You may copy and learn to enjoy those things he enjoys. You may value what your father values or behave in ways he behaves. You, of course, do not copy only your father but rather look to him to provide one alternative way of being in the world.

Definition of womanness. Your father also defines what you as a woman are supposed to be and how you are to behave. He does this first by his relationship with his wife and second by his relationship with you. For example, if he enjoys teaching you how to take a car apart, he gives you the message that this is an acceptable activity for a woman. However, if he takes only your brother into the garage and tells you to help your mother in the kitchen, he gives you a clear message about how women should not behave. If your father plays sports with you when you are young and encourages you to hit the ball as hard as possible and run as fast as possible, he gives you a message that these activities are acceptable for a girl. Your father may also enjoy seeing you dressed up and looking pretty in your most feminine clothes. In this way he gives you permission to be athletic and competitive as well as feminine.

This description of a father's role, both in the family and in the outside world, is the traditional role of men in relation to women in this culture and is in the process of change. More mothers are presenting their daughters with new role models for mastery. You now learn from both your own mother and society at large that you can be successful in the outside world. You can be whatever you choose to be, an electrician, housewife, or doctor. With the change to less rigid sex roles, mothers and fathers together provide dual models for both successful mastery and interpersonal relationships.

Heterosexual love object. There is one way in which a father's influence has not changed—he always provides the first heterosexual love object for his little girl. Your father is the first male about whom you feel sexual. The traditional notion of childhood sexuality is that the child desires genital contact with the opposite-sexed parent. An alternative interpretation is that childhood sexuality is the child's desire for total possession of the parent. According to this view, the desire for possession is experienced as a generalized excitement, as a total bodily excitement, not focused primarily on the genital region. As a small child, you glow with love, excitement, safety, warmth, and good feelings when your parent enters the room. As an adult, you express these feelings along sexual lines with someone other than your father. When you are an infant and toddler, however, these feelings need not be primarily genital or sexual. They may be interpreted as sexual by your parent, or by you as an adult as you review your childhood, but not by you when you are still a child.

Your parents may be well aware of some of the signs of this generalized excitement and sexuality you feel toward your father. For example, you may ask your father to marry you. Such a proposal need not reflect your wish to have your father's penis in your vagina or your wish to do away with your mother. What it may reflect is your desire to have your father to yourself and your annoyance at having to share him with your mother and other people. In order for you to pass through this stage with minimal trauma, your father's response to your expressed wishes must be appropriate; that is, he must let you know that you are desirable and that your feelings are understandable and acceptable. He must also communicate that these feelings will not be acted upon with him. Your father must let you know that you are a sexually attractive person without being seductive or giving you the message that the sexual feelings you both share will be actualized.

One difficulty that your father may have at this point is

that he may become frightened by his own sexual feelings and therefore become rejecting of you. His rejection then makes you feel that your own sexual feelings are frightening and unacceptable. On the other hand, your father may be too seductive toward you and, as a result, you may become overwhelmed by your own sexual feelings. As an adult woman, you may then attempt to resolve these past feelings toward your father in your choice of a sexual partner. You may attempt to hold onto your father forever by marrying a man who is similar to him. Or you may marry a man who is the diametrical opposite of your father, a choice which indicates your panic concerning your sexual feelings toward your father.

The absent father. Your father is important to you whether he is actually in the home when you are growing up or not. If he is absent, you may grow up with your mother's image of men. For example, if your father deserted your mother while she was pregnant with you, you are then reared with your mother's disappointment, sadness, rage, and suspicion about men. As it was in your mother's life, so it seems it must be for you. If, on the other hand, your father died, you may be raised with an unrealistic set of feelings about him. You and your mother together may hold onto a cherished memory of the man who was, and together strengthen each other by remembering how loving, good, and kind he was. Thus you may grow up with an unrealistic image of what to expect from men. If your parents divorce, you must reconcile your mother's feelings about your father with your own experience of him. For example, you may have a very positive, loving relationship with your father, so that your experience with him leaves you with one image. But your mother may be embittered by the divorce and may communicate this to you in a way that creates a different and conflicting image of him. Thus you are caught between your own good feelings toward your father and your mother's feelings of anger and pain.

Despite a desertion, death, or divorce, your father or your image of him plays a crucial role in your life. Under propitious circumstances, he provides a safe place for you to experience your own sexuality and your striving for competence in the outside world. It is important for you to have this rehearsal in order for you to become an adult woman with the capacity for competence in the outside world and the ability to sustain intimate and close sexual relationships.

But the closeness with your father must be regarded as a rehearsal, not a permanent situation. Going from the safety of your home and your loving father to the casual indifference of the outside world is the difficult and slow process of growing up. To resolve this separation in a healthy way, you as an adult must come to know both that you cannot have your father and that you do not need him. You can continue to appreciate him for his fine qualities but at the same time see him as a human being who is not perfect. Your acceptance of him in this way will allow mutual respect to grow between the two of you as adults. Giving up daddy is eased by having had a healthy enough relationship with him that you are able to go beyond that relationship to healthy relationships with other adult men. If the relationship with your father was characterized by either overindulgence or rejection, healthy separation will be more difficult.

Strategies of Dealing with Father

Regardless of your relationship with your father, he represents one half of your world when you are a child. He represents one way of being in the world, one way for you to model yourself or choose to be. You love your father a great deal and recognize his power over you. As a result of all these aspects of being a little girl and living with your father, you want to stay close to him and take part of daddy with you as you grow up and move through life.

This process of growing up is normal and healthy. People grow up to be like their parents. There are many folk sayings which recognize this fact, such as, "The apple doesn't fall far from the tree." Growing up is difficult because you love your father and find it hard to leave him. But growing up means that you have to leave him, and one of the ways of doing this is to take parts of him with you. This process becomes destructive when as an adult you do not have the ability to let go of your father in a healthy manner, and by holding onto him you limit your freedom.

Internalization. One of the ways of holding onto daddy is to internalize him, to become like him. Internalizing is a two-part process. As you do your mother, you see your father as a model and imitate his behavior, attitudes, and ways of being. For example, if your father enjoys watching the sunset and sharing it with you, you may learn to enjoy sunsets and other aspects of your natural environment. These experiences shared with your father lead you to enjoy them later in life when your father is not present. At this point, your behavior is internalized. In other words, first you model your behavior after your father. Later you experience that behavior as part of you, as your own, as a fact about you coming from your own needs and desires. You are not aware that you have swallowed an aspect of your father and are now using it in your repertoire of behavior.

You use the same process in internalizing your father that you use in internalizing your mother. Your father is thrilled by the ways in which you are like him and praises you. You feel his pride and feel good about yourself. You repeat these behaviors to get still more of your father's praise. Thus you become like your father without knowing that you are like him. As a child you take in an aspect of your father and keep it for your own, and in this way you stay close to him.

For example, assume that your father adores wearing red shirts and is thrilled to be able to buy you a red velvet dress. Your father does not tell you to wear red; nor does he teach you to wear red. But you associate the wearing of red with good feelings about him and with his good feelings about you. As an adult you know that red is your favorite color but do not know why. Obviously if you remain fond of the color red but like other colors as well, this internalization does not present difficulties for you. But if, on the other hand, you can wear only the color red and have to decorate your entire house in red, this way of staying close to your father is restricting your freedom.

Identification with the aggressor. Another way of staying close to your father is by identifying with him as the aggressor. Your father has a great deal of power in the family, and you may be frightened both by your helplessness and by certain aspects of his power. One way to deal with this fear is to become like him in those aspects you are most afraid of. In other words, you may internalize the part of your father that frightens you. This is your attempt to become the victimizer rather than the victim. An example of identification with the aggressor is for you to become violently explosive as a way of defending against your father's explosiveness. You see your explosive father as both powerful and in control of you. You, the helpless child, yearn to reverse this situation. Thus in trying to gain independence and self-sufficiency, you internalize the explosiveness in an effort to acquire the power and control for yourself. For example, Laurie, a 19-year-old single woman, had a father who always found fault with her. In fact, he found fault with everyone and everything, until he succeeded in isolating the family from almost all social contact. As she grew up, Laurie discovered that she too found something unpleasant about everyone; nobody was perfect. She had no friends, since nobody was good enough. Laurie became like her father in order to gain the power she had experienced him as having when he verbally attacked her as a child.

A more striking example is Gladys, a 38-year-old white, single woman, who, as a child, had been repeatedly and violently raped by her father. She was enraged both at her father and at her mother for not protecting her from this violation. Understandably, Gladys felt that only men had power. As she grew up, she found it comfortable to wear men's clothes and to look as much like a man as possible. Gladys kept her hair very short. She wore men's trousers and shoes, a man's watch, a tailored shirt and a trenchcoat, jockey shorts, and no bra. Her manner of dress did not reflect her admiration for men; on the contrary, she was terrified of men, hated them, and avoided contact with them whenever possible. In therapy she observed, "I've often wondered why I look like a man, dress like a man, and act like a man, when I hate men so much." In becoming like the person who had hurt her most, Gladys was demonstrating identification with the aggressor. Gladys learned in time that this was the way she had devised in childhood to control her pain, to prevent it from happening again. That is, if she had been a boy, she could have prevented her father from raping her. So becoming as much like a man as possible not only protected her from her father but also kept her close to him in a safe way. In other words, although Gladys hated her father she also loved him. Unfortunately, in becoming like him in those aspects she hated she wound up hating that part of herself. By holding onto her father she was, in effect, keeping a hated thing inside her.

Rebellion. To rebel is another way of holding onto your father, although, taken at face value, your actions appear to indicate that you have let him go. Rebellion is doing the opposite of what your parents tell you to do, or being the opposite of what they are. For example, your parents may see themselves as intellectuals and spend most of their free time reading books. If you, on the other hand, disparage reading and feel that peace and contentment can only be found in sports, your attitude can be seen as a rebellion. It is the extreme nature of your behavior which indicates its rebellious quality. For example, if in your attempt to separate from your family you cut off all family ties, your behavior is extreme. The intensity and extent of the separation indicates that you feel defensive; it is not a true separation but rather a defense against separation.

You may find that rebellion also plays a part in your interpersonal relationships. For example, if your father is a corporate executive, you may rebel against your need for him by choosing as lovers men who are consistently unsuccessful. On the surface it may seem that you are totally separated from your father, but, again, the intensity of the disparity indicates your rebellion. Your need to deny your closeness to your father and your desire for him lead you to choose men who are vastly different from him. You may even fool yourself into believing you are entirely indifferent to your corporate-executive father by consistently choosing men who have not even finished high school. You are rebelling against those aspects of your father which in some way are crucial or important to you, those aspects which somehow encapsulate your image of your father.

Another example of rebellion is offered by Pat, an incest victim, the daughter of an attorney, who came into therapy when she was 24. When Pat was seven, her father came into her room, pinned her arm behind her back, caressed her body, and gently massaged her vulva. After that incident, his sexual contact with her increased and intensified. Initially, each sexual contact was preceded by his twisting her arm behind her back and threatening her. By the time she was nine, he was having oral sex with her and had so aroused her that she was orgasmic. Her body had learned to respond to his sexual prodding. The only love and affection she received in the home were from her father and always in this sexual context. Because of her increasing arousal and enjoyment of the sexual contact, Pat felt guilty. She felt that she was responsible for her father's molesting her. Her guilt was the result of the pleasure that she had begun to feel. She did not know what she had done to make her father act so strangely.

As Pat became pubescent, her guilt increased. Her shame and embarrassment about her father's being sexual with her became overwhelming. Her face took on a hard, angry look as a defense against her feeling of desire for her father and the shame that went along with that desire. Finally, she told her father that he could not touch her any more because she was afraid she might get pregnant. She repeatedly threatened to tell her mother, and when she reached 14 he finally stopped molesting her.

As Pat grew up she plunged into sports and social activities in her high school. These included Future Teachers of America, the Debating Society, and the softball team. From these clubs she progressed to involvement in more feminist-oriented groups. These political groups reinforced her anger and legitimized it. She could be justly angry about women's role in society. Thus she could be angry at all men rather than just at her father. Being angry helped her suppress her sexual feelings for her father. She could not possibly be sexual if she were so angry. She had found a political movement on which to hang her psychological hat.

As an adult, Pat avoided sexual involvements. In fact, all sexual feelings were frightening to her. She was aware that when people approached her sexually she became uncomfortable and wanted to avoid the contact. Therefore, Pat appeared to be an angry separatist who was entirely asexual. The last thing anyone would assume was that Pat was fighting back her own sexual feelings to defend herself against feeling sexual toward her father. But this was in fact the case. Pat had rebelled against her father rather than working through her feelings of wanting him. Although she expressed hatred for him on the surface, underneath she had a strong need for him and a fear of living without him. Her guilt about her sexual feelings and her sexual pleasure with her father had made her repress her love for him and had caused her to become an angry separatist. Removing the guilt enabled Pat to feel both her love and her hate for her father.

Therapy helped Pat get back in touch with the feelings of love and fear she had had as a little girl. At the same time, it helped her to recognize that she was no longer a child. As an adult she was not dependent on her father; rather, she was in a position to leave him and seek fulfilling sexual relationships. In addition, she came to understand that the incest was not her fault, and that she was not "bad" for still having loving, warm feelings toward her father. Thus Pat is an example of a person who used rebellion to hide, even from herself, her positive feelings toward her father. She acted the reverse of how she felt, spending her emotional energy fighting against her girlhood father whom she had not let go.

Repetition of the relationship. Still another way to hold onto your father is to become involved with men who are similar to him. If you are involved with a man who is like your father, then you need never give your father up. This repetition is not necessarily unhealthy. For example, if you see your father as warm, kind, and generous and repeat this relationship by marrying a warm, kind, and generous man, you may find fulfillment.

However, if you repeat painful aspects of your relationship with your father, your behavior is self-destructive. For example, if you had an alcoholic father, you may choose an alcoholic lover as well. Why would anyone who grew up living with the agony of an alcoholic father choose to repeat the experience as an adult? Again, you choose it because you loved your father and he loved you. It does not matter that he came home reeking of alcohol and often beat your mother. He was still your father, and along with your fear of him or hatred for him you felt a tremendous love. So as a grownup you may find yourself inexplicably drawn to men with drinking problems as a way of remaining close to your father. When you were little you had no control or power over your father's drinking or the violent outbursts that resulted from his drinking. You felt powerless to change him or the situation. However, as an adult you may unconsciously believe that by involving yourself with alcoholic men you can control them, reform them. You can be the person who makes them different, and thereby you can symbolically control your father. Indirectly you hope to reform your father who will then be grateful to you and love you unconditionally. Certainly you, as an adult woman married to an alcoholic man, have a sense of yourself as separate from your family of origin. Yet in the recesses of your mind you may be aware that you are living life as your mother did. Through your marriage you are redoing your childhood by symbolically rescuing and changing your father.

Still another way of hanging onto your father by repeating the relationship is to become involved with married men. You may feel safer and more familiar with a married man because your father was married. You may be engaging in a fantasy of winning your father from your mother by taking the married man away from his wife. Or if your father was overindulgent or overly sexual with you, you may seek to hold onto him by being with a man who is like him, that is, one who is married. If you perceive your father as rejecting or unreachable, you may choose a married man who is also rejecting. This may be your attempt to get the love from a married man that you did not get from the other married man in your life, namely, your father. Sadly, your very choice of a rejecting man makes it impossible for you to ever win the love that you want.

You may go through a whole string of married men, or you may attach yourself to one married man for a long period of time, never quite giving up the illusion that he will leave his wife for you. For many women, the attraction is the fact that the man is married; if the man should leave his wife, he then is no longer seen as attractive.

For example, Carol, a 31-year-old white woman, had been involved with a married man for nine years. Her father had been a Marine Corps sergeant in charge of boot camp training. He was a cold, rejecting man who beat her, her mother, and her siblings. Carol felt that she hated her father. She had not seen him for years and said she wanted nothing to do with him. Her lover, Stan, was a professional hockey player who gloried in the violence of the sport. Because he was married, Stan had little time for Carol. Additionally, their times together often ended in physical brawls, one of which once sent Carol to the hospital. Thus she had picked a man who was violent and unreachable like her father. Carol had broken up with and gone back to Stan at least two dozen times. She continued to believe that he would leave his wife and marry her. Stan kept assuring Carol that his relationship with his wife was nonsexual and not important to him. He said that he was staying in his marriage for the children. Then Stan's wife became pregnant again. This was the final blow to Carol and she came into therapy.

How does a woman get hooked into being involved with a man in such a destructive way? Carol became increasingly, though slowly, aware that this man was like her father. What was it about her father that made her need so desperately to repeat that relationship with another man? Logic would seem to indicate that the pain of giving him up and trying a different life style would be easier to bear than continuing on her present course. But Carol, like many of you, yearned to see her parent as perfect and somehow felt that her father's imperfection was her fault. Parents, of course, reinforce this notion in a thousand ways by casual statements such as, "You're driving me crazy," "You're making me mad," "Why the hell did you spill the milk on the floor—look what a mess you made for me to clean up." The message to the child is that the things that go wrong and that distress the parent are her fault. Then, whenever the parent behaves irrationally, the child blames herself.

Thus Carol felt that if she could be perfect, her father would no longer beat her. She tried very hard as a child to be a good little girl, carefully cleaning up her room every day, talking softly, walking around the walls of the room so she would not accidentally trip over her father's feet and enrage him. Though she tried very hard to be perfect, she felt that she had failed because she was not quite perfect enough to keep him from becoming enraged and beating her. Although it was very painful for her to feel that it was her fault that her father was violent, the alternative was even more terrifying. And that alternative was that she was totally helpless and could neither prevent her father from beating her nor change him. The terror that this idea evoked was the terror of death. To keep herself from feeling this terror, she continued to try to be perfect and to attempt to win her father in her adulthood through her relationship with the married hockey player. If only she did the right thing, if only she was perfect enough, she felt, he would leave his wife, be with her, and stop being violent.

In order to give up this relationship, Carol needed to reexperience the terror and vulnerability she had felt as a little girl. She needed to feel that in fact she could not control her father's rage and could do nothing to make him be different. While this realization was too frightening for her to deal with as a child because of her helplessness and dependency, Carol now was not helpless and vulnerable and could live without attempting to control her father or his substitutes. Thus she needed to feel again the pain she felt as a child in order to come to know her strength as an adult.

Sometimes women not only repeat the relationship with their "bad" father but also re-create the feelings of helplessness and dependency they had as children. An example is

Harriet, a 45-year-old white woman who had been in prison for five years for the murder of her husband, Bill. Harriet came from a poor Appalachian family, one of seven children. Her father was an alcoholic, a violent man who would come home at night, drunk, and beat up the family members as they lay sleeping in their beds. He deserted the family when Harriet was ten. Harriet married very young in an attempt to get out of the home. Unfortunately, the man she chose to marry was like her father—alcoholic and violent.

For more than 20 years her marriage was fraught with beatings, poverty, and sudden moves to different parts of the country. Bill took odd jobs such as handyman, janitor, and construction worker. Most of the time, however, he was un-employed and the family was on welfare. They had four children. Over the 20-odd years of marriage, Bill beat Harriet many times. One time he locked her in the closet for four days. She escaped and ran across a snowy field and was hospitalized. Bill came to the hospital, yanked the intravenous tubes out of her arm, and took her home. On another occasion, Harriet was hospitalized because Bill broke her leg. Thus Harriet's life was filled with unceasing violence and inescapable poverty and pain. She had repeated her father-child relationship with her husband. Even though Harriet was now an adult, she had managed to create a situation in which she duplicated the trapped, helpless, vulnerable position she had been in as a child. Harriet hated this position and felt terribly sad and frustrated, but could not figure out a way to live without her husband. She did not know how to take care of herself and her children. At times, when she found her position totally unbearable, she would make tentative attempts to leave him. However, Bill would always find her, beat her up worse than before, and drag her home.

One night Harriet was awakened by a brutal pain. Bill had been out drinking and had come home angry and abusive. She was aware that it was happening again, that there was no way out, that the pain would go on and on. She reached into the drawer of the bedside table, got Bill's gun, and shot him. She could not believe that she had done it. She could not even remember shooting him. But there he lay, on the floor, with blood coming out of his chest, still and quiet at last.

Harriet saw a therapist in the prison and came to understand that she had repeated with her husband her relationship with her father in an attempt to ultimately win her father's love. She also recognized that she had reestablished herself in the helpless, vulnerable position of her childhood. Having gained this insight into her behavior Harriet felt more secure about leaving prison; she realized she could face the world without repeating her self-destructive pattern still another time.

Thus we see how very important your father is to you. You as a little girl loved your daddy so much, cared about him so deeply, that you wanted to have him forever. It was difficult to let go, so difficult that you found many different ways to hold onto him, such as internalization, identification with the aggressor, rebellion, and repeating the relationship.

Getting Free: Dorothy

Dorothy, the professional woman presented at the beginning of this chapter, came into therapy at the age of 35. She had been having repeated anxiety attacks following the death of her indulgent, 70-year-old father. Psychotherapy helped Dorothy to understand the connection between her feelings toward her father and her anxiety attacks.

The process of therapy is analogous to peeling an onion, with the outside layer coming off first, and then successive layers peeling off, exposing each layer underneath. This was true for Dorothy. At first she needed to make the intellectual connections between her current behavior and her childhood patterns. Then she needed to connect these understandings with her feelings so that she could try new kinds of behavior that would be more adaptive for her.

During the first phase of therapy Dorothy needed to learn how her father's death led to her anxiety attacks. She was, in effect, redoing her father's heart attack by having similar symptoms herself. In this way she was able to keep him alive, to keep him there forever. This was an indication of her tremendous need for him. As Dorothy slowly began to get a picture of her childhood, she was able to see that her father had been overly indulgent toward her. He had given her too much attention, favoring her over her siblings and her mother. He had pampered her and overprotected her and had not sufficiently encouraged her independent mastery except in the area of academic performance.

When Dorothy's father rocked his infant daughter on his leg and massaged her back before she went to sleep, he saw this as being loving and close; he did not realize that it was sexually arousing. Obviously, touching between parent and child is not in and of itself inappropriate; quite to the contrary, it creates a sense of security, comfort, well-being, and warmth. Touching is necessary for the child's development of sexuality and individuality. However, there are appropriate limits. The sexual feelings within the parent are what create the problems; that is, the acting out of unconscious sexual feelings on the part of the parent ends up being the seduction for the child. Children evoke sexual feelings in all parents. Parents who feel secure in their sexuality and enjoy appropriate sexual outlets are able to be more comfortable with their sexual feelings toward their children. Parents who have difficulty with this issue fear they will be overwhelmed by their own sexual feelings toward their children. Thus they vehemently repress their sexual and sensual feelings toward their children, which they then act out in an unconscious, seductive manner. This is what happened between Dorothy and her father.

It was the way Dorothy's father touched her and the expression on his face that conveyed to her his arousal. He did not have to use words for her to sense that massaging her back was arousing for him. It was not what Dorothy's father did, it was how he felt when he did it. These feelings were sexual, were communicated to Dorothy, and stimulated similar feelings in her. These sexual feelings for her father became terrifying to Dorothy, for she knew instinctively that these feelings were "wrong." She also feared the rage of her mother if her mother were to know how Dorothy felt toward "her man." Then, just when Dorothy was beginning to explore her own sexual feelings, she learned of her father's affair. This affair with a woman her own age was frightening to Dorothy. On the one hand, she felt almost as if her father were having an affair with Dorothy herself; on the other, she felt rejected and replaced. The affair also intensified her sexual feelings toward her father because it made it seem, for the first time, that sex with her father was really possible.

In order to avoid the intensity of this conflict, and to keep from feeling her sexual feelings, Dorothy totally turned off her sexuality and no longer felt sexual. Even though as an adult Dorothy did have sexual relationships, they meant nothing to her. She did not have any sexual feelings during these experiences but rather felt herself a spectator. Turning off her sexual feelings did not mean she had turned off her affectionate feelings toward her father. In fact, her lack of sexual responsiveness to other men was a way for her to be faithful to her father without being incestous. It was a safe way out. Dorothy stayed close by internalizing him, and being, like him, successful in business.

These are the underlying reasons for Dorothy's anxiety attacks after her father's death. In therapy, Dorothy came to understand these reasons and to see the connections between her past history and her present behavior. In addition to gaining these intellectual insights, Dorothy also needed to become reacquainted with her feelings. Since it is almost impossible to turn off one set of feelings without diminishing the others, Dorothy's suppression of her sexual feelings resulted in the diminution of all her feelings; that is, she could not feel real sadness, real anger, or real happiness. The process of therapy involves repeated focus on feelings. The therapist asks questions such as, "What do you feel when you remember that incident?" or, "What are you feeling now?" or, "What are you feeling about me?" The purpose of these questions is to help the client get reacquainted with her feelings, to look at them and feel them and know they are all right.

Focusing on feelings also encourages the client to be intimate with the therapist. This part of the therapeutic process is essential, for it allows the client to know that genuine warmth and caring between people is possible. It builds trust. It proves to the client that it is possible to be close without being sexual. In addition, encouraging the expression of feelings between client and therapist allows the client to generalize these feelings to other people outside the office. The client comes to feel that if she can trust and feel close to her therapist, she can risk duplicating this closeness with other people.

In Dorothy's case, she needed to feel her present sadness about the loss of her father and her anger at his death. She needed to remember and reexperience the feelings she had prior to her anxiety attacks. She needed to know what her thoughts and fantasies were prior to these attacks, and how these thoughts and fantasies were tied to the past. In the process of therapy Dorothy reexperienced her feelings, coming to a new understanding of them with the help of the therapist's interpretations.

Dorothy needed not only to get in touch with her adult feelings but also her childhood feelings. She needed to reexperience her feelings of closeness to her father and her feelings of dependency on him. In addition, she needed to remember her past sexual feelings for her father. In therapy you do not always have to get in touch with past sexual feelings, because these are usually appropriately buried in the unconscious. For Dorothy, however, reexperiencing her childhood sexual feelings was a prerequisite for further growth, because in the process of keeping down these feelings she had buried all of her sexual feelings and diminished her other feelings as well.

Dreams often help a client to bridge the gap between adult life and childhood feelings and events. Luckily, this was true for Dorothy. In the middle of treatment, Dorothy told the therapist a dream in which she was peacefully walking up a ladder into the sky with her boss who was behind her, gently holding her hand. As she seemed almost to glide up the ladder, she became increasingly aware of the green grass dotted with flowers below and the blue sky above filled with fluffy clouds. In reflecting on her thoughts about this dream, Doro-

thy was able to see that her boss was a stand-in for her father
and that some of the blissful, oceanic feelings she had as she
glided up the ladder were similar to the sexual feelings she felt
as a child when her father massaged her back at night.

This dream helped Dorothy to unlock her hidden childhood feelings. She was able to feel her closeness with her
father and dimly recall her past longings for him. She also felt
the reality of not being able to possess her father. As a child
she could not have him, and now as an adult she could not
have him. And, in dealing with her rage about not being able
to have her father, Dorothy was able to realize that she did
not need her father any more. As a child she needed him,
wanted him, and was dependent on him. This dependency
was a life or death dependency. As an adult she did not need
him in the same way. She did not want him as she had wanted
him in childhood. Now she could take care of herself and her
own needs. Dorothy was able to look at her father as a human
being, a nice, loving man with many positive strengths and
many weaknesses. She did not need to see him as a perfect,
god-like being. Dorothy was now free to explore intimate relationships with others.

At this point in the therapeutic process, Dorothy's therapist encouraged her to risk becoming intimate with people
outside of therapy, to open up and to consider them in a new
light. With this encouragement, Dorothy was able to relate to
others and to appreciate them and their unique qualities,
while at the same time opening herself up to increased involvement. Dorothy slowly became less driven at work, taking
more time to share herself with others. By drawing upon the
sharing she had done with her therapist and the closeness she
had felt to her, Dorothy was increasingly able to take more
risks and to be more open.

The freedom to allow intimate relationships is always the
issue in giving up daddy. Regardless of whether you experienced your daddy as rejecting, overindulgent, or molesting, as
an adult you come to know that you do not need him as you
did when you were a child. You cannot have him and do not
need him. You are separate from him.

4

The Struggle for Survival:
OMNIPOTENCE AND VULNERABILITY

Wringing her hands, Betty looked at her taut, tense face in the mirror. She was a bright, 32-year-old married woman, mother of a beautiful infant son, Don. Betty was a social worker, one of the few black women from her neighborhood who had made it. She told herself over and over again, "Nothing is wrong, nothing is wrong." But she could not control her rising panic and compulsion to check again on her son. So for the fifth time that hour she climbed the stairs to Don's bedroom and reassured herself that he was all right. He had not choked on anything; no one had broken in to kidnap him. Betty then again made sure all the windows in her son's bedroom were secure, and wiped away imaginary dust from the dresser. She sighed, feeling relieved, but knew that her anxiety would mount in a very short time. Betty found that she could not control her fear or her compulsive behavior. Despite the fact that she knew her fear was irrational, it continued to plague her and make her life miserable. She began staying up all night to make sure that Don did not die in his sleep. She could not attend to anything else. She, her husband, and her house all became secondary. Finally, in despair, Betty decided to seek psychotherapy as a way out of her distress and turmoil.

Of five children, Betty was the second child and eldest girl. Her father was a laborer who had moved from the South to take a job as an automotive worker. With him he had brought his heritage of racial discrimination, which caused him to view the world with anxiety and approach every situation with caution in an attempt to protect his family. He was a religious man who spent his spare time at the Baptist Church. He was careful to follow rules, both those of the Baptist religion and those of white society. He wanted to make sure that his children would be safe and secure and that they would be able to prosper and do better than he had done. He was proud of the fact that year after year his family slowly improved their situation. Although Betty's father tried to help the poorer members of the black community through his church work, he kept himself separate from them. He did not want to become like them again. He did not want white society to view him as a "nigger."

Betty's mother worked as a part-time domestic to augment the family income. She too was fearful and quiet, proud of her neat and tidy house. The house and its furnishings were evidence of the security that she and her husband had worked so hard to achieve. Everything seemed proper. The house was quiet, no one screamed, the grass was freshly trimmed, the children were well-groomed and well-behaved. In Betty's family there was a set time for everything; everything was done on schedule. The children ate, took their baths, and went to bed, every night at the same time.

Betty sensed that these routines were necessary to keep disaster at bay. Everything had to be in its proper place. The shades had to be drawn nightly; the children had to be well-behaved; the family had to go to church. It seemed as though these routines would help to prevent disaster. After all, disaster could strike from anywhere; they could never know what the white community might do.

Despite their precautions, disaster did strike. Betty's oldest brother, David, was murdered. Some gunmen held up the store in which David was shopping, they started shooting, and David was killed. David had gone to the store for his mother. He was an innocent bystander. He had had nothing to do with the robbery; there was no reason why he should have been hurt. Yet, at 16, David was dead from a bullet wound. The family was devastated by his death. On the one hand, they could not believe it; on the other hand, they knew this must be the disaster they had awaited all along.

So Betty, her mother, father, and younger brothers and sisters withdrew. The shades were drawn at four o'clock in the afternoon, and the family sat huddled around the television. When they talked it was about how the disaster could have been prevented. "If only I hadn't sent him to the store." "If only he had gone earlier." "If only he had gone later." "If only I had gone to the store." On and on the family went, each of them blaming herself or himself for not being careful enough to prevent David's murder.

Betty went off to college in place of her brother. She majored in social work as an undergraduate and later earned her MSW. She was always a conscientious and good student who enjoyed her work. However, she kept feeling guilty about being in school in David's place. Her first job as a social worker was in the Welfare Department, and her second job was in a men's prison. She enjoyed working and was gratified by her sense that she was making the world a better place.

At age 27, Betty married a Baptist minister. She cared for her husband and felt he was a good man. They were respectful of one another's needs and seemed to be the perfect couple. Her married home life paralleled her life as a child in that she and her husband did not drink, dance, or smoke. Their house was spotless. It was tastefully decorated but was so neat that it demanded a tremendous amount of attention from her.

After four years of marriage Betty and her husband decided to have a baby. Toward the end of her pregnancy, she quit her job with considerable sadness. Betty was surprised to find that she was not totally looking forward to the birth of her baby. She was dismayed by her stretch marks and felt uncomfortable, bloated, and messy. She was afraid of the indignities of the birth process but hoped that her baby would be sweet-smelling, cute, and cuddly. When she first held Don she was alarmed that she did not feel an overwhelming gush of love. Betty had expected that this immediate gush of love would banish any remaining ambivalence about being a mother. When it did not happen, she was frightened.

Betty was careful to take good care of Don. Like all babies, he was very messy and at times smelly. She changed his diapers instantly after he urinated or defecated. Daily she washed two or three loads of diapers. She was dismayed when he spit up his formula, making it necessary for her to change his sheets and all of his clothes. She worked hard to keep the house from smelling as though a baby lived there. She was also aware that her figure did not look quite so good as it had before her pregnancy. Somehow things did not seem to be in their proper place. She could not get her life back in order. Don had entirely disrupted her schedule and her body. Betty's sense of anxiety and impending doom increased. Catastrophe was bound to strike. Something had to happen to this baby, because, after all, tragedy was always lurking around the corner.

Betty felt her fears and concerns were realistic. However, she began to realize that her compulsive behavior and her inability to leave Don alone for even one moment were not quite normal. Her obsessive thoughts about Don's being kidnapped began to weigh heavily on her and prevented her from thinking of anything else. Her compulsion about keeping his room dust free and her fear of his choking made a life separate from him impossible. She was a prisoner of her thoughts and actions.

The Struggle for Survival

When you are born you are totally helpless. You come into the world vulnerable and dependent for your survival on your caretakers. There is no way that you can take care of yourself. Your food, your warmth, your comfort, the love that you receive—all are given to you by others. Without them, you will die. Never again will your vulnerability be so total. When you are an infant, vulnerability is a life-death issue. If people do not feed you, you will starve to death. If people do not protect you physically, you will freeze to death. You cannot even roll over if you are uncomfortable. You are unable to crawl to food or shelter. You are even unable to lift your head and look at the world around you. Biologically you are totally vulnerable.

In spite of your biological vulnerability, you psychologically feel that you are the center of the world. When you cry, someone comes to feed you. When you are cold, someone covers you. When you are wet or dirty, someone changes or bathes you. When you are bored, someone holds you up to see the world. You are aware only of your body. The world is still only dimly available to you. Your body, your feelings, and your needs are the only things that are important to you. They are your only reality. You have no awareness of the mechanics behind the scene. You do not know that you are being fed because your mother knows you are hungry. You assume you are being fed because you are hungry. You are hungry, you cry, you are fed. You do not realize your mother's role in the interaction; you know only your own. You feel you are the center of the world; you feel you control the world. Thus you start your life with a contradiction; biologically you are totally vulnerable, but you feel all-powerful.

As you grow and gain a consciousness about yourself and your world and become aware of yourself as a separate person, your sense of vulnerability increases. You begin to know just how helpless you are. You come to feel dependent upon your caretakers for survival. It no longers feels to you that you are hungry, you cry, and you are fed, but rather that you are hungry, you cry, and your mother, when she gets ready, feeds you. You know that what you want does not happen automatically. You no longer feel at the center of the universe. In fact, sometimes you feel small and insignificant. Your magical power has evaporated. To defend yourself against this frightening vulnerability, you imagine yourself as all-powerful. You remember how it felt to be the center of the world, and you recall this feeling to defend yourself against your sense of insignificance and helplessness. It is not that you consciously decide to change your feelings in this manner, but rather that this is how it happens. You use the feeling of being all-powerful, that is, omnipotent, to counter your feelings of vulnerability.

For the rest of your life you struggle with these two polarities, omnipotence and vulnerability, opposite ends of a continuum. Starting at infancy, omnipotence is used as a defense against feelings of vulnerability. For example, as a child you may witness a violent thunderstorm and that night imagine that you are a dinosaur roaring through the woods. You deal with your fear of the thunderstorm by imagining yourself to be a very powerful, large, indestructible creature. Another common example is for you as a child to feel so special, so omnipotent, that you think the sun follows you wherever you go. This behavior is not at all unhealthy; rather, it is your way, when you are a child, to feel unique and special in a world where you really are very vulnerable and helpless.

The use of omnipotence as a defense is not limited only to childhood. For example, as an adult flying in an airplane which develops engine trouble, you may feel totally vulnerable and powerless to effect any change. One way you might deal with your overwhelming sense of vulnerability is to imagine yourself as a World War II ace pilot who brings the plane down safely. Obviously, in this fantasy of competence and mastery you are using omnipotence to defend yourself against your fear that the plane will crash and you will die.

The ultimate vulnerability is death, and in the end all omnipotent feelings are defenses against death. As an infant, you were totally helpless and powerless and would die if left on your own. Similarly, when your parents became angry you were at their mercy. You had no way of gauging the intensity and depth of their anger. You always felt it as overwhelming and beyond your control. Under very stressful circumstances, you may even have worried that your parents might harm or even kill you. You were totally vulnerable. Now that you are an adult, situations which stimulate your vulnerability cause this past vulnerability to surface as well. Again, the greatest terror is death. It is true; you are all mortal. We will all die. To be concerned about dying and frightened in dangerous situations are realistic reactions. Obviously, being high above the earth in a plane with a faulty engine calls forth the fear of death. Death is the inevitable terror, both uncontrollable and guaranteed. Because you never know when or how you will die, you put huge amounts of energy into controlling the anxiety that is evoked when you think about death.

The Development of Mastery

Although you cannot prevent death, you learn to deal with the anxiety that it creates. Much of your intellectual and physical development is devoted to mastering and diminishing the intensity of this anxiety and terror. Even though you cannot control death, you can increase your competence and mastery in the world. These new physical and intellectual skills diminish your feelings of vulnerability. Physically you learn to feed yourself, clothe yourself, and move freely through the world. Simultaneously, you progress in your ability to think, and this enables you to both further master your world and deal with your emotional vulnerability.

Physical mastery. When you are an infant, you cannot even get food to your mouth, but by 18 months you are able to feed yourself with a spoon. At that point you are not as dependent on your mother to feed you. She still has to prepare your food, but you can get it from the table to your mouth. By the time you are nine, you can make a sandwich for yourself, so your dependency is decreased again. When you are a teenager, you can prepare a hot meal for yourself and your family. So once again the progression of years brings increased mastery and decreased vulnerability. By the time you are an adult, you can not only prepare your food but also earn the money to buy the food and drive yourself to the grocery store in your own car. Barring external disaster, you will never again face the possibility of starving to death; one vulnerability is eliminated.

Similarly, as an infant you are unable to keep yourself warm when you are cold. Your mother must come and cover you. When you are a little older and are cold, you can take your blanket and wrap it around you for warmth. As your coordination increases, you are able to dress yourself. Your fingers are sufficiently competent to button your buttons, snap your snaps, zip your zippers, and tie your shoes. This physical skill means that you can now manipulate your environment to keep yourself warm. As your physical coordination increases through adolescence and adulthood, you can choose to develop a variety of complex physical skills, such as sewing to clothe yourself or building a house to shelter yourself.

Sports may also offer the means for diminishing vulnerability. For example, when you run you may experience feelings of power and competence. As a result of feeling in control of your body, you may feel centered and in control of your life. Running is increasing in popularity today, perhaps because it allows an individual to experience greater mastery in a world in which individuals have minimal power.

Intellectual Mastery

Magical thinking: In addition to developing physical mastery, you learn to feel less vulnerable in the world by developing your intellectual capacities. This cognitive growth starts in early childhood with what is known as "magical thinking." There you are, at age three, your pink-and-white cake decorated with clowns and birthday candles. You are told to make a wish and that if you blow out all the candles in one breath, your wish will come true. You close your eyes and wish for the doll that you saw in the store window. You take a deep breath and are able to blow out all the candles. Later that day when you open your presents, what do you find? Lo and behold, there is the doll you had wished for. You were told that if you did the right thing and were a good little girl, your wish would come true, and so it did. Thus you begin to believe that your wishes can come true, and society supports this belief. Many popular songs, such as "When You Wish upon a Star," and numerous myths, such as Santa Claus, reinforce this notion. Thus society colludes with you in the development of magical thinking. You come to feel that thinking it makes it happen. This is the basis of magical thinking.

As a child you learn to cherish your good and positive wishes and to be anxious and scared about your bad ones. For example, suppose your mother punishes you and you inwardly wish her dead. If something then happens to your mother, you feel a tremendous amount of guilt, fearing that you hurt her with your thoughts, that your wish harmed her. However, even if no harm comes to her, you cannot be certain that it will not in the future. Magical thinking persists because sometimes your wishes come true and you lose sight of the fact that your wishes do not make the reality. There is always an understandable causal connection. Reality, not magic, makes things happen.

Superstition: As you grow older, you find that other children share some of your magical thoughts. Remember when you were in the first grade, skipping to school with one of your friends, and you chanted the rhyme, "Step on a crack and break your mother's back"? This is magical thinking that has, because of group usage, become superstition. At first you may use this rhyme as a way to deal with your own vulnerability about separating from your mother and having to walk to school without her, but it develops a life of its own. It becomes something you share with your friends, a way of being part of children's culture.

However, not only children use superstition to keep bad things from happening. Many of you as adults share numerous superstitions, such as bad luck being associated with Friday the 13th or black cats. It is obviously easier to avoid a black cat than to control all the bad things that might happen to you. Superstition gives you the illusion of control.

Religion: The most structured and formalized type of magical thinking and superstition can be seen in formalized religions. In the Catholic Church, thinking a bad thought is tantamount to doing it. The Church's position is that if you give in to the pleasure of an impure thought, it is the same as acting on it. In the same vein if you go to confession and say ten Hail Marys, all the sins that you committed are wiped away. In Judaism, the mezuzah around your neck or on your door is there to prevent tragedy from happening. In some fundamentalist sects, the "laying on of hands" is believed to cure illness. The ritual in all religions includes phrases to keep evil at bay. Similarly, some of you are committed to eating only certain "health foods" in the hope that you will never become ill. Thus both traditional and modern-day religions give you some sense of power and control over your environment. In an attempt to feel less vulnerable and less helpless, you look to religion as a way to explain your world and to protect yourself against evil forces.

As mentioned above, magical thinking is the precursor of all intellectual development. It is the first way that you as a child use your mind to diminish your vulnerability and make sense of your world. Simultaneously, you gain more realistic mastery over your world and begin to understand cause and effect. As you learn how and why things work, you are able to give up more of your magical thinking. This is possible because reality intervenes and because your greater intellectual development allows you to feel more powerful and more capable of influencing your environment. For example, by the time you are eight years old you know that wishing for a birthday gift does not make it appear, even if you blow out all the candles. You know you have to ask your parents for the gift or buy it yourself. The world works by physical cause and effect, not by magic. Mental causes do not create physical effects. In sum, increased physical and intellectual skills reduce your sense of vulnerability and helplessness by increasing your mastery and competence. You do not need to rely so heavily on omnipotence as a defense because you can cope with reality.

Intensifying the Struggle for Survival

Omnipotence and vulnerability are universal issues; they are impossible to avoid. Because you are born helpless and dependent, you have issues that center around vulnerability and omnipotence and must develop some strategies for dealing with these two extremes in your life. Certain childhood experiences foster the intensification of this conflict, making it more difficult for you to discover a happy medium between these polarities.

An overly rigid upbringing. One such experience is to have had an overly strict and rigid upbringing, as did Dora, age 22. Dora was the daughter of an orthodox rabbi and his devoted wife. As far back as she could remember, there had been strict rules about proper behavior and about what she could and could not do. She could not eat certain foods; she could not go to school on certain days; she could not always romp and play. Dora knew that what seemed to her to be small transgressions, such as mixing up the silverware or drinking a glass of milk while eating a meat sandwich, would make her parents very angry. In addition, her father always seemed so cold and distant, so preoccupied with his studies and his congregation. Dora felt that there must be some "right thing" she could do that would make her father more attentive, more fun, more like her friends' fathers. So Dora grew up believing that everything was either right or wrong. She learned that if only she could figure out what to do, then everything would run smoothly. On the other hand, if she did the wrong thing, catastrophe was likely to strike. She grew up feeling that she must know all the rules in order to be omnipotent. If only she could figure out how to be perfect, she could make her world perfect too. Conversely, when something bad happened Dora felt guilty and tried to figure out what she had done wrong.

Dora reached a crisis when she completed a BA in psychology and was unable to find a job. She felt that her inability to find a job was her fault, that she must be doing something wrong. After all, if she were good enough, perfect enough, smart enough, and tried hard enough, she would find an interesting and challenging job. As a result of her inability to find a job, she sought therapy in an effort to allay her guilt and figure out what she was doing wrong. In therapy Dora learned that her guilt was a defense against her feelings of worthlessness, her feelings that she must be an incompetent and bad person if she could not get a job, if she could not rise above the economic situation.

As Dora progressed in therapy, she became further aware

that her feelings of worthlessness were her way of dealing with her need to be omnipotent, which was, in turn, a defense against her feelings of vulnerability. The reality was that Dora could not change the economic situation; she could not change the number of psychologists already in the job market; she could not sell herself simply because there were no buyers. Dora could not make happen what could not happen; she could not be omnipotent; she was powerless in this situation. Dora had to deal with and admit to this powerlessness. However, her lack of power here did not mean she could not be powerful in other aspects of her life. In other words, she could get a job in another field if she so chose, or go to graduate school and get a degree that would make her more marketable.

Thus Dora needed to learn that there were ways in which she could increase her mastery while giving up her need for omnipotence. She could not change the world, but she could function within it. Dora learned that the rigid rules of her childhood did not guarantee happiness; in fact, these rules did not work, for there were no absolutes.

A chaotic upbringing. In contrast to Dora, 30-year-old Ruth had been brought up in a chaotic household. Her childhood was dominated by her mother's drinking and her father's violent outbursts. She was totally unable to predict or prevent the chaos of her parents' verbal and physical attacks on her. Some days Ruth would return from school and find things as they should be, her mother smiling and sober and dinner already prepared. Other days Ruth came home to find her mother passed out on the sofa and no food in the house. She had no way to predict her reality. Clearly, Ruth, as a child, was totally helpless and vulnerable. There was no way she could change her parents or modify their capriciousness. Yet Ruth could not believe that there was nothing she could do to make her parents behave like the parents of her friends. She denied the capriciousness in her life and believed that she could and must control her parents' behavior. This was her only way of regaining a sense of power and control. She felt that changing her parents' behavior was her only chance for happiness. Thus Ruth came to believe that she had the power to make her parents sober. Maybe if she said the right things to her mother in the morning, her mother would not need to drink any more. Maybe if she cooked dinner, her father would not be angry at her. Maybe if she cooked something different, his anger would abate. Ruth thought that it was just a matter of figuring out exactly the right thing to do. As an adult, Ruth always felt guilty. She believed anything that went wrong was her fault, whether in relationships or in everyday living. She felt it was up to her to prevent all catastrophes.

Ruth needed to realize that she could not, as either a child or an adult, change her parents. She was powerless to make her parents different. She wanted them to be the perfect parents, for this would have made her feel safer and less vulnerable. But the reality was that her parents were not perfect. She did live in a capricious household and there was nothing she could do to change that. As a child she had been helpless and dependent; this was her reality. As an adult Ruth needed to know that she was no longer helpless and vulnerable. This did not mean that she was omnipotent, for no one is omnipotent, but rather that she had certain skills and masteries which enabled her to cope with the world. She was no longer dependent upon her parents; she did have control over her life. But she also had to recognize that although she could never control her parents nor could she make them different, she did not need them to be different because she was no longer a helpless child. She was no longer dependent upon them for nurturing and love, and certainly not for her survival. She could accept her adult vulnerability without needing to feel omnipotent and, at the same time, know that she had been helpless and dependent as a child. That was over now. She was a capable adult, not omnipotent, but competent in her world.

The child as parent. Still a third environment that fosters the struggle for survival is a situation in which your parents are unable to fulfill their parental role and look to you to parent them. Unfortunately, you know that you are unable to parent your own parents; thus you feel doubly vulnerable.

Not only are you vulnerable because you are a child but also because you have parents who are unable to protect you. The message you receive from your parents is that you must protect them, that you must be omnipotent. You thus have an exaggerated sense of your own power and importance.

Such a child was Tina, who had cared for her younger siblings, cleaned the house, and prepared the meals. During Tina's childhood her mother was either immobilized by depression or in the hospital. Her father was absent much of the time, overworked and harried; his time was consumed by his work and his attempts to deal with his wife's depression. Tina became the parent for her younger siblings. She never had the time to be a child herself. She had gone from being a helpless infant and toddler to having the responsibilities and chores of adulthood. Vaguely she knew that she was unable to be an adult and that she was doing a poor job of caring for her younger siblings. She could not even take proper care of herself; how could she possibly take care of them? Try as she might to keep the house neatly organized and to cook the meals, she was aware that she was not doing it well. Tina had to act as though she were more capable, more competent, and more powerful than she was. In time she could almost believe that she was as powerful and omnipotent as she pretended to be.

Illness within the family. Wendy also had a childhood which fostered her inability to know the boundaries of her power. When she was ten years old, her mother, ill during most of Wendy's life, died of cancer. Wendy's father was a caring, loving man who looked after his wife and expected Wendy to be understanding and helpful in the care of her mother. Wendy frequently felt angry about her mother's illness. It did not seem fair to her. All her friends had mothers to do things with, to curl their hair, to go to school plays, to listen to sad stories, and to be generally healthy and involved with their daughters' lives. The more Wendy wanted and needed her mother to do things with her, the sicker her mother became. Wendy dealt with her mother's inabilities with increasing anger, and it seemed to Wendy that it was her own anger that made her mother weaker and paler.

Then, when Wendy was ten, she was thrilled to have the lead in a school play. She wanted both her parents to be there, and they promised to attend. Her mother knew it would be difficult but would try to be there for Wendy's special day. The night of the play Wendy was excited and enthusiastic; she felt like an important, special person. The play went very well and Wendy took her bows with much pride. When she looked for her parents, however, they were not there. She was enraged, furious at her mother. How dare she promise to come and then not show! How dare she not allow her father to be there! How could her mother do this? Wendy wished her mother would simply die. She could not believe how much she hated her. Still enraged and crying, Wendy went home. When she arrived there, she found out her mother was dead. From then on, Wendy was terrified of thinking ill of people. She was afraid that her thoughts might harm them. Even though she knew it did not make sense, she was afraid that if she thought mean things about another person, that person would be hurt. She was convinced that her thoughts had killed her mother and could kill again.

This issue again came to the fore for Wendy 17 years later when her lover was planning a vacation. Wendy felt very angry about her lover's leaving her but could not deal with these angry feelings because she was sure that to put them into thoughts would mean her lover would die. So she tried to think of other things, to occupy her mind in order to distract herself from her anger at her lover which she feared might destroy him. The whole time that her lover was away she was terrified that he was going to die. Her terror was so intense that she called him frequently to assure herself that he was all right. She knew she did not have that kind of magical power; yet she could not avoid or diminish her fear. Nothing seemed to help. She was constantly terrified, still believing that her thoughts created events.

All of you have issues that center around vulnerability; all of you use omnipotence to defend yourself against vulnerability and to deal with this issue. Some childhood experiences itensify the conflict between vulnerability and omnipotence. If you had a chaotic upbringing or a major illness or death in your family, you were made to feel vulnerable. If you had an overly rigid or strict upbringing, or had to fulfill the parental role, you were made to feel omnipotent. If you were raised within any of these circumstances, you will find it more difficult than others to resolve your feelings of vulnerability and omnipotence. Some upbringings increase your illusion of omnipotence and some increase your sense of vulnerability. These circumstances intensify your need to use omnipotence to defend yourself because they increase your sense of vulnerability. Because conflicts around vulnerability and omnipotence are universal, these issues reemerge in adult life.

Omnipotence and Vulnerability in Everyday Life

A disabled car. All of you have had the experience of needing to get to an appointment on time. You rush around the house getting ready, concentrating on not being late. You get into your car and start down the highway. Two miles out of town you hear a sudden clunk and your car stops. You pull off the road and get out of your car, open the hood, and look despairingly into the engine. You have no idea what you are looking at, no idea what could possibly be wrong. You are stranded and will be late for your appointment. You have no idea how much money it will cost to fix your car or how you are even going to get into town. You feel totally helpless; you are clearly dependent on others to bail you out of this situation. You need to figure out how to get into town, get your car towed, arrange to repair it, and contact the person with whom you had your appointment. You are enraged. You do not know at whom to be enraged, but you are enraged nonetheless. Your omnipotent defense has been challenged and you are angry because you feel there is nothing you can do about your situation. Of course, the reality is that you are not totally helpless. There is something that you can do in this situation. And, in fact, as you arrange to have your car towed and repaired you begin to feel less helpless and more in control. Your anger surrenders to a growing sense of power and control as your adult skills help you to handle the situation.

An airplane ride. Another example of vulnerability in everyday life is what happens to many of you on an airplane. You drive to the airport, check in your bags, and walk nervously to the gate. You know that you have to take this flight to get to your sister's wedding which you really want to attend; but you also know that you hate flying. You walk onto the plane, fasten your seatbelt, and stare nervously out the window. You sit there and become increasingly aware that in just a few minutes you are going to be at the mercy of the pilot and this machine. What if one of the engines should fail? What if the pilot is hung over and not quite alert? You do not even like to ride in a car with someone else driving, and now you are about to trust your life to a complete stranger and a big, complicated machine. At takeoff you sit there shaking, gripping the armrests, hoping that everything will go well and it will be over soon. Clearly the issue you are faced with here is that you are out of control and vulnerable. If the engine should fail or the plane catch fire, the chances of your survival are minimal. You have put your life into someone else's hands. You are totally dependent on someone and something else for your survival.

Your hurt child. Another situation which may restimulate your conflicts concerning omnipotence and vulnerability is one in which your child is hurt. A scene in the movie *Kramer vs. Kramer* illustrates the depth of feelings possible when your child is injured. In this scene the child falls off a jungle gym and hurts his eye. The father is terrified. He picks up his child and runs with him to the hospital. His child being hurt restimulates the father's own vulnerability, his own fear of death, and his fear that his child is permanently and tragically damaged. He was unable to prevent this accident; he was unable to protect his little boy; he was unable to be an omnipotent parent. He had failed in what he most wanted to do. His omnipotence was challenged and he felt guilty.

A robbery. Still another example of having your omnipotence challenged is illustrated in the following scenario. You are on your way home after a long day's work. You have turned off the freeway and onto a five-mile scenic drive to your home. You pull into your driveway, walk up to your house, unlock the door, and find it empty. At first you are dumbfounded, and then you realize your home has been burglarized. Your personal space has been violated. You are enraged. Someone unknown to you went into your home without your permission and took your belongings. You are enraged and powerless. You had thought your home was your safety, your security, your sanctuary; and now someone has invaded it. Your mind rushes. Who has done this terrible thing? Why did it happen to you? What could you have done to prevent it? If only you had had a burglar alarm. If only you had had a dog. If only you had come home earlier. If only you had not stopped for that drink. You are looking for what you could have done differently in an attempt to regain some sense of power. Being "ripped off" puts you back in touch with the total sense of vulnerability that you lived with as a child. Feeling that you could have done something to prevent the robbery reinstates some sense of control.

Loss of a job. Your omnipotence can also be challenged if you suddenly lose a job without just cause or for no reason directly related to you. Let us assume, for example, that you are 50 years old and have worked as a secretary for a construction company for 20 years. Suddenly, much to your surprise and dismay, you discover that the company has gone bankrupt and are without a job. To make matters worse, this bankruptcy means that you have lost all your benefits, your retirement plan, your pension, your medical insurance, everything you had worked for and relied upon. You are now 50 years old and back in the job market. How could this possibly have happened? It seems totally unfair and unjustified. You feel at the mercy of forces beyond your control. You have no power whatsoever; you feel entirely helpless, powerless, and vulnerable.

A suicide. Your sense of omnipotence is also threatened if you are a psychotherapist whose client commits suicide. Imagine that you have been seeing a 40-year-old woman in therapy for the past three months. In her last session, she told you that she just discovered that her husband is going to leave her. She seemed, however, to be handling the news fairly well and assured you that she would not need to see you for an extra session that week. You encouraged her to call if she felt she needed to talk with you. The next day you get a call from her husband. Your client has killed herself. Your immediate reaction is disbelief and shock. You feel sad and think, "What did I do wrong? How could I have saved her? What should I have done differently?" Your next response is, "I will not do therapy any more. I'm a bad therapist. It's all my fault." You struggle with guilt. You struggle with what more you should have done; you feel totally helpless. It is over now and very final. There is nothing you can do. There is no going back. It is finished. Your client fired you without your consent. In spite of your help, she took death into her own hands. You were helpless.

Getting Free: Betty

Betty, whose life was discussed at the beginning of the chapter, came into therapy because of her excessive concern over her infant son, Don. She was constantly terrified that he might choke to death, be kidnapped, or become ill; as a result of her fears, she had almost made herself a prisoner in his room.

Betty sought out a well-respected woman therapist in her community. The first issue that Betty dealt with was that of race. Because her therapist was white, Betty was reticent about trusting her. Betty quietly tested her therapist to assure herself that she would be treated as a respected equal. It is difficult for anybody to come into thereapy because it means opening up to a strange person. This process of opening up is made more difficult when a racial difference exists between therapist and client. This was especially true for Betty, given her family's concern about their helplessness as black members of American culture and their belief that white society might attack them at any time. Betty trusted her therapist's credentials, but needed to test her racial stand. The therapist brought up the issue of race and the two of them explored it.

Therapy proceeded at a relatively slow pace beginning, as usual, with intellectual insights. Betty's first insight concerned motherhood. She realized that her son Don was indeed totally helpless and dependent upon her. She felt she should be the perfect mother and protect him from all danger. After all, that was what mothers were supposed to do.

Betty's second insight was that Don reminded her of her brother David. David was the first-born son, as was Don. Their names both began with the same letter. David had been brutally shot, and Betty still retained tremendous feelings of sadness, helplessness, and rage about his murder. Betty still felt that she should have prevented David's death; now she felt doubly responsible for keeping her baby Don from harm. She had to make everything perfect so that nothing bad would happen to him. Betty also felt guilty about the praise lavished on her for being a mother and producing such a beautiful baby. This guilt was reminiscent of the guilt she felt about David's death. She remembered the praise she had received for going to college when she had only gone in David's place.

In the process of dealing with David's death, Betty was able to realize that her family had felt helpless in the face of white society. This sense of helplessness existed prior to David's death. The family felt that, try as they might to control their lives, much of their fate was determined by the whim of white society. When life had become intolerable down south, Betty's terrified father had brought his family north, only to find that his job was dependent upon the white foreman, the white-owned company, and, finally, the white economic structure. He felt that his life was not in his control. He controlled what he could, but he felt it would never really be enough. Essentially, he was still a sharecropper.

Betty grew up with this message. She felt that her life was never her own, that she could not control what happened to her, that white society might swoop down at any time and take away her power. She tried to control this feeling of powerlessness by adopting the routines and rituals that her family had instituted. In other words, if she were perfect, if she did everything just as it should be done, perhaps she could avoid disaster. This is a perfect example of magical thinking at work. Betty felt that if she were able to keep her son's room spotless, she could keep him safe and secure forever. And, as is frequently the case with regard to an adult's magical thinking, Betty's logic had an element of reality. Keeping Don's window locked might help prevent his being kidnapped, but it was, of course, unlikely that anyone would want to kidnap Don.

As Betty became increasingly aware of these intellectual connections, she became more in touch with her feelings. When she first came into therapy it was hard for her to feel anything but her anxiety. Slowly she was able to learn that her anxiety was a screen for other feelings. Her therapist spent much time asking Betty, "What would you be feeling if you were not feeling anxious? What would you be doing if you were not checking on your son?" Thus Betty was able to see that her anxiety was a screen for her anger and sadness. In making the intellectual connections between her fears for her son and David's death, Betty was able to get back in touch with her feelings of sadness, rage, and helplessness about David's murder. She was able to see that her current anxiety was a screen for these overwhelming feelings. Even after David's death, Betty's family had not encouraged the expression of feelings. They had never given way to intense mourning because of their fear of being out of control. Betty's family had denied their anger and sadness to avoid feeling vulnerable. As a result, Betty was unaware of her own feelings of anger, sadness, and vulnerability. Experiencing her son's helplessness mirrored her own past helplessness which she wanted to deny. These denied feelings began showing themselves as anxiety. Betty had pushed down her feelings and, in so doing, had created a pressure-cooker effect; she needed to use more and more energy to keep herself unaware of her feelings. The longer she continued to deny her feelings, the more elaborate her rituals had to become in order for her to keep those feelings out of awareness.

One day Betty began her therapy session by reporting that she was feeling extremely anxious. Her therapist encouraged her to look at what she was feeling anxious about. Did anything happen recently? Was there any feeling she was trying to avoid? Was there something in the present that reminded her of something in her past? Betty shared with the therapist that this was the day following the anniversary of her brother David's death. The therapist then asked Betty how she felt about the anniversary, and Betty replied that she was not aware of any feeling except her anxiety. The therapist suggested that perhaps Betty was feeling sad about her brother's death. At this point, Betty, much to her surprise, burst into tears. She was even more surprised to find that her anxiety lifted almost instantly and gave way to sadness. Betty sobbed about her brother's death as she never had before, not even at the time of his murder. She could not believe she still had so many tears and so much sadness about an incident that had happened so long ago. Betty was mourning her brother, and her ability to feel her sadness freed her from her overwhelming anxiety. Betty learned that her anxiety was a screen for her feelings of sadness. Though she continued to be anxious, she had periods when she could be in touch with her feelings without the defensive screen of anxiety.

Almost without realizing it, Betty had begun to make some behavioral changes. One reason for these was that Don had grown older. She no longer needed to worry about his dying in his sleep. In addition, her increased understanding and growing ability to tolerate her feelings made her more comfortable.

As Betty became more in touch with her present feelings, she was able to recall her childhood feelings as well. At the same time, Betty was beginning to toilet-train her son Don. This was very difficult for her. She wanted him to be a good little boy and to be quickly and easily trained. Yet the messiness and the odor, not to mention the extra work, bothered her tremendously. She could almost sense his shame when he had an accident. Don tried hard to please his mother; he wanted to be a good little boy, but sometimes he could not get to the toilet in time. When accidents occurred, she saw his woebegone expression and could feel his sense of shame.

Something about her son's shame helped Betty to remember her own shame as a child. It seemed that she could never do things quite right. She could not make her bed neatly enough. Sometimes she put the fork on the wrong side of the plate. She never seemed to be proper enough, clean enough, or well-groomed enough. She guessed that her first experience of shame must have centered around her toilet training. After all, her mother bragged about Betty's being toilet-trained at nine months old. Underneath her sense of shame was her feeling that unless she did everything right, she was not lovable. Of course, she could not do all things right as a child, so she inevitably felt unlovable and unloved.

Betty's feeling of not being loved heightened her sense of vulnerability. Although everyone has feelings of vulnerability, the love you get from your parents makes you feel more secure, less at the mercy of whimsical fate. Betty had not experienced this security. Her family had felt that they were in fate's hands and had had a difficult time giving Betty the reassurance and love she needed. Betty was able to make the intellectual connection that she must have felt particularly vulnerable and at risk when she was a child. Her parents had cared for her physical needs meticulously, believing that this was the way to love a child. Yet it had not been the love that Betty needed. She had not felt the warmth and unqualified acceptance which would have diminished her sense of vulnerability.

Therapeutic progress is a matter of a client's taking two

steps forward and one step backward. As Betty became more in touch with her feelings about both her childhood and her brother's death, she also got in touch with her sense of vulnerability. She would progress making clear-cut behavioral changes, but periodically she would become frightened by her feelings and would regress. Toward the end of therapy, Betty began reexperiencing her feelings of vulnerability and sadness, and she defended herself against these feelings by becoming enraged at her therapist. After all, she had made all these intellectual connections and many behavioral changes, and she still did not feel "fixed." She was angry at her therapist for not fixing her. Her therapist was supposed to be the professional with all the answers, yet she still had not made everything perfect. Part of how Betty let go of her need for omnipotence was to hand all her power to her therapist. As Betty became more in touch with her feelings of vulnerability and sadness, her need for omnipotence was restimulated. This time she defended against her vulnerability by surrendering her yearned-for omnipotence to her therapist. Betty gave her therapist the power and responsibility to make life perfect for her.

Betty's therapist helped her to see that neither total vulnerability nor total omnipotence is the reality. Just because Betty was not totally omnipotent did not mean that she was totally vulnerable. The reality lies somewhere in the middle. Nor did Betty need an omnipotent ally; such an ally is both impossible and unnecessary. The therapist helped Betty to see that she could be in control of her own life. Although she could not have complete control, that did not mean she was out of control either. She could develop her personal skills for dealing with her world and could keep her life pretty much in control. She could have her feelings and not be overwhelmed by them. She could be a good mother, a good wife, and could deal with the chance events that occur as a natural part of everyday living. Betty gradually came to realize that chance events, or accidents, did not render her totally vulnerable or at the mercy of fate. Betty's therapist helped her to take back her own power and to know that she did not need the therapist to do it for her. Betty was able to feel her own power and mastery skills. Betty was free.

Feeling appropriate adult power is the issue in dealing with omnipotence and vulnerability. You are not a helpless infant. You cannot have omnipotence in controlling your life, but you can have courage, strength, and power.

5

Anger and Sadness:
THE CHICKEN OR
THE EGG

Sarah ran crying out of Ed's apartment. He just didn't understand her. He wasn't able to give her enough, even though they had been lovers for nine months. Strangely, though, by the time she reached her car she felt very calm. In fact, she felt nothing, only numbness. She drove past the Smithsonian Institution on the way to her apartment, reflecting that it was now one year since she had left her home in the Midwest to take a good job with a national wildlife magazine. As she drove on, she was suddenly struck by the impulse to drive her car into oncoming traffic. This impulse terrified her. She pulled off the road, trembling. This was certainly not the first time Sarah had thought of suicide. In fact, she had been hospitalized for suicide attempts twice before, once when she was 18 and again when she was 22. But she had thought that was all over now, that her life was well put together. Sarah sat shaking, scared and disappointed. She knew herself well enough to know that it was time to take herself back into therapy. Therapy had helped her before, and she believed that it could help her again; help her to work out her anger and sadness so that she would not act out and turn them against herself.

Sarah was born into an upper-middle-class Jewish family from Kansas City, Missouri. Her mother was a housewife, an attractive, outgoing woman who spent large amounts of time on social gatherings and community affairs. At home she was volatile and easily excited; Sarah was never sure whether her mother would be peaceful and warm that day or ranting and explosive. Although usually she was demanding and critical, sometimes she would cuddle Sarah and tell her how much she loved her. Sarah was confused; she felt that her mother was dangerous. Sarah never knew when or how badly she might be attacked. She simply could not trust her mother whose anger seemed so excessive and capricious.

When Sarah was five years old, her mother gave birth to another daughter, after which she experienced a severe post-partum depression. Her mother was never treated for her depression but lay around waiting for the depression to pass. So Sarah experienced a double loss; first she lost her mother to the new baby, and then she lost her to depression.

Sarah's father was a successful neurosurgeon. He loved his work and dedicated most of his time and energy to the development of his skills. He was highly esteemed. Because of the demands of his work, he was fairly removed from the family. When he was present he was easy to be around, but he was rarely there. He cared for his daughters, but only when his work was completed. His main contribution to their rearing was to encourage their academic success.

Sarah was a good little girl. She was not a particularly attractive child, but she was studious, polite, and shy. In high school she never felt as if she really fit in. She did not date much but achieved good grades and took part in some extra-curricular activities. As a teenager she was moody, but this was attributed to normal adolescence.

At 18, Sarah went off to the University of Chicago to major in ecology. Living in a dorm with a new roommate proved difficult. She found it hard to fall asleep at night and would often awaken too early in the morning. Sarah struggled to keep her mind on her school work. Occasionally she even embarrassed herself by falling asleep in her classes. Her desperation increasing, she went to the student health center where she obtained some sleeping pills. Sarah knew that something was wrong but did not know quite what. She felt somehow removed from herself, as though she hardly knew herself any more. She did not look forward to anything in her future or in her present life. Everything was bland, gray. She seldom felt angry; she seldom felt excited. Sarah felt nothing but her depression.

As Sarah went into finals she was able to mobilize herself to study harder. She wanted to do well and so drew upon all her energy to study hard and to force herself to be alert when she went into her exams. However, Sarah was aware that she was not functioning as well as she had in the past. She just could not override all her feelings of blandness and indifference. And then came her biology test. She had studied hardest for this test and felt she knew the material well. The teacher handed out a list of many questions, directing the class to write five or six sentences on each question. Sarah dutifully obeyed the professor's request. When the exam ended she had answered only half the questions. She looked around at her classmates and discovered that most of them had finished the test but had written only two or three sentences in response to each question. When Sarah realized that she had done poorly on this exam, her depression and despair increased. As she walked out of the classroom, she was aware of a sudden impulse to put her hand through the glass door. Her impulse startled her and, although Sarah resisted it, she was shaken. Sarah went home feeling alone, isolated, and desperate.

When her grades came out, Sarah could hardly believe it. To her, two C's and three B's meant total failure. She could not believe she had done so badly; she had even received a C in biology. The professor had not given her any credit for answering the questions in just the way he had requested. Sarah did not know what to do. She felt burdened; she felt there was no way out. She went home and swallowed all of her sleeping pills and lay down on her bed. Shortly thereafter her roommate discovered her with the bottle of pills by her side. Sarah was rushed to the emergency room where her stomach was pumped. The hospital recommended that she go into psychotherapy.

Sarah did not want her parents to know about either her depression or her suicide attempt, so she chose to go into therapy at the student health service. Her therapy was mostly supportive. She liked her therapist and felt the therapist cared about her and sincerely wanted to help her. The therapist's support enabled Sarah to get through the remainder of the year and to put her life back in order. She was able to pick up her grades, felt less depressed, and became more involved in her work. At the same time, Sarah met a man with whom she fell madly in love. As her involvement with him increased, Sarah began to feel better and soon terminated therapy.

The remaining three years of Sarah's college life were relatively uneventful. She continued to be a fairly good student. She felt more involved in life and more in touch with her own feelings. She was involved with her lover and devoted much time and energy to him and their relationship. However, she knew that when they graduated from college he would be leaving her. He had made it clear that he was going on to graduate school and did not want to commit himself to an ongoing relationship. He also found Sarah too demanding and clinging and did not want a permanent relationship with her.

Sarah felt that she would be able to handle the upcoming separation. When the time came, however, it seemed to her that too many changes were occurring at once. First, graduating meant that she had to leave her familiar college life. Second, she had been unable to find a job and, as a result, was feeling increasingly anxious and inadequate. Third, she felt abandoned by her lover. Her depression mounted. This time Sarah thought that she really wanted to die; she did not want to go on, she was too unhappy. It seemed to her that life would never be what she wanted, that it would always be a series of disappointments, one after another. No matter how hard she struggled, it all led to the same misery.

Sarah got into the bathtub, ran the water, and slashed her wrists. A friend who had been concerned about her became alarmed when Sarah did not answer the phone. She knew that Sarah was in the apartment, and when Sarah did not answer her door she called the police. Sarah was rushed to the hospital. This time the suicide attempt could not be hidden from her parents. They were notified, and Sarah was hospitalized for three months at Menninger's, where she was given antidepressant medication. After discharge, Sarah continued psychotherapy as an outpatient. The following year Sarah went to the University of Kansas to study journalism.

Sarah's therapy helped her to learn that she turned her anger at other people on herself; she hurt herself rather than becoming angry at the people she loved. These insights allowed her to feel better and mobilize her energy to get her into graduate school. Although she was wary of entering into a serious relationship with anyone, she was a good student and enjoyed her work. She felt more enthusiastic and optimistic about her life than she had for a long time.

Two years later, when Sarah was 25, she landed an exciting job with a national wildlife magazine in Washington, D.C. She was apprehensive about making another move and again putting herself through numerous separations but felt that the job was too good an opportunity to refuse. Much to Sarah's delight, she handled the move with little trauma. Three months later she became involved with Ed, a Ph.D. biologist who also worked on the wildlife magazine. Sarah was very excited about her willingness to become involved with someone again. She had great hopes for the relationship. She felt that Ed would give her everything she wanted and needed; she believed that he would be the answer to her life's quest for love and fulfillment. Life seemed wonderful until Ed appeared to withdraw; then Sarah felt devastated. "Why won't he let me move in with him? I want to be with him all the time; doesn't he love me? Doesn't he want these things too, or is he just using me? Is he too going to abandon me? How could this be happening to me again? How could I again be feeling suicidal?" Sarah knew enough to know what these questions meant. She needed to get back into therapy.

Understanding Anger and Sadness

All human beings feel sadness and anger, starting in infancy. Both are primary emotions. Sadness hurts. It is a big, open wound. You feel alone, not understood, not cared about, not valued; you feel as if you are bleeding. Sadness comes over you like a pervasive wave; your tears are an expression of the depth of your pain. It is the only feeling that you are aware of when you are feeling it. There is no room for anything else. Those moments of acute sadness and despair become your total world. Sadness comes from the pit of your being. It is the totality of your life for that minute, an overwhelming, crushing weight.

For you as an infant or toddler, love is protection. Lack of love makes you feel vulnerable, and this vulnerability contributes to your sense of sadness. You may feel sad and frightened when you are vulnerable. When you are a child, indications of love are physical, concrete. For example, for Christmas you want a particular doll; you have your heart set on it. But Christmas rolls around and you do not get the doll. You feel sad because, at the age of five, not receiving the doll is equivalent to not feeling loved.

When you are an adult your sadness may arise from many different sources, such as disappointments, diminished self-esteem, empathy, lack of love, and loss of love. For example, you may feel disappointed if you have been planning and looking forward to a vacation for many months and for some reason beyond your control the trip is canceled. You feel disappointed; you feel sad. The trip was something to which you looked forward. You feel sad and disappointed that it will not happen.

You may also feel sad if you watch a friend mourn the loss of her lover. You care about your friend and feel for her. You watch her cry and identify with her. You feel sad about her pain and may cry too. Feeling sad through empathy is something that many of you experience. You may cry at movies; you may cry if you hear about an animal being hurt. You may feel sad about social injustice. Empathy is one of the major ingredients in all close relationships. To feel empathy, you must be able to get out of yourself and care about the other person. Not only do you share others' sadness this way, but you also empathize with their joy, excitement, and sexuality.

You may feel sad if you suffer a blow to your self-image, ranging from the relatively unimportant to the most traumatic. For example, you may feel sad if you have lost a hard-fought campaign to be president of the Junior League. You wanted this very much but you did not achieve it. You experience some loss of self-esteem. You thought you were going to win; you felt you deserved to win; yet you did not. You question your opinion of yourself, wonder if you overestimated yourself. Your self-esteem has been hurt.

A much more traumatic experience is to lose a breast. This loss of a body part represents a loss of self-image. A piece of your body, something that was part of you, is forever gone. You must alter your image. Your physical integrity is challenged. You feel overwhelmingly sad and lost, lonely and frightened. In mourning the loss of your breast you have to say goodbye to a piece of yourself. In time, when the mourning process is completed, you will develop a different sense of yourself and a different sense of your body's integrity. You will then have a new feeling of self-esteem and a new body image.

Feeling insufficiently loved or appreciated also may engender a sense of sadness. Suppose you have reached your mid teens. Your friends have boys calling them; they are going on group movie dates; they are having fun with boys and feel sought after and desired. You do not. No one is calling you; no one is asking you to spend an evening at a movie; no one is asking you to take a walk on a balmy spring night and listen to the crickets. You feel unwanted, undesired, and unloved. It seems to you that you have felt this way all your life; you have never felt loved. You feel sad; you wonder if you ever will be loved. You never felt loved by your family, so maybe you will never feel loved by anyone. You wonder if you are unlovable.

Losing someone you love is still another situation which may result in your feeling sad. Suppose you have a very good friend. Over the years you have been very close and have shared a great deal. Suddenly she moves halfway across the country. You do not want her to leave, but you know that she will and that you will have to mourn your loss.

The most intense feelings of mourning and sadness are stimulated by the death of a loved one, regardless of whether this person is a parent, lover, or child. Suppose you have been married for 20 years and your husband suddenly dies of a heart attack. You feel you have lost part of yourself. You feel overwhelmed by your sadness. You feel totally at loose ends. You cannot believe this has happened. A person who was so crucial in your life is suddenly not there any more. He has vanished. His hairbrush, his bathrobe, and his smell still linger in the house, but he is not there. Never again will you be able to talk with him. Never again will you be able to love him. You have not even been able to say goodbye. You cry and cry and cry. You feel you will do nothing but cry for the remainder of your life. But, of course, that is not how the mourning process works. First you feel overwhelmingly sad, and then you also begin to feel your anger. You get in touch with your anger at your husband for leaving you so precipitously, leaving you with the burden of managing your life without him. And so, for a long while, your sadness and anger intermingle, but you are still primarily preoccupied with him and with his death. Slowly you begin to include other people and other things in your life; you know that you must manage your life and continue without him. Although your sadness may linger for a very long time, you eventually feel less preoccupied with your husband and more able to turn your attentions elsewhere and ultimately to be happy again.

Some of you will respond to the above situations with sadness; some of you will respond to these same situations with anger. At its most extreme, anger wells up inside you like a volcano. You feel physically strong and ready. Your mind may be crystal clear, or your mind may be pounding with emotion, making logic difficult. You have the sensation of heat, as if you are a steam kettle about to explode. You want to lash out at the situation which is angering you.

As your sense of your own power grows, so does your potential for feeling angry. As a child you may want to play with a certain toy, but your mother feels that the toy is dangerous and takes it away. You are angry and scream out against this challenge to your power. Your anger is an attempt to regain your lost power.

How you deal with and feel about your anger are determined by how your parents dealt with your anger and their own. Unfortunately, most parents are terrified of their own anger and unwilling to tolerate anger in their child. As a result you can easily grow up frightened by your anger. It may make you feel out of control. You may be afraid that you could actually act on your feelings and hurt someone. You may believe that by expressing anger at another person, you will cause that person to strike back at you. Because anger is so terrifying to you, you use many defenses to control it. Sometimes you may deny that you are angry; sometimes you may turn your anger into sadness and cry; sometimes you may laugh nervously, make hostile jokes, or get a headache. Because anger is so frightening, it is difficult for you to deal with it in its purity. Hence you turn it into something else that feels safer to you.

Yet only by allowing yourself to feel and explore your anger can you learn how safe and productive your anger can be. You can be angry without hurting or killing someone, or being hurt yourself. Feeling enraged is different from acting out your rage by hurting someone. There is a vast difference between how you feel and how you act. Feelings do not have to be acted on. Even fantasizing about killing someone does not mean you are a violent person or that you will act on your fantasies. You always have a choice as to how you will act on any feeling. Your fantasy of hurting someone may be a safe way of discharging your anger. Other ways of feeling and discharging your anger may be through sports, plunging yourself into your work, art, or writing, punching a punching bag, cutting up vegetables, screaming, or talking about your anger.

Feeling anger can be positive; it is not in and of itself destructive. Angry feelings will not hurt you; they will not hurt other people. In fact, you can use your anger to energize yourself for creative and intense endeavors. You may use your anger to fight for yourself and to determine your own life. The insistence on maintaining a realistic sense of your power necessitates the healthy use of your anger as well as a sense of yourself as a controller of your destiny. Suppose another person has just been given a part in a play for which you have yearned. You may shrug your shoulders, feeling intense sadness; you feel diminished, not good enough. You decide to give up and never return to acting; you will never try to act again, not even as a hobby. You are reinforcing your sense of sadness and vulnerability. Or you may feel angry, determined to show them all how wrong they are. You are a good actress, yes, even better than the person who was chosen. Of course you will try again, work hard, and next time you will win the part. In this case you have affirmed your fighting spirit, using your anger to enhance a sense of your own worth and power.

Some of you will probably say that you never get angry but that you are often sad. Frequently anger and sadness are screens for each other. You may cry when you are angry or scream when you are sad. However, as a woman you have probably been socialized to express your sadness rather than your anger. You are brought up knowing that there is little payoff in your being angry. In this society, men are stronger than you, both physically and in status. From the beginning you know that your father is stronger than your mother, that your brothers are stronger than you, that the boys in your neighborhood can overpower you physically. Additionally, you learn that you should not even try to beat up the neighborhood boys. After all, that is not ladylike. It is not considered proper for you to be as big and strong as the boys. If you get into a fight, the behavior considered appropriate for you is to cry and run home to your mother for comfort. Girls do not fight, they cry. Crying is seen as feminine, the proper and cute thing to do. Crying gets you protection and elicits love and care from your family. While your brothers are learning that physical aggression and assertiveness get them what they want, you are learning that being feminine, soft, tearful, and helpless is most productive for you. If ever you cross the line of differentiation between boys and girls, at best you are considered a tomboy and at worst you are punished for your unladylike behavior.

This prohibition against being angry does not cease with childhood. As an adult you learn that angry women are seen as "castrating bitches." This may be the most derogatory term that can be used to describe a woman. The very words "castrating bitch" call to mind a man-eating monster. Men are threatened by women's aggressive or assertive behavior and often retaliate by ridiculing such behavior. For example, many of television's situational comedies poke fun at successful, career-oriented women, portraying them as hostile, aggressive, man-hating nags. You are likewise taught that an angry woman will not "get" a man. No man will love you if you are angry and hostile; no man will care about you if you ever become angry at him. You will never get the love you so desperately want if you are assertive and insist on taking care of your own needs. Thus you have learned not to be assertive yourself, but to hope that the man you love will be assertive for you and protect you. You hope that he will take care of your needs, accepting and loving you forever. Thus women's manly heroes and fantasies are often men who embody this aggressive, almost violent ideal, such as football players, cowboys, business mavericks, detectives, policemen, and even criminals.

Because you have been socialized to cry rather than to express your anger, it is not surprising for you to feel as though you are never angry but always sad. You screen your anger with your sadness. For example, suppose you are an art student who has worked long and hard on a portfolio which you present to your teacher for evaluation. Your teacher takes a brief look at your drawings, tears them up, and throws them aside. She yells that your work is pure garbage. Your immediate reaction is to run from the room crying. You feel hurt and devastated. But is it possible that this is not all you feel? Is it possible that your tears and sadness are a cover for your anger at the injustice and insensitivity of your teacher? After all, she destroyed your creations. She was there to evaluate, not destroy. She attacked you. You were probably feeling both sadness and anger, but you were using your tears to cover your screams.

Through the years, cultural factors have reinforced women's expression of sadness and denial of anger. For many of you, this is your characteristic style. Recently, the women's movement has validated women's anger and you as a woman are beginning to feel more comfortable with your anger. You are becoming increasingly aware of your oppression and lack of equality. You are beginning to feel that your anger is justified and appropriate; that you have good reason to be angry. In this society, men have had and continue to have the power.

You are not paid equally for the same job; you are politically underrepresented. Although you do not have the money or power in our society, you carry the major responsibility for child-rearing and maintaining the family. The dreams you had hoped to realize by surrendering your power to men and taking a secondary position have not come true. Men, in fact, do not worship you or take care of you. They do not make you feel good about yourself or give you a purpose for being. They do not act out your dreams for you. You have given up a great deal and have received little in return.

As you learn that your anger is legitimate, many of you try to feel more comfortable with it. The popularity of assertiveness training testifies to your need to feel comfortable with your anger and to learn how to use it productively. Because the women's movement has validated and legitimized your anger, it becomes more likely that some of you are feeling more comfortable with your anger than with your sadness and may now use your anger as a cover for sadness. Anger, after all, does not hurt. For example, you explain to your husband how important it is to you that he not go bowling this Friday night so that he can spend some time with you alone. But he refuses to change his plans and goes bowling anyway. Perhaps in the past your reaction to this situation would have been to cry and to feel sad, rejected, and unloved. Now your reaction may be one of intense anger. You may yell and scream at him, feeling as though you have been attacked rather than rejected. In this instance you may actually have been feeling sad and hurt because your husband did not want to spend time with you, but you defended yourself against these feelings by becoming angry. You were using your anger as a screen for your sadness.

Louise, age 24, offers another example of using anger to cover sadness. When she was 20 her first lover left her for another woman. Louise did not give herself time to mourn the loss of this relationship. She avoided feeling her sadness and bereavement. Instead, she briefly felt enraged at his betrayal. Then her rage vanished and Louise acted out her feelings of anger by becoming promiscuous. She picked up men, had sexual intercourse, and discarded them. She was using men for sexual service, acting out her rage by treating them the way she felt she had been treated by her lover. Louise was covering her sadness. Instead of working through her bereavement at the loss of her lover, she acted out sexually and thus avoided her sadness.

Situational and Transferential Anger and Sadness

Your feelings of anger and sadness may be triggered by a present situation or be carried over from a past situation. That is, your feelings can be either situational or transferential. It is not the incident in itself but the intensity of feeling it evokes that is important when trying to differentiate between these two types of anger. Suppose your boss sexually harasses you on the job. If you are feeling situational anger, you will be angry at your boss for his inappropriate behavior. You will take a firm stand, making it clear to him that you will not tolerate this behavior. On the other hand, if this incident with your boss brings out your transferential anger, your reaction will be quite different. You will be angry, but your anger is being stimulated not only by the present situation but also by some experience in your past. Suppose, for example, you had been molested by your father when you were a child and your boss's advance unconsciously recalls this to you. You are enraged; you can hardly stand; you feel dizzy; you feel like vomiting. You want to strike your boss and are terrified at the immensity of your anger. You are terrified that you will lose control. You leave the office quaking. You are not sure you will ever be able to return. You cannot bear the sight of your boss and do not want to see him again. The intensity of this rage indicates the transferential aspect of your anger.

Most of the time situations which evoke anger are simultaneously transferential and situational. Again, suppose that you have been sexually harassed by your boss. Although you were not molested by your father, you do have unresolved anger directed toward him. Then, your reaction to your boss's sexual harassment is again intense anger. You have a hard time letting go of this anger and continue to feel it for several days. However, you will not feel like vomiting, passing out, or attacking your boss. Your reaction is somewhere in the middle, somewhere between the first two examples.

For many of you, anger is such an overwhelming and frightening feeling that you try not to feel it at all, regardless of whether it is situational or transferential. You may feel that the expression of even a little pique is akin to a big explosion. It all seems dangerous. However, as you begin to differentiate between types of anger and discover their source, you are less frightened by your anger. You then have some power to deal with your anger productively. In other words, if you examine your anger and realize that it is primarily unresolved anger toward your father, this knowledge enables you to respond more appropriately. You do not act on your anger because you know it is misplaced. On the other hand, if you are clear that your anger concerns only the immediate situation, then, of course, it is legitimate. You can act on your anger if you so choose. Thus differentiating between situational and transferential anger facilitates the management of your life. It allows you to understand, own, and use your anger to maximize your control over your life.

Sadness may also be transferential. With transferential sadness you feel sad, but it is a heavy sadness. You seem to be sadder than the incident warrants; you seem to be overreacting. For example, your new puppy dies. You sob and cry, blaming yourself for not taking adequate care of her. You miss her desperately. Yet you knew her for only a few weeks. A month passes and you are still crying about your puppy. In the midst of crying you recall your grandfather and how much you loved him. You remember him carving a horse for you, cuddling you during thunderstorms, and singing you songs. You were too young to go to his funeral, or so your parents thought. Now with the death of your puppy you are mourning your grandfather for the first time. You have transferred the sadness about your grandfather's death to the death of your puppy. Yes, you are sad about the puppy. But the depth and duration of your sadness is not about this puppy; it is about your grandfather. Carrying transferential sadness is like carrying five suitcases on an overnight trip. When you avoid sadness, you pack your suitcases too full and the slightest jar may break them open and cause the contents to come spilling out.

Sadness and anger are inevitable feelings as you journey through life. They start in infancy and are often together, hand in hand. Whether you use your sadness to cover your anger or your anger to cover your sadness, the two are Siamese twins.

The Price of Burying Anger and Sadness

Anger and sadness, like all emotions, need to be felt. If you are free, you can feel all your emotions including anger, sadness, joy, pleasure, sexuality, sensuality, and contentment. Burying anger or sadness may result in either depression, anxiety, or psychosomatic illnesses.

Depression. Some of you may find it easier to be depressed than to feel either your anger or your sadness. Depression may grow, enveloping you with a blanket of despair and self-doubt. The weight is so heavy it diminishes your ability to move, sleep, or eat normally. Yes, even your physical being is affected. You may be unable to sleep, and you may lose weight; or you may sleep continually and gain weight. You may be unable to concentrate, unable to finish tasks, unable to accomplish even the necessary routines of your daily life. Immobilized, you wallow in yourself, in the morass created by your own thoughts, in the messiness created by your own inability to care for yourself. If you have such a serious depression, with physical as well as emotional changes, medication may be helpful to you.

Incidents of serious depression seem to run in families. Whether such depression has a biological, chemical, or genetic basis or whether it is learned in families is an unresolved controversy long explored by researchers. Maggie Scarf's book, *Unfinished Business,* devotes much attention to this issue, examining all sides of it. However, if you are a woman with serious depression, the nature/nurture controversy is less important to you than receiving the help you need. This help may include medication and an understanding of those psychological and environmental factors unique to you which triggered the onset of your depression. Psychotherapy gives you the tools with which to manage your depression. For most of you, your depression is not so overwhelmingly intense or pervasive. It is a sense of the blues, a mild depression which many of you feel at some time in your life. In these cases, depression may be a defense, a screen against anger, sadness, and other feelings. You do not want to feel your anger and sadness; instead you are depressed.

Depression is not synonymous with sadness; it is the dampening down of all feelings. When you are depressed you feel heavy, burdened. It is a muting of all feelings, mixed with self-criticism. Underneath the depression is a welling up of anger and sadness. In the attempt to avoid experiencing your feelings, you push them down and thereby create a pressure-cooker effect. The more you push them down, the greater is their potential for exploding. As with a pressure cooker, the pressure builds up and more force is required to keep it down. The best way out of this pressure cooker is to allow yourself to experience your feelings gradually. You need to know that your feelings are all right; that you will not explode.

An example of the use of depression as a defense against feelings can be seen in the movie *The Rose*. Bette Midler portrayed a rock star who always felt either enraged or depressed. She acted out her anger with the use of drugs, outbursts of temper, and misuse of her power. When Rose was not feeling powerful or angry, she felt depressed. Underneath her depression were overwhelming feelings of sadness. She did not feel loved. She substituted adulation for love. The crowning blow came when she returned to her home town for a concert. There, especially, she longed to receive the love and acclaim that had been heaped on her elsewhere. It was in her home town that she had experienced her greatest humiliation, and she wanted to turn her teenage agony into an adult triumph. But this was not to be. Even the owner of the corner drugstore where she had gone as a child did not recognize her as a famous rock star. When this happened, she did not feel her sadness but rather screamed at him in rage. She continued to maintain her rage as a cover for the vast sadness inside her. When her rage subsided, she was left with depression. She was so depressed she was unable to mobilize herself to get to her concert on time. Her depression was finally so overwhelming that she numbed herself with drugs and died.

Rose's anger was a defense against her sadness, and her depression was a defense against both. To her it seemed safer to feel her anger than her sadness, and it seemed safer still to be depressed. When she began to feel her rage going out of control, she would turn her anger inward and become depressed. It was not that Rose consciously planned to deal with her feelings in this manner, but rather that she unconsciously played them out in this fashion. Underneath Rose was a vulnerable, lonely, sad woman who covered her feelings of vulnerability by expressing anger. She used her anger to feel more powerful and less vulnerable and alone. However, it did not work for her. It did not make her all-powerful. When anger and power failed, she became depressed.

Anxiety. Burying anger or sadness may, for some of you, result in a sense of anxiety. Here your anxiety functions as a defense, as a screen to hide your feelings even from your own awareness. This was the case with Janet, a 35-year-old woman who was afraid to leave her home. She experienced intense anxiety and distress if she tried to walk out of her house. Janet, the mother of two small children, was a housewife who said that she loved her husband and enjoyed being a wife and mother.

Initially, Janet started feeling apprehensive about leaving her house at night, fearful that she might be attacked or raped. There had been a rape in her neighborhood and this increased her fear. Janet was not sure that she was able to go about safely in the world. She felt very vulnerable. She had a fight with her husband and the next day was afraid to go shopping. Maybe someone would attack her, even during the day. She saw no connection between her fight with her husband and her increasing reluctance to leave the house. A short time later, her son was in a fight at school. The principal called Janet, concerned about her son's behavior, and made an appointment with her for a conference. Janet was unable to go for the appointment. She felt responsible for her son's outburst of anger. Where had all his anger come from? It could not have come from her; she had taught him never to be angry. She herself was never angry. She became terrified; she was not sure what she was afraid of. Her terror was nameless. She only knew that she was paralyzed with fear and could not leave her house. She felt immobilized with panic. She felt if she walked out the door her heart would burst.

What were the factors which led Janet to become a captive in her house? Janet felt vulnerable because she could not control either an anonymous rapist or her son's behavior. In addition, she was unable to feel or express anger at her husband. When her husband screamed at her, she did not defend herself; she only cried silently. Janet never felt anger; her son seemed to be acting it out for her. It was his acting out of her anger that intensified Janet's fears; it was her own anger that she was afraid of. Seeing her son's anger intensified her terror of her own anger, the anger she had so carefully smothered all these years.

When Janet was growing up there were dire consequences to expressing anger. It simply was not allowed. Her family did not get angry; they projected their anger onto the world and saw the world as aggressive, angry, and threatening. Thus to Janet the world was very frightening. In therapy, Janet was able to look at what her life had become. She was not really happily married. She was not really happy staying at home and being a housewife. She felt trapped, doomed. There was nothing exciting to look forward to. She became increasingly aware that underneath her feeling of entrapment was her anger, all that stored anger that she did not know how to express. She was angry that her husband was not more exciting. She was angry that her children needed her so much. To her it seemed easier to view the world as angry, hostile, and aggressive than to deal with her own anger; it was easier for her to feel anxious than to own her anger.

Psychosomatic illness. Not expressing anger or sadness can also result in the development of illnesses such as headaches, ulcers, asthma, or colitis, all of which have a psychological component. You have all seen Excedrin Headache Number 9 on television and know that headaches can result from daily stresses. You may become angry at your children's messiness and respond with a headache. This is a very common form of psychosomatic illness, and for most of you it is not incapacitating. You do what the commercial suggests; take an aspirin and forget it.

Unfortunately, not all psychosomatic ailments are so easily dealt with. Often incapacitating physical conditions result, causing severe physical distress and impairment. People who have such disorders rarely are aware of the psychological underpinnings. Usually the ulcerated patient does not feel her anger but sends it to her stomach to eat away at her stomach walls. Similarly, many migraine sufferers translate their anger into their heads, while asthmatics translate it to their lungs.

You may somaticize anger, turning it into a physical ailment, by taking it out on your bowels. This is called colitis, or spastic bowel syndrome, and is characterized by frequency and urgency of bowel movements. Colitis is a disease clouded with shame, a disease which sometimes necessitates such radical surgery as an iliostomy or colostomy.

Mary Jane is an example of someone with colitis. When she was ten years old, her family moved. She had to leave her friends, her five-year-old dog, and the security of her room and school. She did not want to move. She had just begun to feel comfortable in her old school where she knew all the teachers and most of the students. Suddenly her family moved. The task of making new friends, finding her way to the new school, and meeting new teachers seemed overwhelming to her. She was upset, frightened, and shy, generally feeling out of place. Everyone seemed too busy to pay attention to her. No matter what she said or did, they would not have allowed her to stay in her safe, familiar neighborhood. She was not able to control her life. Soon after the move, she found herself unable to control her bowels. She had to run to the bathroom again and again during the day. She felt totally ashamed. She was afraid to go to school because she might have "an accident." Her parents responded with much concern and attention. At first they thought she had the flu, but when her symptoms did not go away, they became alarmed and began taking her to one doctor after another. She was mortified when the doctors probed and prodded her in secret places. She wished she could get control of her body again.

Mary Jane felt out of control and powerless in her life and soon became out of control in relation to her own body. Just as her family made decisions about the specifics of her life—where she would be, whom she would be with, and what she would do—so her bowels began making decisions about where she would be, what she would do, and when. Her bowels were a metaphor for her life. In addition to feeling vulnerable about her life circumstances, Mary Jane was also angry. However, her anger was never recognized or validated. She was never listened to, never allowed to express her anger in words, so she expressed it with her bowels, controlling her family in the process. It was as if she was saying, "Shit on you." She wanted to shit on the world.

Mary Jane's feelings of vulnerability and anger were expressed through her body. Rather than feeling her feelings, she unconsciously expressed them in bodily distress. Mary Jane's case concretely illustrates how destructive it may be to avoid feeling your anger and sadness directly. This is in contradiction to the popular notion that the expression of feelings is in and of itself dangerous. It would have been better for Mary Jane to express her rage directly rather than to let it destroy her body. Likewise, it would have been less destructive for Janet to feel her anger and use her power to diminish her sense of helplessness than to make herself a prisoner in her own house. And, again, it would have been less destructive for Rose to experience her sadness than to act out her anger and kill herself.

Getting Free: Sarah

Sarah, whom you met at the beginning of this chapter, went back into therapy after the reemergence of a suicidal thought. She had been in therapy twice before and had learned about depression. She knew that it was hard for her to be angry at those she loved. She knew it frightened her and so, instead of feeling anger at others, she turned those feelings on herself.

Sarah had also learned some skills to keep her depression under control. She knew there were things she, as well as other depressed people, could do to keep herself from going into the depths of a serious depression. She had learned that when she began to get depressed, she needed to seek out people who cared about her. She needed to be with people who gave her a sense of being a valuable, lovable person. She needed to try to have fun, no matter how impossible that seemed. Sometimes she had difficulty getting up in the morning and readying herself to go out into the world. Yet this was something she had to do. It was crucial for her to keep busy; if she were unable to do things with other people, she needed to do them by herself. She could go to the movies alone; she could go window shopping alone. When Sarah had been in school, she had known it was crucial for her to keep up on her studies. She had also learned it was not healthy for her to sleep too much. She knew that excessive sleeping in and of itself could make her feel more depressed. Just as being immobilized fed on itself, so did going out and interacting with people feed on itself. The more she kept herself busy, the easier it was for her to be active, and the better she felt. In addition to continuing the routines of life and reaching out to others, Sarah learned the value of various physical activities. She learned that repetitive, rhythmical activities could ease the onslaught of depression. Running, swimming, roller skating, walking, volleyball, racquetball—any physical activity—could diminish depression; and Sarah was a good runner.

When Sarah came into therapy for the third time, she was not a novice. She knew a lot about herself and about what strategies worked for her. The therapeutic task was easier this time. There was less for Sarah to put together. Sarah felt that the majority of her difficulties stemmed from her relationship with her lover, Ed. She shared with her therapist Ed's repeated declarations ·of love and his complaints that she was too dependent, too demanding, too clinging. Sarah could hear Ed's words but could not feel what they meant or believe that he loved her. If he really loved her, he would give her what she wanted. If he really loved her, he would commit himself to marrying her or, at least, allow her to move in with him.

Shortly after starting therapy again, Sarah went to see a movie with Ed. The movie centered around the death of the main character's mother. Sarah felt devastated by the movie, experiencing an intense amount of sadness and pain. It seemed very important to her to spend the night with Ed; she felt she needed him tremendously. She needed him to take away her pain and make her feel secure. Unfortunately, Ed had a commitment to spend the night at his sister's home and he felt that he could not break the commitment. Sarah was inconsolable. She could not believe that Ed would reject her when she needed him so much.

When Sarah discussed this incident with her therapist, the latter wondered aloud if there were some connection for Sarah between the loss of her own mother and her feelings for Ed. This idea seemed to click for Sarah. Suddenly she had a greater awareness, more of a "gut" feeling about the neediness she had felt as a child and the neediness she felt in relation to Ed. Sarah's therapist asked her if she had felt this sense of sadness and loss in the past. Sarah thought for a while and remembered feeling this same sense of sadness and loss when her mother had gone to the hospital to give birth to her sister. Sarah had been sent to her grandmother during this time and had felt alone and isolated from the family. When she came back, her family was there, crowded around her newborn sister. She looked in the bassinet and could not understand why such a big fuss was being made. That creature in there did nothing but cry and demand their mother's attention. Shortly thereafter her mother became depressed. She lay around the house doing nothing; she could barely feed the baby. She paid no attention to Sarah. Sarah was afraid that her mother would never come back and be the way she used to be.

This memory brought a wave of feeling over Sarah. She felt the experience all over again. She felt loss, sadness, and abandonment. She remembered that when her mother became depressed, she feared that she had lost everything. Her mother might never again be there for her. Her mother might never again love her as she had before. Sarah felt alone and isolated. She felt cast out, abandoned; she felt waves of terror. She understood then why she needed so desperately for Ed to spend the night with her after the movie. He was supposed to take away her pain. He was supposed to make sure she never felt abandoned and alone and isolated again. He was to prevent her from ever experiencing loss of love. Sarah had made an important connection. She learned that she had emotionally lost her mother when she was a child, that she still felt this loss, and that she expected Ed to replace her mother.

The next several months in therapy were spent looking at other ways in which this pattern repeated itself, other ways in which Sarah expected Ed to satisfy her unfulfilled childhood needs. For example, Sarah had a terrible day at work. She came home wanting Ed to spend time listening to an account of her day. When he was too preoccupied to listen, she felt this as a rejection. Each time she felt sad or needy she thought of running to Ed. She wanted to run away from her sadness; she wanted Ed to make her happy and fulfilled. Although this pattern did not start with Ed, Sarah was now able to see it more clearly. She could see that she looked to Ed to provide her with the love and affection she had not received as a child. She wanted Ed to take away her years of sadness over the loss of her mother's love; she wanted him to give her what her mother had not.

A visit to her parents' home in Kansas City stimulated the next breakthrough in therapy. Now that Sarah was living apart from her family, she could see many interactions which she had not seen previously. She could see the extent to which her father had been absent, how uninvolved and distant he still was from the family, how all his contact with her was confined to asking her about her job and her achievements.

She became increasingly aware of her anger toward him and struggled to be civil to him. At the same time, she noticed that her mother was, as she had always been, volatile and capricious. Although Sarah had gone home determined to want and need less from her mother, she still felt hurt by her mother's criticisms and violent mood swings. She still felt put off balance by her mother's unpredictability. She felt like a little girl again, scared and vulnerable.

When she returned to Washington, Sarah had much to work on. First, she was now more in touch with her anger and could allow herself to feel it without turning it inward on herself or outward on Ed. She knew she was angry at her father; she was angry at him for not being available to her both when she was a child and now as an adult. She felt cheated and angry. Sarah's therapist suggested that perhaps Sarah was also feeling some anger at her mother. Yes, in addition to her fear of her mother's capriciousness, Sarah also was angry that she could not rely on her mother to be a consistently warm and loving person. This interpretation helped Sarah to connect with some of her buried feelings. Yes, she was angry at her mother. In fact, she had been angry at her for giving birth to her younger sister and then becoming depressed. Even before that, Sarah had been angry; her mother could not be counted on. In fact, Sarah had not been able to rely on either of her parents. Their love had been inconsistent. She had translated their inconsistency into her own unlovability. As a result, she sought constant reassurance from Ed that she was lovable. She was trying to win from Ed that which she had not felt from her parents.

Sarah's last task in therapy was to mourn that which she had not received from her parents, and to then go beyond it. She needed to feel her anger at both of her parents for not giving her the love she wanted and deserved as a child. She needed to feel her sadness about herself as a child for not feeling loved or lovable. She needed to feel this pain again and again until she could finally be free of it. She did not need to find someone in the present to fulfill these past needs; that was neither necessary nor possible. No one in the present could make up for that which she had not gotten in the past.

And, as an adult, she did not need those things any more. She needed to let go of her past anger and sadness. She needed to see her parents for what they really were, to forgive them, and to realize that they had done the best they could and that it had to be enough. She had to forgive them and then let go of them. She needed to start living in the present and enjoying her adult life. When she was able to forgive them, she could then recognize what they had been able to give her, recognize the ways in which they had loved her, and see them as human beings with both human frailties and strengths.

Sarah felt her anger and sadness. She felt sad about her childhood deprivations and her fear that she was unlovable, she felt angry that she had not received the caring she had deserved as a child. As a result of Sarah's working through these unhappy feelings, her depression lifted. Life would always entail both sadness and anger, but she was now able to permit herself love and happiness as well.

6

Intimacy:
THE ABILITY TO LOVE

DEAR HARRY,

This is intended as a short note to tell you of my caring and my intention to file for a divorce from you. Please don't blame yourself. I have had several affairs in the last six months and I am not sure why. I'm not sure of anything except that I will soon be divorced for the third time. This seems really crazy in view of my lifelong desire to be a happily married woman. I feel very confused as to why I am doing this, but I know I will do it.

Love, JAN

As Jan sat in her darkening hotel room, she felt unsure of herself. She knew only that she had to send this letter to Harry. She felt confused and perplexed as to what was motivating her, but slowly sealed the letter, wrote their address on it, and stamped it. Jan then began reviewing the 29 years of her life, trying to make some sense out of them. She wanted to understand the patterns that kept replaying themselves over and over like melodies in a blues symphony. Somehow Jan felt as though she were reciting lines from a play, as though she were acting a role she was powerless to change.

Jan was reared in a middle-class Catholic family. Her father was a salesman for a chemical company and his job necessitated frequent moves from town to town. He was a social extrovert who was always the life of the party. He knew a great many people with whom he had superficial friendships but was not close to anyone; no one really knew him well. Jan was raised on her father's grandiose plans for the family. He wanted them to live better than they did and always had a new scheme for being the salesman of the year and making a lot of money. Though he was immensely enthusiastic about each of his schemes, he was never able to bring any of them to fruition. Similarly, he went from one job to another, always imagining that he could make his mark in the new job, that somehow this time he would strike it rich. Although he was a natural-born salesman, he could never bring his ideas to reality; he could never actualize his goals.

Jan's mother was a housewife, very much devoted to her husband, supporting him in all of his wild schemes, and never losing faith in his ability to make his dreams their reality. She always relied on his decisions for the family, feeling that he was much brighter and more capable than she. Independent thinking was not something Jan's mother felt capable of, and, besides, her husband "always knew best." Because of the frequent family moves, she was always in the process of packing or unpacking the household and hence had no time to develop her own separate life. She never met the neighbors or made friends. Her family and her husband were her whole life. Jan's mother had been reared in rather unusual circumstances. Her own mother had died when she was five, and she had been raised by her father and older sister. She did not talk much about her mother's death or her childhood and tried to convince herself that those things were in the past and did not matter any more. Although Jan's mother had managed to fill her adult life with all the symbols of successful womanhood, one could sense in her that some indefinable spirit had been crushed.

Jan had a sister ten years her senior. Following the birth of this sister, Jan's mother had experienced a series of miscarriages, which led her to believe that she would never have another child. By the time Jan was conceived, her mother had given up the idea of having more children and was not prepared for being a mother again. Although she had seemed devoted to her eldest child from the beginning, she seemed less giving with Jan.

Jan had vivid memories of her childhood. Her mother had

very definite ideas of how things should be done: a place for everything and everything in its place. There was a right way to do everything. Jan's mother dutifully taught Jan the proper way to complete tasks. But no matter how hard Jan tried, she was unable to meet her mother's expectations. And when she failed, her mother would turn on her with fury. When Jan made a pie, her mother told her the crust was not flaky enough. When Jan learned to sew, there was always a stitch out of place or a dart that needed redoing. When she did not do things to her mother's liking, Jan was told that she was no good. Her mother took it as a personal rejection when Jan did not do things perfectly, and she heaped criticism on her. Jan felt that she could never be good enough, do enough of the right things, or love her mother in the right way to receive the praise she so desperately sought.

One of the memories which Jan recalled with waves of shame and anger was an incident following her entry into first grade. Jan had wet her pants in the morning and her mother had insisted that she attend school wearing the same wet pants, exposing Jan's shame and humiliation to the world. Jan felt devastated; she felt that this marked her as a bad, terrible child. She felt, too, that the world would recognize her badness and would be unable to value her, just as her mother did not value her.

Despite Jan's difficulties at home, she proved to be popular among her peers. Like her father, she had an easy time socializing with others and making friends. She was an attractive girl who, in fact, bore a striking resemblance to her mother. She was of average intelligence and with little effort consistently received average grades in school. Even Jan's frequent moves did not detract from her ability to develop friendships and gain popularity. Shortly after she began high school, Jan caught a glimpse of one of the school's football stars. She fell for him at first glance and immediately felt that her life would be fulfilled if only she could be his wife. He asked her out and, to Jan's great delight, fell in love with her. It was a dream come true for Jan. She became a cheerleader in order to be near him during his practices and games. Despite her passion for him, she abided by her mother's dictates and maintained her virginity until she married him a week after graduation.

For the first six months, marriage was the bliss she had always sought. Sex was fantastic. She could hardly let her husband get out of bed in the morning to go to work, and she spent her days imagining what it would be like when he returned home in the evening. While he worked, Jan watched soap operas on TV and prepared elaborate meals for him. Her life became a routine of cleaning their small apartment, watching television, preparing meals, and looking forward to the time when he came home. She hid from her own awareness a vague sense of growing dissatisfaction. Was this really all her life was to be—television, cooking, and the nightly thrusting in bed? For even sex had become less important to her. Somehow over the months she had ceased to look forward to it as much. The newness of it had worn thin; no longer an adventure, it had become a tiresome routine. Jan realized that she was bored; she could hardly face another day. Even the soap operas failed to intrigue her. One evening during dinner she announced her decision to get a job, but her husband was adamantly opposed; he was the man of the house and she was to stay home while he worked to support her. Without further consideration, Jan knew what she would do. The next day she packed her clothes, moved out, and filed for a divorce.

Jan's mother was furious with her for breaking the rules. Marriages were sacred; people did not get divorced. Jan had made her bed, and she was to stay in it with her husband. Her mother refused to speak to her and, in fact, had not spoken to her to this day. Jan was not aware of being in the least upset about the loss of her mother. She told herself that her mother had never cared for her anyway, and this just formalized their break.

Jan got a job as a saleswoman and enjoyed being out on her own and supporting herself for the first time in her life. During her periods of anxiety or unhappiness about being alone, she went out with friends or to a bar where she met men who were attentive to her. And so her life went on for the next three years. She went from one relationship to another; they were all the same. There was an initial burst of passion, an opening thrill accompanied by wild lovemaking, followed by irritability and boredom. Jan was grateful that she had not married any of these men during their periods of wild abandon, for they all had soon grown stale and uninteresting.

Then, when Jan was 23, she met Fred, an instructor at a community college. Fred seemed completely different; he was stable and intellectual. This time there was no wild passion, no hours of lovemaking. He obviously cared about her and respected her. He was interested in her mind rather than her body and wanted her to realize her intellectual potential. He became her mentor and, following his advice, she began school. Shortly thereafter, they were married. Jan became interested in the same type of art that Fred liked; she read the same books; she liked the same music. She worked hard in college to please him. They were always together and people commented on what a good relationship they had. Of course, their relationship held no excitement, no flair, no intense feelings. But after all, Jan reasoned, this was what mature marriages were like. Certainly stability, love, and caring were more important than excitement or short-lived thrills.

Jan graduated from college and took a job as a manufacturer's representative for a china company. Shortly thereafter she met Harry, a colleague. As soon as she saw him she felt that same wave of excitement, the same certainty that she had felt about her high school sweetheart. If she could marry Harry she would be fulfilled. Jan could not stop herself; soon she and Harry were involved in a passionate affair. She ignored her relationship with Fred. She and Harry spent hours in bed while Fred waited at home, wondering what had happened to their marriage. Harry himself was married and the father of three children, but he too was swept up by the passion and quickly moved to divorce his wife so that he and Jan could be together. It was again like a fairy tale come true; Harry was everything she wanted in a man. He was everything she wanted to be herself. She could hardly wait until their divorces were final so they could spend every day together. At 28, Jan was married for the third time.

Now here she sat in the dark hotel room, recalling all the men in her life. It seemed as if she had become a different person with each of them. First she was the enthusiastic cheerleader turned passionate wife, then the hip bar-hopper, then the adoring college student, and finally again the passionate wife. Jan looked at the way she had been with each man; she had always tried hard to please each one, wanted to spend all her time with him, and each time was convinced that this man was her fulfillment in life. With each new man she thought that she had finally found the permanent love she wanted. And yet each time that love had seemed within her grasp, she had turned away from it. How could she turn away from the love that she wanted so desperately? In search of an answer, Jan entered therapy.

Mother and Father Revisited: Reaping the Fruits of Separation

It is impossible to talk about love and intimacy without talking about your relationship with your parents, since your relationship with them is the foundation for all your relationships. Your adult experiences of and potential for intimacy are based on your experiences with early caretakers. Your relationships throughout life—those intimate, loving, close, frustrating, or fused relationships—are variations on the theme that you and your parents developed together.

Fusion: A Mutant of Love

The origin of all the issues that arise in your life concerning fusion is your relationship with your mother. It is with her that you are originally fused, biologically tied. Obviously, you are fused prior to your birth when you share the same body. At that time, you and she are one. Immediately after your birth until you are about six months of age, this fusion continues. You do not recognize yourself as a separate person. You and your mother are one. You mold your body to hers; there is no boundary between you. Her breast is your lifeline; her body gives you life and nourishment. You are at one with her, and it is this oneness which makes you feel safe, secure, and loved. An oceanic feeling exists between you and your mother. You feel the waves of her love, keeping you safe and secure. All of your life is peace and contentment. This fusion is both necessary and inevitable.

As you become older and more separate from your mother, your relationship with her remains crucial and influences your ability to relate to other people in your world. If your mother remains consistently loving and giving while fostering your developing sense of independence, you feel safe and secure within yourself. You go out into the world without needing to give parts of yourself, without wanting to fuse and return to the blissful feeling of oceanic oneness with your mother. If, on the other hand, your mother is not able to be sufficiently loving and giving, you may spend your adult life seeking the blissful feelings that you had with your mother during your first months of life, but were too soon lost. Similarly, if your mother is overly smothering and cannot let you go, you may find it difficult to go beyond her scope, and you may repeat fused relationships in your adult life. The reverse may also be true; you may be so terrified of repeating the fusion with your mother that you are unable to form close relationships and may always "run scared" from intimate relationships. Thus if you do not get enough love and attention as a child, or if you are smothered and not permitted to go outside of the realm of your family, your chances of having problems that center around fusion increase dramatically.

Fused relationships are common occurrences. For you as an adult, fusion is the loss of the sense of yourself as a separate being. It is the giving over of your identity to another person. Fusion is a feeling that you and another person are molded into one larger entity; you and the other are one being. You feel that you cannot survive without the other person. The two of you feel like one. Your interests are the same; your perspective on life is the same. When the other leaves, you are not sure you can survive. You feel as if you may die. Your entire life is bound with the other person's. Separations are gut-wrenching experiences; you feel as though you have been abandoned. When you are not with the other, you are obsessed about that person, going over and over in your mind all the nuances of each word and each look that have passed between you. Your entire life is woven around the time you will spend with the other person. Your friends, your hobbies, your interests, even your job, recede in importance. You will sacrifice anything for the other person.

Still, you carry with you a feeling of insecurity; a feeling that you are not loved enough, that you are not really safe, that you are not cherished. You do not feel loved because you are no longer yourself, because you have given away yourself and have become the reflection of another. You no longer have anything of yourself to love. You are like Cyrano de Bergerac, giving up yourself, your life, so that your loved one can be happy. It matters not what happens to you; all that matters is that your lover is happy. Your feeling is that the other person is paramount. The reality, however, is that you do not love this other as a separate, unique human being; rather, you love this person for what he or she can give to you. You are hoping that your lover will be able to fill your unmet needs. You are hoping that with this person you can recapture the oceanic bliss that you once shared with your mother. You are longing for the return of a feeling rather than the mutual, interdependent love of a separate person. You are not valuing the other for himself or herself, but rather for what he or she can give to you. This person is a substitute for your mother.

Although fusion can create much pain and suffering, fusion can also provide you with some of your most exhilarating and fulfilling moments. Temporary closeness and fusion in which two bodies are molded as one and during which your lover anticipates that which will most arouse you is an example of fusion during sexual contact and is in the service of healthy pleasure. It is a time when your separateness and your unique individuality are put on the shelf for awhile and you and your lover are one body, fulfilling, at the same time, one another and yourself. You are one body, one spirit, one soul sharing the same sexual pleasure.

Many of you as mothers recapitulate your own fusion as an infant through the fused relationship with your infant. Then you, as a mother, are fused with your baby, and the oceanic feelings which you had as an infant are again rearoused by the suckling pleasure of your own child. Here again, fusion is a necessary and healthy aspect of human relationships. Thus fusion is a double-edged sword; although it may create in relationships that which is the most painful and traumatic, it may also create in relationships that which is the most blissful and passionate.

The Electra Complex

You, as a three-year-old child, enter the Electra period having already experienced in toto your mother's psyche. The relationship with your mother, whether fused, rejecting, or healthy, has set the stage and dressed you in a costume with which to play out the drama of the family romance. By the time you are three you are increasingly able to perceive and involve yourself in the world around you. You have a sufficient sense of yourself and enough personal strength from your relationship with your mother to permit a close relationship with another human being, and this human being is usually your father.

Now your father takes on a new interest. Previously he was more in the background while your mother played the role of the primary caretaker. Now you become aware of and aroused by the intriguing differences between your parents. Your increasing awareness of these sexual differences creates strange sensations that reside in your genital region and become linked with your feelings toward your father. Then you attach your genital, sexual feelings to the nearest man in your world, and that man is usually your father. Now you want your father all to yourself, just as in the past you wanted your mother. For the first time, you respond to your mother with a mixture of jealousy and competition, competing with her for your father's attention and love. This web of entangled, intense feelings—mixtures of lust and longing, jealousy, hatred, as well as fear of disappointment and rejection—is called the Electra complex. It is an intense family romance. The Oedipal complex, about which so much has been written, is the male counterpart of the Electra complex.

If you are raised in a traditional family, you are with your mother all day. Your father's return from work signals dinnertime for the family. An excitement about your daddy being home prevails, and you feel thrilled to see him. Some of these feelings of intrigue and excitement are localized in your genitals and, hence, are called sexual. But you are also interested in your father as a separate and special person, as someone more novel than your mother with whom you have spent most of the day. He is the most interesting person in your life. When he comes home he does not need to concern himself with the daily, mundane household tasks but can spend time playing games and talking with you. You are his princess just as he is your prince. Yet you are extremely aware of the difference between you, an unseen wall that you greet with a mixture of fear, fascination, and curiosity. You are uncertain as to the nature of this difference; you are unsure of how his body works; you do not know what all this means.

You are also keenly aware that your father treats you differently from the way he treats your mother. You see the subtle changes in your mother when your father comes home and how differently she relates to him than she does to you. Suddenly your mother is not the person in power and authority. She is, at best, equal with someone. At worst, she may become a child in relationship to your father. You watch diligently this relationship between your parents. From your watching, you learn how they are with each other, how they communicate, how they express warmth and affection, anger and sadness. You watch and learn and model.

As you continue to grow, your sexual feelings toward your father recede as newer and more available males enter your life. You may develop crushes on your cousins, movie stars, or the handsome sixth-grade boy in your school. Unconsciously knowing that your sexual feelings toward your father are taboo and cannot be acted on, you move to others and soon forget that you ever had such feelings. It seems almost impossible to you that you ever felt such intense longing and excitement at the mere sight of your father. As you become a teenager, these feelings seem totally impossible to you. This is a period in which you see your father in the bleakest light, and, by so doing, are able to overcome your lust for and dependence on him. It is a period in which your sexual feelings become available for other men. Yet, like a recurring melody, the drama of your unique Electra complex is repeated throughout your life.

Lovability: Your View of Yourself

You, like everyone else, question your lovability—question whether you are a worthwhile, lovable person. If from the beginning of your life your parents treat you with love and respect, you are likely to grow up feeling lovable. Loving parents instill within you a sense of your own lovability and value. You know how much your parents appreciate you, how much they respect you; and thus you know that you must be a good, worthwhile person who is able to give and to receive love. If your parents are smothering and praise you for everything, never objectively evaluating your strengths and weaknesses, you are likely to grow up wondering if you are really being loved for yourself. You may wonder if people really see you as you are, or if they are loving some idealized image of you. You may wonder if you are a basically lovable person or if you are being loved because of your appearance, your achievements, or your position.

If, on the other hand, your parents are basically unloving, ungiving, or rejecting, you are likely to grow up feeling unlovable. You feel that you must be a terrible, unlovable person because you are not able to win your parents' love. You feel that you must have an evil core; you must be the "bad seed." Because you feel unlovable, you are terrified of letting anyone come close to you for fear that they will see just how bad you are. You feel, "Anyone who really knew me could not possibly love me." You struggle through life with a core of self-hatred and self-doubt, a sense of badness, a feeling of being a terrible person. You may keep to yourself because you fear that if you are not alone, others will see your "badness." Feeling so totally unlovable colors your entire life, making it difficult for you to feel worthwhile. You feel instead that nobody has ever loved you and nobody ever will.

For most of you, the issues you face concerning lovability are not as all-encompassing and appear in milder form. You may be concerned that the man you love will find another woman more attractive or more intelligent than you. You may care for someone more than that person cares for you, and this may challenge your feelings of lovability.

Those of you who do feel loved may have questions about why you are loved: Am I loved because I am basically a lovable person, or because I am easy to get along with? Am I loved because I am good looking? Is it because of my achievements or because I take care of people? The issue for you may be whether it is the essence of you that is loved or whether it is what you do that is loved. Or the issue may be whether you are loved because of who you are, because of what you may become, or because of what you do for others.

Trust: *Your View of Others*

How you as an adult will view other people is predicated on how you and your parents view each other when you are a child. If your parents treat you lovingly and consistently, then you are likely to greet other people as though they too are loving and friendly, as though they too can be trusted. Your family is a microcosm for the world; your parents are prototypes for other people. If from your earliest months your caretakers are sensitive to your needs, both physical and psychological, then more likely than not you will view the world as a safe and secure place and view other people as trustworthy. Your parents must feed you, clothe you, and keep you warm. They must share your joys and wipe away your tears. They must be there for you in a consistently warm and loving manner, reinforcing your notion of them as reliable and constant. As you view your parents, so too will you view other people in the world. You also watch your parents' relationship to see how they relate to one another. Are they considerate of each other's feelings? Do they love each other and support each other? Do they nurture each other's growth and development? If they provide a model of consistent love and security, it is likely that you will approach others with the assumption that they too are trustworthy. In addition, you watch how your parents relate to others outside the family. Are they friendly and outgoing, enjoying a variety of different people? Do they act as though they trust others? Do they assume that other people can be counted on? You sense whether they like and trust others and, if they do, feel more sure yourself that other people are reliable and trustworthy.

If, on the other hand, your parents do not treat you with the respect due a separate, sensitive human being, you will be more likely to assume that other people too are dangerous, that other people too will disregard your feelings and be insensitive to your pain. You may assume then that other people consider only themselves and pay little heed to the needs and feelings of others. Similarly, your distrust of the world is increased if you see your parents being insensitive to one another or approaching the world with a mixture of suspicion and distrust. Then you too may feel that the world is a frightening, unpredictable jungle.

The reality is that the world is not a jungle, nor is it totally safe and secure. The reality is somewhere in the middle. During the course of your life you will meet people who will care for you and treat you with respect, people who are responsible and moral and behave with integrity. You will also meet people who are lacking in integrity, who care only for themselves and have no concern about the damage they may cause or the pain they may inflict on others. Your parents can be most helpful to you if they can teach you that there is much ambiguity in the world; that there are many differences among people. This lack of absolutes is, of course, difficult for you as a small child to understand. However, as your experiences of people and of the world increase, you become more capable of distinguishing the differences between people and more able to understand that people are neither all bad nor all good.

If, as an adult, you experience other people as untrustworthy, it will be difficult for you to involve yourself in an intimate relationship. You may keep yourself distant from others, for fear that closeness will bring pain. You may wall yourself off from others, perhaps presenting a prickly exterior or a wall of indifference. Your lack of trust necessitates your avoidance of closeness. Of course, the more you present yourself with a hard and tough façade, the more people will stay away from you, further convincing you that people are dangerous and not to be trusted. This becomes a self-fulfilling prophecy.

On the other hand, if you experience people as basically trustworthy, you are more likely to allow yourself to risk becoming intimately involved with others. This does not mean that you will never be hurt, but rather that you will know that being hurt is part of the risk of intimacy—a risk that must be taken in order to reap the benefits of an intimate relationship. This pain will not immobilize you or drive you into a shell. You will deal with your pain until you are healed and again ready to risk the vulnerability that accompanies closeness. This does not mean that you trust people indiscriminately, throwing yourself into any and all relationships, but rather that you see others as basically trustworthy and are able to make an intelligent decision about another person's ability to be close and humane.

Early Expressions of Intimacy: A Circle

What you have learned from your early caretakers, how you feel about your own lovability, and how you gauge the trustworthiness of others set the stage for your journey through relationships. You have amassed a repertoire of skills, knowledge, and intuitions about the workings of yourself and other people. You have already formed an incipient view of the world and your place in it. Now you are ready to begin relating with other people, refining your conception of yourself and your relationship to others. You begin tentatively experimenting with your ability to relate and carefully assess the results.

Now your siblings, your friends, your race, religion, sex, socioeconomic status, and physical appearance all begin to make an imprint on your life, to make an impact on your ability to relate with others. If, for example, your siblings treat you with love, respect, and compassion, you are more likely to grow up feeling as though people are friendly and trustworthy. If you are born with a physical impairment, however minor, you are more likely to doubt your own lovability. Or if your parents divorce when you are quite young, it may be more difficult for you to experience the world as a safe, secure place.

Frequently, factors such as your sex, race, socioeconomic status, and experiences with siblings and friends reinforce the themes of your early childhood. As you expand your experience of the world and develop a sense of yourself, you also develop expectations about the world's reaction to you. Often you behave in ways which reinforce those expectations, making them self-fulfilling prophecies. For example, if you have a sense of yourself as a separate, lovable human being, and a sense of other people as trustworthy, you will navigate the world in a friendly manner. In turn, your friendly, trusting approach to the world and other people will make it more likely that people will be friendly and trusting toward you. You will reap what you have sown. If, on the other hand, you do not see yourself as lovable or other people as trustworthy, you will greet the world with suspicion and hostility, making it more likely that other people will withdraw from you. Again, you reap what you have sown, becoming further convinced that people are hostile, unloving, and untrustworthy. Thus your experiences in childhood may result in self-fulfilling prophecies which influence your ability to relate in the world.

Suppose you as a child are playing on the playground with one other friend. You are feeling bad about yourself and are feeling unlovable. You may say to yourself, "No one likes me; only one kid will play with me." Feeling bad about yourself and critical of your playmate, you are likely to behave in such a way as to alienate the friend. When your playmate leaves you to be with another, your notion that you are unlovable and that other people are not to be trusted may be reinforced. Your suspiciousness and defensiveness are increased. On the other hand, suppose you view yourself as lovable and other people as trustworthy. You will be more likely to say, "I have one friend, and we are really close and have lots of fun together." You are likely to treat your friend in such a way that your friendship will be enhanced, and, as that friendship blossoms, your view of yourself as lovable and other people as trustworthy is further reinforced.

Of course, not all experiences confirm earlier expectations. Sometimes new situations impinge upon you and change your view of yourself and the world. Suppose you are well loved at home and have a sense of the world as safe. Much to your dismay, when you go out in the world you discover that others treat you unkindly, poking fun at your buck teeth and freckles. Even your teacher seems to treat you with less enthusiasm than you expected, giving you less attention than she gives to the other children. These new experiences change your self-image. You puzzle about your lovability and question whether the world is as trustworthy as you thought. On the other hand, suppose you grow up in a family where you do not feel special and are not certain how safe the outside world is. As you tentatively approach the world, you find that your superior intelligence brings you much attention and praise. You feel lovable and special; other people appreciate you and seem to be trustworthy. Here again, your self-image and view of the world have changed because of your experiences with the world beyond your family. A myriad of incidents and experiences contribute to your increasingly complex and changing self-image. And this self-image, evolved from the new data about your lovability and others' trustworthiness, determines your relationships with others.

Unhealthy Interpersonal Stances

From childhood on, you carry into every human interaction your experiences and anticipations which, in turn, influence your present interactions, increasing the likelihood that your initial expectation will be reinforced. For example, if you experience yourself as unlovable, you may isolate yourself from people, fearful that permitting closeness will expose your "badness." Then, when people do not reach out to you, you feel even more unlovable and isolate yourself still more. Similarly, if you have unresolved sexual feelings about your father, you may love an older, ungiving man, trying to seek from him that which you did not receive from your father. But if he sees you simply as an "easy lay," rather than as an important, meaningful person, you may become more determined to win from other men what both he and your father have been unable to give you. You may then begin pursuing many older men, trying still harder to symbolically win with your father. In this manner your earlier experiences can snowball, further hindering your ability to develop close, intimate relationships.

A clinging vine. Ann could not enter a relationship without becoming a "clinging vine." At 30 she sought therapy when her current lover said that he would have to end their relationship if she did not stop clinging to him and smothering him. Ann did not want their relationship to end. She was terrified that it would leave her totally devastated and incapable of functioning. This was the third man who had complained of her clinging to him; the first two had left her. Ann began to wonder what she was doing to destroy her relationships. What was she playing out from her past? Ann did not want to experience again the searing pain of a separation. She could remember only too vividly the pain of past endings when she could not eat, sleep, or work efficiently. She had felt panicked. She had been anxiety-ridden and had felt endangered, although she knew that nothing catastrophic would happen to her. She also had found herself wanting to go back home to her mother, who would not hurt her or cause her pain. She remembered her mother's warning that people outside the family were not to be trusted. Only the family was safe; other people could be hurtful and dangerous.

Ann's first lover was a man she met during her freshman

year in college. She arrived at school intent on carving out a career for herself, not on finding a husband or lover. However, much to her surprise, she was soon head over heels in love with a fellow classmate, and her schoolwork plummeted. Ann thought of nothing but him; she could not bear to be separated from him. She talked with him constantly, cutting her classes to be with him. They ate together, slept together, spent practically every moment of their time together. Other people jokingly began to call them Siamese twins.

After a while, Ann's lover began to feel crowded; he told her he needed more time for himself and his studies. Ann felt terribly anxious when she was not with him and spent every moment waiting and longing for the time when she would be with him again. As time went on, she became increasingly demanding of him. If they were apart, she wanted him to call and let her know where he was. She could not understand how he could want to spend time away from her. As Ann became increasingly dependent and demanding, her lover felt increasingly trapped. He no longer felt like his own person; he did not feel free. As he began taking more time for himself, Ann became increasingly anxious. She thought perhaps she had been wrong; perhaps she could not really trust his love for her. Maybe her mother was right after all; maybe safety could not be found outside the family.

This relationship continued for a year and a half, during which time Ann became increasingly clinging and perpetually anxious, while her lover became increasingly distancing. Finally, he told Ann that he did not want to continue the relationship because she was simply too demanding and dependent. He loved her, but just could not cope with her. Ann was devastated. She felt as though her world had ended. She was constantly anxious. Her heart pounded so hard that she felt it would explode. Her stomach was in knots. Ann entertained the notion of going back to the safety of her home and enrolling in a local college, but on the advice of a close friend decided against it.

In time, Ann resolved her confusion about her lover's leaving by telling herself that it was all his problem; he was deficient in his ability to relate intimately. She had thought that, like her mother, he would care for her and love her forever. Having discovered that this was not true, Ann decided that she would have to be more careful the next time. Maybe no man could be trusted. Maybe they were all like her lover, unable to love and care for a woman.

Ann threw herself into her schoolwork and her female friends. She promised herself not to become involved with a man for a long time. She was going to be cautious enough to guarantee that she did not feel this pain ever again. And, in fact, that is exactly what Ann did. She finished her undergraduate and graduate career without any further sexual involvement. Sometimes she felt lonely; sometimes she felt vulnerable; sometimes she felt incomplete, as though she were not whole without a man. But she did not open herself up to a new involvement until after beginning her first job. Then she decided to again try relating to men, still wondering whether they could be trusted, still fearing that they could not.

Now, a new variation of the old theme evolved. Ann would go out with a man for the first time, holding herself somewhat distant and wondering if she could trust him to love her as she wanted to be loved. After the first date she would invariably find herself involved in some crisis which necessitated the immediate attention of the new man in her life. In her mind, Ann greeted each new man with the question, "Is he the one who will love me forever and satisfy all of my needs?" So, albeit unconsciously, in order to test each one she became involved in a crisis. In one instance she called a man the day after their first date, very distraught about a car accident, needing him to take her to the hospital and to help her with the insurance forms. In another instance she called a new date, upset about her uncle's death and wanting a ride to the funeral. Each time she presented herself as helpless and needy. These were just two of the crises that Ann needed help with. Of course, most of the men did not pass Ann's unconscious tests. They hardly knew her; why should they be available to her in situations that called for the aid of an intimate friend or family member? Why should they put away their own lives and devote hours of their time to a stranger? It did not make sense. Their "failure," of course, reinforced Ann's notion that men were basically untrustworthy and incapable of love.

Additionally, as these men disappointed Ann and her dependency needs remained unmet, she became more clinging and more demanding. A snowball effect was thus created. Ann wanted her dependency needs met. As she became more clinging, men became increasingly rejecting of her, thereby increasing her dependency needs. Her response was to create even more difficult tests, which men read as indications of the extent of her neediness. And they fled in terror. What Ann did not realize was that on an unconscious level she did not really want a man to stand by her for, if she had, she would have chosen one who needed to be needed as much as she needed to be dependent. In other words, both her fear of fusion and her need to reinforce her image of men as untrustworthy predominated; otherwise she would have found a man who wanted to be needed as much as she wanted to be taken care of. Their needs would have hooked them together. This hook-up might have been less than healthy but would have insured that they stay together. Consistently choosing men who fled from her neediness reinforced her unconscious fear of her own need for fusion while intensifying her conscious quest for a "trustworthy" man.

Finally Ann found a man who passed her test and she allowed herself to trust again. The relationship evolved as before, and soon she was repeating all of her demands. Not surprisingly, this relationship too was ended by the man, leaving Ann further convinced that men were untrustworthy and unable to love. Once again Ann lived a life of caution, avoiding all sexual relationships and throwing herself into her work.

Through her job, Ann met a man who became a fairly close platonic friend. They enjoyed their time together, having dinner or going to the movies. They both appreciated the friendship. With time the sexual attraction between them increased and finally they decided to sexualize their relationship. Ann was frightened but hopeful. Here was another chance. She was going to try again, although she had not put him to the test. However, she had known him for a while as a friend and felt him to be a kind and loving man.

Slowly it all began to repeat itself. Ann's thoughts were always on her new lover, wondering what he was doing when they were apart, worrying about his caring for her, feeling lonely for him. She lived for their time together. Again she became clinging and demanding. She fawned over him, washing and ironing his shirts, tidying up his apartment. At first he was flattered by her attention, interpreting it as proof of her love, but soon he began to feel smothered. When he tried to explain these feelings to her she reacted with dismay and terror, wondering if he were rejecting her, wondering if he were unable to love. These feelings were only too familiar to Ann. Her lover encouraged Ann to go into therapy. He believed that it was not men who were unable to love her, but rather that her demands were insatiable. Knowing that her experiences with men could no longer be attributed to chance, and possibly not even to the inability of men, Ann began therapy.

Ann learned that she behaved in such a way that what she feared the most was guaranteed to happen and what she wanted the most was doomed to failure. Ann's mother smothered her and taught her not to trust other people. She rewarded her dependency and clingyness with attention and love. Ann's relationship with her first lover restimulated her childhood dependency needs which she then acted out with him. This intense dependency drove him away, proving to Ann that men were not reliable. Believing that men were unable to satisfy her needs, she withdrew from all men. When Ann felt able to embark on a new relationship with a man she created tests which were impossible to pass, tests which were both premature and excessive. And as the men failed these tests, she was again convinced of their untrustworthiness and inability to meet her needs. These failures then stimulated even greater demands by Ann, which further drove the men away. Ann needed to realize that she was not the helpless child that she once was, that adults do not respond to clingyness in the same manner that her mother responded to her as a child, and that she no longer needed her mother as she had needed her as a child. Lastly, Ann needed to learn that love is not equivalent to fusion, and that demanding to be cared for like a child undermined her chances of being loved and valued as an adult.

Running hot and cold. Samantha, age 24, is another example of a woman who was continually replaying and embroidering a childhood script. When Samantha was eight she spent hours putting on her mother's makeup, dressing up in fanciful costumes, and dancing for her father, who sat entranced as his daughter, exotically and seductively dressed, pirouetted for him. Now Samantha at age 24 spent hours applying the most exotic, expensive makeup. In fact, sometimes she even had a bevy of attendants to style her hair and dress her. Her job as a fashion model involved hours of pirouetting, dancing, and posing in front of the camera. Samantha was living out her childhood fantasy. She was doing as an adult that which was most thrilling for her as a child. Yet, while she was replaying the best of her childhood, she was replaying the worst as well.

Samantha vividly remembered a gnawing sense of discomfort during her childhood dancing for her father. Even though he doted on her and applauded her during these performances, she knew that this was the only time that she would have him. If she brought him her school work, a skinned knee, or a concern about a playmate, he would invariably dismiss her, telling her to talk with her mother. He was too busy for such mundane concerns; yet he was obviously proud of her physical beauty and never tired of showing her off to his friends. Samantha was aware that her father related differently to her mother. He attended to what she said and indicated interest in her concerns and well-being. Samantha knew she was not as important, or at least important in a less complete way. She could not measure up to her mother, except in her appearance. Samantha's beauty was outstanding; it always commanded attention.

Not surprisingly, Samantha chose modeling as her career, using her greatest asset to insure both financial security and, she hoped, love. And, sure enough, her beauty reaped success in both areas. She became a sought-after model with a rapidly growing reputation; and men fell at her feet. They adored her with puppy dog eyes, wanting to follow her to the ends of the earth. Most of the men Samantha attended to were at least ten years her senior, if not more. She did not know why, but she found young men boring and older men fascinating and sexually exciting. The men were intrigued with her; she became their toy, their playmate. Thus Samantha had unconsciously repeated the relationship with her father by choosing men close to his age who experienced her in the same way as he had, as a prize to be displayed to the world. She was not a real human being to any of them, simply a beautiful object.

These relationships did not exactly parallel the one with her father. Once she was involved with a man, their relationship ran hot and cold, alternating between extreme passion and extreme hostility. Each new relationship took off like a rocket, soaring to the heavens with passion and love, and just as quickly surrendered to violent fights and agony. Then Samantha found her lover disgusting and heaped criticism on him. He was not good looking enough, he was too hairy, his penis was not long enough, he did not make enough money, or his table manners were obnoxious, etc., etc. Everything was wrong with him; nothing was right. Her prince had turned into a frog. She responded with disgust, wanting to end the relationship. Her disgust would then give way to rage, and a huge fight would ensue. The fight was in turn followed by a reawakening of attraction to those very qualities in him which were so disgusting an hour before. Then they would find themselves making wildly passionate love, reminding Samantha of the skyrocketing delights of their early days together.

Samantha's relationships were characterized by intense passion, followed by criticism and rage, and finally punctuated with passion. In choosing men like her father, Samantha was acting out her Electra conflict. Although she wanted to win from these men more genuine love than she had received from her father, these relationships were so reminiscent of her relationship with her father that they unconsciously called forth her sexual feelings for him. As she allowed herself to become closer to each new man in her life, she also became increasingly but unconsciously frightened by her incestuous feelings. She then defended against these feelings by fighting to create distance from her sexual feelings. Thus her critical and argumentative attitude with her lovers was her mechanism for creating the distance she needed to feel safe from her sexual feelings for her father. Then, given the reestablishment of distance, Samantha felt safe enough to desire her father in the form of her lover and again sought the closeness she had just destroyed.

Unknowingly, Samantha was behaving in ways which insured that she would not develop the kind of relationship she wanted. First, she snared all of her lovers with her beauty. This was her calling card. Unfortunately, most men interested in her for her beauty never looked further. Like Samantha's father, all her lovers wanted was a beautiful woman on their arm as proof of their masculinity and prowess. They cared only for her externals, with no regard for her as a person. Whether she was a worthwhile human being was irrelevant. Hence Samantha's attempts to find a man who loved her beyond her beauty brought only disappointment. In addition, despite her beauty, few men could tolerate Samantha's extremes of passion and distance. Although initially exciting, the extreme passion, followed by blood-curdling arguments, soon became too much to bear. She simply was not worth it to them, and they left her. With each new disappointment, Samantha's hurt and desperation deepened, restimulating the childhood pain of her father's dismissal. In response she would make herself all the more beautiful, attempting to ensnare still another "daddy" who would love her forever.

Samantha used her beauty, the childhood quality which brought her both her greatest pleasure and her greatest pain, and replayed it again and again. She sharpened it, she heightened it, she used all her adult skill and intelligence to refine it. It brought her increasing pleasure, increasing wealth, increasing pain, and increasing loneliness. It seemed to her as if there were no way out of this circle.

Ann and Samantha continued to relate in adulthood the way they had learned to relate in childhood, despite the fact that their interpersonal styles prevented them from receiving the love they wanted and deserved.

Like Ann and Samantha, you may not receive the love

that you want and deserve because you behave in ways which inadvertently prevent others from loving you. Additionally, you may be so focused on the love that *you* want, that you may forget the love you need to give in return. You may be so concerned with your lover's meeting your needs and filling you with love that you are insensitive to his needs and wants as a separate person. Becoming so caught up in yourself that you ignore your lover's feelings may also result in your being deprived of the love that you desperately yearn for.

The Anatomy of a Love Choice

When you truly love another human being, you love him for the unique, separate, special person that he is. You love this other not because he is an extension of you, not because he can make the world right for you, not because he can protect you from all harm, and not because he is a stand-in for a parent or past lover. You love him because he is himself and because you enjoy, respect, and admire him. You want to share your life together, watching one another's growth, development, and exploration of the world. You know he is a separate person. His feelings and needs are important to you, almost as important as your own. The progression of years bring sustained interest in one another and increased contentment, understanding, and compassion.

There are many reasons why the person you love is so special to you. Many of the reasons are simply because of who he is. Some of the reasons are because of the unconscious memories he brings forth in you. Perhaps he reminds you of a loved grandfather. Perhaps you feel with him some of the same good feelings you felt with your father. Perhaps his smile and his interest in you remind you of your mother. Perhaps his hobbies are similar to your grandmother's. Perhaps you and he are able to play together as you had played with your brother. This is not to say that you are consciously aware of this person's similarities to the important people of the past, but rather that you feel a certain comfort, familiarity, or joy that brings feelings of safety and security.

Shirley fell in love with Luis when they were both seniors

in college. She first saw him in the student union and was fascinated by this tall, dark, Mexican man. He seemed remote to her and yet intently involved with his friends. Shirley sensed that he was self-aware but not self-absorbed. Luis, too, had noticed Shirley, thinking that she was not American because of the unusual way she dressed. The next semester, Shirley, an anthropology major, registered for a course in Latin American cultures and was pleased to see that Luis was in the class, sitting next to her. Soon they were having intense conversations about each other and themselves, using the content of the course as a springboard to explore one another's cultures and lives. Luis was disappointed to learn that Shirley was an American, but this did not prevent him from asking her out. After all, she was Jewish, and that helped a bit.

Soon they were involved in an intense, passionate love affair. Love felt wonderful. Shirley awoke each day excited about both Luis and her life, a life in which she felt even more fulfilled since she had met Luis. When he leaned over to kiss her, she responded with joy and excitement. His smile warmed her. Even mundane tasks assumed an air of excitement when shared with Luis. She felt perpetually "high," as though every day were a party. Shirley felt her life was happier, more exciting, and more fulfilled than she had ever dreamed possible. Sexually, Luis was the most exciting man she had ever been with. They spent hours making love, sharing sexual fantasies, and exploring one another's bodies. As they explored each other's bodies, so they explored each other's minds, trying to give and take all of each other. They spent hours talking, revealing their innermost thoughts and their dreams for the future. They were fascinated by their different histories and, at the same time, impressed with the many similarities in their lives. Although they had come from widely different backgrounds, they shared many similar attitudes and reactions to life.

With time, Shirley realized her commitment to Luis. He was a human being whom she cared about very deeply, a special human being who could give so much to both her and the world. Luis was a sensitive, warm, caring man, able to engender respect and admiration from others as well as from

Shirley. She knew that she was committed to him as a person and that, regardless of what happened to them as lovers, she would always care about him and his well-being. Luis also was committed to Shirley. He had at last met a woman with whom he could share his passion as well as his soul, with whom he could be open in a way he had never dreamed possible. He wanted to plan a life together with Shirley.

What were the elements that contributed to Shirley's involvement with Luis? Most importantly, Luis was a fine human being, a loving, open, and warm man, who was sensitive to both Shirley and other people in his life. Additionally, Shirley and Luis shared many of the same political beliefs, aspirations, and values. There were, however, unconscious elements which created a special intensity and bond between them. In many ways, Luis represented the actualization of Shirley's unconscious life. Shirley was well aware, for example, that all of the women in her family had married men from a different class or religion. Her great grandmother had been an upper-class German Protestant radical enough to marry a poor Catholic and migrate to America. Her grandmother, following in her own mother's seemingly radical footsteps, had married a Jewish doctor, and Shirley's own mother had surrendered the riches of her family to marry a poor Jewish man. Thus it was engraved in Shirley's unconscious that women marry men who are from a different class, religious background, or race. In choosing Luis, Shirley had opted for a man who was different in all three of these aspects. This choice, though it seemed a departure from the family, was in fact an acceptance and internalization of the family norm. She was unconsciously modeling the women in her family in an attempt to strengthen her bond with them. Additionally, like Shirley's mother, Luis was a warm, loving, giving, and affectionate man. Thus being with Luis was reminiscent of the best times that Shirley had had with her mother, times when the two of them spent hours talking and discussing the world of ideas. Even though Shirley had had a close and sharing relationship with her mother, she had always felt that she was second in preference to her younger brother. In some ways, then, Shirley's relationship with Luis allowed her to finally win her mother. She could be number one with the person who on an unconscious level partially represented her mother.

Shirley's relationship with her father had always been more complicated for her. She knew that her father felt the most alive when he had conquered a woman by bedding her. She had witnessed her father's blatant flirtatiousness and her mother's distress at his infidelity. Shirley had made a conscious decision to marry a man who was as committed to monogamy as she was. And, in fact, this was true of Luis, who considered monogamy a crucial factor in an intimate relationship. Shirley also remembered how much time her father had spent away from the family working. Although he had been raised in a poor family, her father was a self-made man who had amassed a fortune as a businessman. Luis had no aspirations for such materialistic success; rather, he wanted to make his mark as a writer and contribute to bettering the circumstances of the Chicano people. Hence in his values, ethnic background, and personal aspirations, Luis was very different from Shirley's father. In choosing a man who was this different from her father, Shirley was expressing her anger at her father while at the same time protecting herself from the feelings stimulated by the family romance. She was also protecting herself from reexperiencing both her mother's pain and the pain of her childhood.

On the other hand, although Luis was different from Shirley's father in many important ways, they shared some similarities. They both loved books and, in fact, her father's main avocation was reading. Both men were ambitious, although the focus of their aspirations differed. They were both intent on making their mark on the world, gaining the respect of other people, and leaving their footprints on the sands of time.

As mentioned earlier, Shirley's relationship with Luis encapsulated more than her relationship with her parents. She had always felt very close to her maternal grandparents; and by what might be a chance occurrence, her choice of Luis further tied her to her loving relationship with them. Her grandmother spent most of her time writing poetry and had even had a small volume published. Her grandfather, though he supported his family as a physician, had been a radical communist in his youth and was still involved with radical politics. Thus Luis, a writer who was active in the Chicano left, also shared some of the characteristics of her grandparents and allowed Shirley a continuing connection with them.

Luis then represented many things to Shirley. By choosing him she was able to hold onto the positive aspects of both her parents and her grandparents while avoiding the uncomfortable elements that originated from her childhood family romance. The bonds that linked Shirley to Luis were bonds that originated in her childhood, bonds that intensified their relationship and quickened their commitment.

Pictures of Dyads

Of necessity, a relationship always involves two people, each bringing into the relationship a unique history and set of experiences. You meet each other, and your experiences and personalities mesh into a new entity, moving you into another dimension and creating a "relationship." This relationship is both greater than and different from the sum of its parts. Some of you complement each other, others clash. Some of your difficulties mesh in such a way as to insure that both of you will remain forever united in pain. Others of you are able to be together in a way that is mutually satisfying and growth inducing for both of you, a way in which the many aspects of your personalities contribute to the "workableness" of the partnership. There are, of course, many problematic relationships in which one or the other of you is in a great deal of pain or feels stifled or oppressed. How these relationships work and why you remain in them can usually be explained in terms of the unconscious elements being played out in the dyad. For example, one such relationship might be called a mother-child relationship. One of you is the caretaker, the giver, the mother; the other is the needy, dependent, clinging child who looks to the other partner to make the world safe. Such a relationship will work so long as the child remains a child and the mother wants to continue mothering. If the mother, however, should tire of the role, or the child should grow up, this previously workable relationship would become dysfunctional. You frequently, though unconsciously, seek out a complementary partner; those of you who need to play the child role will seek out a mother, whereas those of you who need to play the mother role will seek out a child. This search is unconscious, with neither of you specifically articulating what you are looking for or exactly how you mesh with that person. It is a popular truism that "love is blind," that you do not see aspects of yourself being played out in your relationships which are clearly visible to others.

Dyads can be described by delineating the unconscious elements being played out between the partners. For example, some of you need a triangular relationship, one in which three people are involved. In this case, because of your past family romance, you consistently maintain a three-person relationship in which you or your partner is involved with a third person. These triangles are a recapitulation of the triangular relationship that you experienced with your parents. Another dyad can be referred to as the "George and Martha" relationship, illustrated by Edward Albee's play, *Who's Afraid of Virginia Wolf?* The couple in this play, George and Martha, alternated between fusion and distance created by cruel and vicious verbal games. Their fusion created a sense of safety and oneness which surrendered to terror when the fusion became too intense. Their rages then created the distance they needed as a defense against their fusion.

A third dyad, the "dual fused" relationship, is one in which both of you are totally intermeshed and interwoven, negating any sense of separate identity for either of you. You are one within the relationship, rather than two separate people interrelating. Another dyad can be seen in "the nonrelationship relationship," consisting of two of you who really are terrified of intimacy and incapable of a commitment to a real relationship. You may be afraid of fusing and losing yourself to another, or fearful that you yourself are not lovable. As a result, you join with a partner who is equally afraid of intimacy; you both act out the motions of a relationship but really have no intimacy or mutual interdependence.

In the sadomasochistic dyad, one of you unconsciously needs to be hurt and punished while the other needs to be expressing rage and hostility. At the core of both of you lies a tremendous amount of self-hatred, with one of you turning your hatred inward and the other turning it outward. "Inequality" describes yet another common dyadic relationship, in which one partner feels committed, involved, and loving, while the other remains aloof, distancing, and unavailable. If you are in the powerless position, you may feel totally unlovable and, like Woody Allen in his movie *Annie Hall,* you feel that you would not want to join any club that would have you as a member. If you are in the powerless position, you may be there not only because of problems with lovability but also because you are trying to win in the present that which you were not able to win in the past. You hook yourself up with a partner who plays the part of your most rejecting parent. This is your attempt to attain the unattainable love of that parent who has rejected you. You may be in the powerful position of this dyad for a variety of reasons: as a defense against fusion, an identification with the aggressor, or an unresolved family romance.

The seesaw relationship. The seesaw relationship is exemplified by Tom and Tanya who had been "seesawing" since high school. When one was up in the relationship, the other was down. When the one who was down went up, the one who was up went down. They continually alternated in their commitment to the relationship. When Tom was involved and committed, Tanya was disenchanted. Tom would then seduce Tanya back; and as soon as he succeeded in winning her back, he became disenchanted. Now it was Tanya's turn, and she would use her wiles to seduce Tom back into the relationship once again. Of course, her success was followed by her own loss of interest. One was always being seduced and the other seducing. No one could win, although it always looked as if one were on the verge of winning.

During one of their swings, Tanya became involved with another man. This time, Tom resolved that the relationship was over. As soon as Tom made his decision, Tanya terminated her fling with the other man and fervently committed herself to Tom, protesting that he was the only man for her. Tom was ecstatic; he had finally won her just when he feared complete loss. Tom and Tanya eloped. The next morning Tom found himself feeling overwhelmingly trapped and wondered how he could have done such a thing. And so the seesaw continued, for now it was Tanya's turn to pursue the seduction. The process continued, only the content had changed. Tom and Tanya spent their next five years trying to decide whether to divorce or have a child. The seesaw did not stop swinging, the topics were simply altered.

If you are involved in a seesaw relationship, you are afraid of closeness and need to defend yourself against it by being involved with someone who is as frightened of closeness as you are. You maintain a stance of always working toward closeness but never achieving it; the closeness is never actualized. This fear of closeness can originate from several sources. Perhaps you are terrified of fusion, fearful that if you ever allow yourself to be close to someone you will totally lose yourself and your identity. Thus as soon as you start to get close, you back off in an effort to save yourself from obliteration. Doubts about your own lovability may also perpetuate a seesaw relationship. Perhaps you feel that if someone really knows you that person will not be able to love you because he or she will know your terrible secrets. A seesaw relationship can also develop from unresolved family romance issues in which being close to someone makes you feel too incestuous. In this instance, your lover may represent one or the other of your parents and create in you the need for distance as a defense against the closeness which you unconsciously interpret as incest. The seesaw is in perpetual motion, always trying to find the proper balance but never reaching it.

The rescuer and the victim. Roz had been working as a secretary at the men's prison for two years when she noticed Kevin, a new trustee, who had begun to do typing and filing for the prison administration. Kevin was very attentive to Roz, smiling warmly and offering pleasant words. He was a tall, good-looking black man who carried himself with much grace and appeal. Roz was flattered by his attentions. She knew he was "just a convict" but enjoyed both his interest in her and his charm. Roz liked Kevin and found herself responsive to his warmth. This, in and of itself, was new for Roz, who usually felt insecure with men, despite knowing that she was attractive and bright. As the days wore on, Roz learned more about Kevin's life. He had been raised in the black ghetto and at a very early age had become addicted to heroin, after which his every waking moment had revolved around getting his fix. Because he was uneducated, unskilled, and unemployed, he became a thief to finance his habit. Roz realized that she felt very sorry for Kevin. She had been warned about prison con artists but was sure that he was different. He had had such a sad life; and it seemed obvious that he wanted to make something of himself, that he had plans for his future. He wanted to leave the prison, "stay clean," and complete an education which would allow him to find a satisfying job. All he needed was someone to help him, someone to care for him, someone to love him. Roz knew she wanted to be that person.

Roz was the rescuer in this relationship, a role she played for several reasons. She was one of three girls in a white, middle-class family and had always felt herself to be the least pretty and the least intelligent of the three. Her grades never seemed good enough and she was never as popular with boys as her sisters were. Her father seemed to prefer her two siblings. He was freer with them and more able to give of himself and his time. When Roz was with her father, she sensed his discomfort. Roz had an ally in her mother but perceived her mother to be in a position similar to her own—with little power in the family. Her mother, like Roz, could take care of others but could not feel fulfilled or strong within herself. Roz felt uneasy around men and people in power. They made her feel small and insignificant, so she shied away from them. Now here was Kevin: a man who obviously needed her, who made her feel special, who gave her life a new meaning. What she did not realize was that she also felt he was inferior to her in that he needed her more than she needed him. In this instance, she was clearly in the position of power. This relationship allowed her to play the role of her father. In addition, her relationship with Kevin allowed her to unconsciously repeat her relationship with her mother. She was mothering and rescuing Kevin just as her mother had done for her.

From Kevin's perspective, he certainly was the victim and was urgently in need of a rescuer. He had felt oppressed and maligned by society all his life; he perceived himself as the poor victim with no choice and no responsibility for the ills that had befallen him. As the helpless victim, he looked to Roz to provide him with the lucky break that he believed he needed and deserved. At another level, Roz represented the fairy godmother who could give to him in a way that his own mother had not. She could rescue him and adore him. She could make everything all right and give him a new chance. For Kevin, it would be like being born again.

Rescuing is a variation of the mother-child relationship, in which one of you is more powerful and takes care of the less powerful person. Needless to say, not all rescuing takes as dramatic a form as it did with Roz and Kevin. You may be trying to rescue a man from his depression or his aloofness. You may be trying to bring him out into the world, nurture him with your love, and watch him flower. You may want to rescue him from his poverty or from his unloving and hostile family. You may want to provide a place where the two of you can be safe together.

Or perhaps you experience yourself as the victim, the one who is weak and helpless, looking for a knight in shining armor to rescue you. You may feel as though the world is dangerous and unpredictable and that you need help to navigate your life. You may want someone to rescue you from your depression, your sadness, your overwhelming anxieties, or other burdens. You may look to a man to free you from your drug dependency or from your fear of leaving home.

The victim-rescuer relationship is a complementary relationship in which the needs of both of you are being satisfied. One of you needs to save, the other needs saving. One of you is in power, the other powerless; one of you feels superior, the other inferior. This relationship works well enough so long as the balance of power remains unchanged, so long as the rescuer remains the rescuer and the victim remains the victim. If, however, the victim outgrows the need to be rescued and the balance of power changes, so must the relationship. If the relationship is based on something more substantial than this unconscious bond, then the relationship might withstand the change in the balance of power stimulated by the growth of one of the partners. If, however, you as the rescuer can relate only to a victim, you will leave the relationship to find still another victim. In either case, the rescuer-victim relationship, like other dyads, presents a picture of how individual personalities interlock, making a relationship an entity unto itself, greater than the sum of the two personalities involved.

The overreactor and the corpse. Barry and Brenda were in the process of moving, and Brenda, as usual, was hysterical. She felt overwhelmed by all of the arrangements that had to be made and did not know what to do first. She did not know how to prepare the children for the move or how to say good-bye to her neighbors. There was so much to do she did not know where to begin. They had to purchase a new house, sell the old one, pack everything, and contact a mover. Though Brenda had made similar moves several times in her married life, it all seemed new to her; it seemed as overwhelming as it ever had. She knew that her husband had to move whenever his company transferred him, but she certainly wished some-one—maybe even he—could be more helpful. She felt that she could not cope with all that had to be done. Although Brenda's husband was very efficient about executing the details of the move itself and, in fact, reassured her that he would be happy to contact the movers and handle the house arrangements, Brenda did not feel that this was enough. Somehow he just was not upset enough; he was not concerned enough. He did not understand what a major change this was for her. He did not understand her trauma and her pain; he just told her to calm down. She wished he would be more responsive. She wished he would understand. There was just so much to be done.

Barry could not understand what was distressing Brenda.

To him, it was all very simple. You just made lists of all the tasks to be done and crossed each one off as it was completed. There was nothing to get excited about. They would have no trouble selling the house or finding a new one. Barry believed that the children would adjust easily to the move. He could not understand what the problem was or why Brenda was so upset. For Barry, one needed only to be rational and since his wife knew that every two or three years meant a job transfer, she should just accept that as part of their life. It was not a big deal and certainly nothing to be alarmed about or fret about. He could not understand her distress.

Brenda and Barry are examples of the "overreactor" and the "corpse." Brenda overreacted to everything, becoming so hysterical and distressed that she had difficulty accomplishing the tasks at hand. She was overwhelmed by her life and in a continual state of crisis. Of course, much of this crisis functioned to distract her from her underlying feelings. For example, Brenda was probably very angry at both Barry and his company, but she avoided her feelings by becoming hysterical, dashing wildly about and emoting to the world, hoping someone would respond to her distress. Barry never became excited, never felt intense joy or intense pain. He was always rational, always on an even keel and in apparent control of his life. Together they seemed to compensate for one another's lacks. She apparently felt enough for both of them, and he apparently used his rational coping skills to prevent their family from falling apart. The reality, of course, was that neither was feeling much of anything. His corpse-like stance was a defense against any feelings. And her extreme emotionality defended her against really experiencing human feelings of pain, joy, or suffering. She never sat still long enough to feel anything.

Thus, the overreactor and the corpse needed each other because separately neither felt like a whole human being. Although Barry was not aware of it, he was totally incapable of feeling and allowed his wife to do all of the feeling for both of them. Similarly, Brenda used Barry as an anchor to guarantee that she would not disintegrate into a puddle of feelings. Given the socialization process in this culture, usually the overreactor is the woman and the corpse is the man, but this is not a hard and fast rule; the roles can be reversed.

The individuals in these dyads have complementary needs which are satisfied within the relationship. They unconsciously search and find each other, their needs intermeshing as each partner attempts to diminish her or his pain within the relationship. Thus the choice of your partner is an expression of your history and your personality; it is a choice made to enhance your pleasure and diminish your pain but may often do the reverse.

Shirley and Luis Revisited: The Day-to-Day Workings of a Relationship

Many factors are involved in the day-to-day workings of a relationship. A healthy relationship allows sufficient separateness for both people. It allows physical separation, time alone, separate friends, and separate interests. It requires mutual love and respect and involves the acceptance of unresolvable differences along with a willingness to compromise. In a healthy relationship, both of you feel safe enough to be; you and your partner share your weaknesses, your innermost fears, and your needs. A healthy relationship includes support and interdependence, as well as fun and sex.

Shirley and Luis have now lived together for four years. As they slowly shared their inner selves with each other, their sense of closeness increased; as they shared each other's fears and secrets, their trust in each other was enhanced. Of course, this was not always a smooth process, without its bumps and pains. Sometimes they hurt each other. Insensitivity and careless criticisms were all the more crushing from someone who was so important, so deeply loved. These wounds required the healing salve of still more openness in communication, still more willingness to listen and hear the other.

The ability to listen and communicate empathically is part of a group of interpersonal skills that is put to the test again and again in an intimate, long-term relationship. Shirley and Luis each brought many of these skills into their present relationship, skills which they had learned in their past involvements with parents, siblings, friends, and lovers. They were able to use their skills in dealing with issues that arose both within their relationship and external to it. Differences about food, television, and house decorating styles all required a tolerance of individual rights and an ability to communicate clearly and openly. If either Shirley or Luis were hurt by someone outside their relationship, their ability to trust and accept each other helped them discuss their difficulty and facilitated problem solving. One of them would put aside immediate self concerns and devote emotional and psychological energy to the other, feeling empathy and offering comfort and support. In addition to their ability to love and trust each other, Shirley and Luis were able to be open, accepting, tolerant, and empathic, thus easing the difficult times and making their relationship all the more meaningful and rewarding.

Using the security they gained from their relationship as a springboard, Shirley and Luis had used their years together to expand themselves, both professionally and personally. Shirley had supported them both while Luis obtained his M.A. in creative writing. She had worked with the understanding that her turn was next. And, as planned, after he graduated and began his teaching career at a community college, Shirley enrolled in a doctoral program in anthropology. They both felt they had grown in their careers. They enjoyed sharing their separate adventures with each other and valued the support they received from one another. Clearly, though they shared many things, they also maintained separate interests and separate lives. Luis spent an increasing amount of time with his students and on his writing, while Shirley devoted herself to her program in anthropology and became involved in the local woman's crisis center. Through their separate interests they each developed separate friendships, some of which they shared as a couple and some of which they enjoyed individually.

Shirley and Luis continued to share political interests and involvements. Luis taught Shirley more about the Chicano culture, while Shirley educated Luis about feminist concerns.

They enjoyed talking politics and involving themselves in various political groups. They also discovered their love of gardening and spent time planning for and growing their vegetables.

Unlike many couples, Shirley and Luis found that splitting up household chores was not difficult. They did not have to negotiate. They did what they preferred and what they could do in the time available to them. And what they did not have time for simply did not get done. They knew what their priorities were, and household chores were not among them.

In most ways, Shirley and Luis also had little difficulty dealing with issues about money. They pooled their income and spent it as was necessary. They were also flexible about which one of them would support the other at any given time. However, one area concerning money was not so easily handled and, in fact, proved to be an irreconcilable difference between them. The issue was Luis's determination to make financial contributions to his family on a monthly basis. Luis knew his family's financial stress. He knew that they had made many sacrifices to raise him and felt appreciative of their support as he moved beyond their sphere. He felt he wanted to repay them in some meaningful way. Although Shirley understood Luis's feelings, she felt that they too needed the money; they could hardly afford to see a movie or go out to a restaurant for dinner. She did not want to be impoverished. It was not that she begrudged his sending them money, but rather that she felt the amount was beyond their budget. Although they had empathy for each other's position, there was no way out of this dilemma; Luis was determined to send the money, and Shirley could not change his mind. They agreed to disagree.

Although Shirley and Luis, of course, had some irreconcilable differences, most of their differences were resolvable. The expression of anger was one such difference. Shirley had a tendency to scream when she was angry. She ranted and raged, which helped her dissipate her anger. Luis was appalled by this behavior and felt that conflicts should be resolved rationally. Yelling did not seem necessary or productive to him. When Shirley became angry, Luis withdrew. His withdrawal further enraged Shirley, causing her to scream still more. Realizing that their expressions of anger were hurting one another and creating a problem in the relationship, they agreed to compromise. Luis agreed not to withdraw and Shirley agreed to try not to scream. Shirley also agreed to respect Luis's request for time out if he felt too overwhelmed by her anger. They would then separate for ten minutes before reuniting to work out their conflicts. This arrangement worked out well for both of them, exemplifying a difference in style that they were able to resolve.

Luis's and Shirley's relationship was sometimes work, mostly fun, and almost always fulfilling. For both of them, it was a quiet, serene, and sometimes passionate island punctuating the end of busy, hectic days. Additionally, the strength they received from one another allowed them both to grow outward, developing as individuals in relation to their own separate worlds.

Getting Free: Jan

For Jan, whose story begins the chapter, the major intimacy issue was fusion. She would fall instantly and madly in love only to become quickly and totally bored. This boredom was a defense against her need for fusion. With each new lover, Jan surrendered her entire identity, her entire self, longing desperately to fuse. Shortly thereafter she would become terrified of the fusion and, needing to create distance, she would become bored and then involved with another man. Over and over again, Jan's therapist made these interpretations to Jan. It was very difficult for Jan to experience her boredom as a defense against fusion rather than as a natural result of the lack of variation in her life. She felt she just needed more variety and excitement than most people. Jan also found it difficult to believe that she would fuse with men in an unconscious attempt to get from lovers the intimacy and warmth she had not received from her mother. She had believed for a long time that her mother was totally irrelevant to her. How could she possibly want anything from her mother?

Although it was difficult for Jan to accept many of her therapist's interpretations, she became immediately and totally involved with both her therapy and her therapist. Between sessions she found her thoughts turning to her therapist and frequently rehearsed what she might say to her. Furthermore, Jan became involved in repeated crises that necessitated a call to her therapist at home or a request for additional appointments. Soon Jan was calling her therapist almost daily and asking for at least one additional session a week. The therapist believed that Jan's urgent calls and crises were more of Jan's attempts to win the love and attention she had not received from her mother. In other words, Jan was behaving toward her therapist as she behaved toward her lovers. She wanted all of her; she wanted all of her time and attention. She wanted her therapist to love her and be with her always. When her therapist began setting limits on Jan's calls and requests for appointments, Jan responded by decreasing her demands. She did what her therapist wanted but was resentful of the limits. However, as Jan stopped acting out her anger by being demanding, she began to feel her anger and became increasingly enraged at her therapist. She experienced her therapist's limits as an angry rejection.

The focus of Jan's therapy then became the relationship between her and her therapist. Jan was very angry at her therapist. She felt that her therapist was being hostile and rejecting by not being available to her at all times. Before long, Jan put her mother's face on the therapist. In other words, she began to experience her therapist as critical, rejecting, and unavailable, just as she had experienced her mother. Despite Jan's feelings, her therapist continued to be warm, giving, and supportive while at the same time maintaining her limits. Simultaneously, the therapist focused on Jan's difficulty in allowing herself to be close and intimate. She focused on Jan's relationship with her mother and wondered if Jan did not feel terrified that all close relationships would end in rejection and hostility. She also looked at Jan's relationship with men, pointing out, first, that Jan consistently left them before they could leave her, and, second, that Jan consistently fled from closeness because it terrified her, even though that is what she consciously wanted. They also explored the timing of Jan's increasing demandingness with her therapist; when they were beginning to get close, Jan had become intensely demanding. The demandingness itself was a distancing maneuver. Unconsciously Jan knew that her increasing demands would bring limits by the therapist, which would then anger Jan and result in greater distancing.

Little by little, Jan began to feel that her therapist really did care about her, even though she would not allow a fused relationship. Jan began to sense that intimacy and fusion were not the same; one could be in a close, caring, warm relationship without fusing with the other person or giving oneself up. As Jan was able to experience this difference, she was able to allow genuine closeness with others in her life. She was learning to be close but healthily separate.

Your close relationships can bring you great fulfillment and joy as well as much sorrow and pain. In these intimate relationships, all that you are and all that you were come into play, impacting on your view of yourself and your approach to the world. Knowing that you are lovable, feeling that others are trustworthy, having the ability to give and receive love and the interpersonal skills to maintain your relationship, all intertwine, enabling you to find the fulfillment of sharing yourself with another. Despite the difficulties of intimate relationships, opening yourself up to loving and being loved can provide you with some of the most satisying, exhilarating experiences of your lifetime.

7

Sexuality:
THE UNVEILING

There Merry lay, her mind tracing the vague shadows on the ceiling from the light in the hall. She felt that one part of her had split off and was watching herself mechanically perform, each thrust and moan timed to perfection, while Jeff moved over her trying to please. "Funny," she thought guiltily, "now it seems unreal, like acting. But fucking my tricks seemed more intense, more pleasurable." Merry was unable to stop the images of her work as a prostitute. As if she were watching a film, she saw herself performing an assortment of acts with grinning men. These images did not, however, heighten her arousal. She could not capture her past pleasures as she now performed again, but this time with Jeff, the man she loved.

Merry increasingly found herself reviewing her past life as a prostitute and often used these memories to escape from her everyday life. A part of her reveled in her past and was annoyed at herself for dwelling on it. She felt that in some ways her prostitution had paid off; it had financed her college degree which had enabled her to secure a good job working with computers. Now she even had a steady, loving relationship with Jeff. However, Merry feared that her life as a prostitute had left its mark; maybe it had changed her in some vital way. Merry felt as if she were torn in two, a part of her seeking the socially acceptable role as a career woman and spouse, while the other part yearned for the excitement of the street life and the sexual pleasure she had been able to achieve with her tricks. In an effort to resolve this dilemma, Merry decided to go into therapy.

Merry, an only child, grew up in a family which was considered the poor relation of an upper-class, southern Catholic family. While her cousins lived in mansions and had what appeared to be unlimited funds, Merry's family struggled to make ends meet. Her father was a gambling addict who had gambled away his inheritance. Her mother barely managed to keep a veneer of gentility over their poverty. Since it was unthinkable for her to work outside the home, they relied on donations from their wealthy relatives to keep the family afloat and hide their shame. Thus the family colluded in pretending that everything was all right, while, in reality, bankruptcy was just around the corner.

Merry felt as though her early childhood had been happy enough, but that her world had begun caving in when she started school. Everyone in her small home town knew how poor her family was. They somehow knew that her father gambled; they teased her unmercifully about the dress she wore day after day and her lack of lunch money. Merry felt alienated and different and tried to talk with her mother about these feelings. But her mother just told her not to pay any attention to these "commoners," reminding her, "We are descended from the founders of the city, from the most aristocratic of families." Her mother also assured Merry that their fortunes would change, that things would be better tomorrow. Merry found herself wanting to escape from the daily misery of her life and spent more and more time alone in the garden, fantasizing about more pleasant worlds.

Merry was the apple of her father's eye. He spent hours playing with her, using his warmth and imaginative powers to charm her. He promised her the world. Together he and Merry would journey to their fantasyland where she was the princess and could have her every wish. On the other hand, Merry could never count on her father. His promises never came true. He would promise Merry to be home for a walk in the park and then show up the next day. When she complained to him, he was contrite and apologetic, only to repeat this pattern shortly thereafter.

One of Merry's most poignant experiences occurred when she was in the second grade. Her family was preparing for

Christmas, which was always a fun, exciting holiday. The day before Christmas her father went out to buy "the biggest Christmas tree in the world." Somehow, though, he never came home; he just never got around to bringing the tree. Merry was crushed, but her mother seemed unaffected. She laughed at Merry and said, "No, tomorrow isn't Christmas. Christmas isn't until next week." Then Merry's mother went cheerfully on her way, preparing for the Christmas that was to occur next week. But Merry was old enough to know that Christmas was indeed on December 25th, as always. Again her mother had tried to sweep reality under the rug in order to cover up for her husband and present the world through rose-colored glasses. Merry felt torn. On the one hand, the fantasy world seemed prettier and more palatable, and brought hope for a "normal" Christmas. On the other hand, she was confused and distressed by her mother's obvious deceit.

This incident highlighted Merry's relationship with both her parents. Her father promised her the world, but never carried through. He was charming and affectionate but not truthful or reliable. Her mother altered reality to maintain the façade that everything was perfect. Even her relationship with Merry was secondary to maintaining the illusion. In order to maintain the pretense of a normal, happy family her mother would sacrifice anything, even her relationship with Merry. And so Merry could not count on her mother either. She could not look to her mother to confirm reality or to help her know how to deal with it.

Needless to say, the relationship between Merry's parents mirrored the relationship they had with her. That is, they both attempted to maintain the façade of a loving, caring couple who never experienced anger or disappointment. Merry's mother never got angry at her husband for whittling away the family money or for his chronic broken promises, or for all the disappointments he had heaped on the family. She responded to him with superficial gushiness which seemed to lack depth and genuine feeling. Merry's father was always charming and courteous to his wife, never coming to grips with his need for greater intensity and passion. Their relationship appeared to be ideal while, in reality, it was nonexistent.

As Merry grew older, she began to pity her mother. She knew that her mother, in her inability to change reality, lied to herself and the world to create the reality of her dreams. Merry was determined to change her own life. She did not want to be like her mother whom she felt so sorry for. She did not want to be pitied. She became increasingly determined to attend college and better her life. She knew she would have to finance her own college education, but felt no obstacle would be too great for her to overcome.

The summer before her freshman year, Merry was working in a neighboring town to earn money for her college expenses. She knew her salary would not cover everything when school started, but she planned to supplement it by working during the school year. After work one evening, she went to a bar for a drink with a friend. At this bar, an older, distinguished-looking man picked her up. Merry was flattered by his attention and attracted to his sophistication. Wanting to "do it" and rid herself of her virginity once and for all, she went willingly and eagerly to his motel. A sexually experienced man, he proved to be a mechanical but adept lover. The earth did not move underneath Merry, but neither was it an unpleasant experience.

Afterwards Merry felt that she had won a small victory in losing her virginity and moving further into adulthood. As the man dropped her off in front of her apartment, he pressed a 50 dollar bill into her hand. At first Merry was startled by the money and looked at it unbelievingly. Then she experienced a sense of elation. What an easy way to make 50 dollars! What an unexpected windfall! This must have been how her father felt when he won at gambling. And then the guilt washed over her. She felt she had crossed over a line, that she had done something wrong. She had violated her upbringing, her mother's wishes, and 18 years of her life. But then she thought, "I have gotten away with something. It's my secret. I can prostitute myself and not get caught. I can win at this." What a convenient solution to the dilemma of her life! Money, power, and adulthood, all rolled into one. At that moment Merry knew she had made her decision. She would turn tricks to finance her college education.

When she moved on to college, that is exactly what she did. She developed a secret life in a secret world where she turned tricks on the weekends. She kept this secret life and world separate from her life as a college student. Each Monday morning she took off her eyelashes, makeup, and elegant clothes and put on her levis and crew-neck sweater, changing from the high-class call girl to the typical college coed.

Merry found herself looking forward to her evenings with her tricks. She developed a steady clientele and even looked forward to seeing some of them. She felt herself to be the apple of their eye. They doted on her, adoring her youth, beauty, and charming personality. She was getting what she wanted from them and looked forward to their time in bed. Her work was actually becoming fun. And then one night, much to her surprise, she had an orgasm. She had not thought it possible for her to come, let alone with one of her "johns." Wondering if other prostitutes experienced orgasms, she struggled with a vague sense of having broken the rules of her profession.

As a college student, Merry maintained high grades. She devoted much time to her studies, and when she became tired she used amphetamines to energize herself. Maintaining life both as a college student and as a prostitute kept Merry constantly on the go, never allowing her time to think or feel. Uppermost in her mind was that she had to get through college; she had to be different from her mother.

Merry graduated from college and found a good job as a computer programmer. She quit "tricking" because her life as a prostitute had served its purpose: financing her education. Now she could use her degree to earn the money she needed. She no longer had a legitimate reason to prostitute herself. Shortly after beginning her new job, she met Jeff and they slowly fell in love. In time, they sexualized their relationship. Merry did not tell Jeff about her previous life as a prostitute. That was something in the past and could not affect her relationship with him. Although Merry had been to bed with many men, she was incredibly shy with Jeff. When they made love she felt as if it were her first time. She did not know what to do with her hands; she did not know what to do with her body. She was amused at herself for feeling so virginal but accepted the feeling as evidence of her love for Jeff.

However, as their sexual relationship progressed, Merry was not able to relax and enjoy it. She was unable to be orgasmic with Jeff. In fact, her sexual pleasure with him began to diminish. It became more and more mechanical, and she looked forward to it with less enthusiasm. Making love seemed a big bother. She hated these feelings and did not want to believe that sex with her tricks had been so much more pleasurable.

As Merry's life became more settled, she found herself able to feel more than she had in the past. As her relationship with Jeff became more intimate, she found herself increasingly disturbed by the secret she was keeping from him. She also felt guilty about having been orgasmic with her tricks but not with the man she loved. She felt she was a "bad person." How could she possibly have been a prostitute, even for the money? She worried that she might be sexually perverted. Merry's guilt was overwhelming. She had been caught by herself; she was paying the price for her prostitution. In an effort to work out her guilt, Merry began therapy.

Journeying Toward Adult Sexuality

The sexually free woman is able to allow sensual pleasure as well as to allow and own sexual pleasure. Sensual pleasure derives from your five senses. When you walk through the woods on a lovely fall day and are able to enjoy the smell of burning leaves, the sight of the gold and red leaves against the blue sky, the crackling of the twigs under your feet, the feel of your body moving in the brisk fall air, and, later, the taste of homemade cider and donuts, you are experiencing sensual pleasure. The same is true when you allow yourself to enjoy a bubble bath—floating in the warmth of the water, luxuriating in the feel of the foamy bubbles and the smell of the perfume. To allow yourself sensual pleasure means enjoying the silkiness of the cream you rub on your legs, your arms, and your breasts. It means reveling in the feel of the clean sheets rubbing against your freshly bathed and creamed body. Sensual pleasure involves being able to lie and caress without sexual tension, while enjoying skin against skin. Allowing sensual pleasure means that you feel good enough about your body, free enough about your body, to glory in the physical part of you and your world.

Allowing sexual pleasure is different from owning sexual pleasure. Allowing sexual pleasure, while not owning it, means giving over to someone else the responsibility of making love to you. You lie there and allow your lover to pleasure you. You turn yourself over to him, giving him the responsibility of bringing you to orgasm. He must know what to do and when. He must know if you like your clitoris massaged. He must know when you are ready to be penetrated. He maintains an erection until you are satisfied. You turn your body over to your lover and he makes you come.

Owning your own sexual pleasure involves assuming responsibility for your sexual pleasure and your orgasm. This can occur either through masturbation or when making love with another person. When masturbating, you can decide what you want and be responsible for getting it. When making love, you may tell your lover what to do to increase your pleasure. You may let him know when you want to be entered. You may request that he have oral sex with you. You may use your sexual fantasies to heighten your arousal. You are equal participants in receiving pleasure and giving pleasure.

The sexually free woman is able to both allow and own sexual pleasure. Sometimes you may turn yourself over to your lover, allowing him to pleasure you. At other times you may direct his lovemaking and request certain behaviors or sexual adventures. Sometimes you may encourage him to turn himself over to you and allow you to orchestrate the sexual symphony. You are free to explore avenues and expressions of your own and your partner's.

It is possible to allow sexual pleasure but be unable to own it, and vice versa. For example, you may be able to turn your body over to your lover, insisting that he be responsible for your orgasm, but be unable to ask for anything specific to heighten your pleasure. On the other hand, you may be able to own your own sexual pleasure but never allow someone else to pleasure you. For example, you might be able to have an orgasm while masturbating but be unable to allow someone to bring you to orgasm. Or you might insist upon always being the conductor and never give the baton to your partner.

To some extent, being able to own your own sexuality with a partner is learned behavior. An inexperienced teenage girl is going to have difficulty talking about sex with her fledgling lover. Since this is a new arena for her, she does not know what is going to please her. She cannot tell someone else what she likes if she does not know herself. She still feels shy about exploring her partner's body and allowing her own body to be explored. If both partners have some sexual knowledge, they will be able to talk about their sexual feelings and desires with greater ease. At this point, too, having a lover with whom you have a good, close, intimate relationship can make the journey toward owning and allowing sexual pleasure easier. In this case, you feel safer in exploring your feelings, your fears, and your body. Thus journeying toward adult sexuality is influenced not only by intrapsychic factors but by interpersonal, educational, and cultural factors as well.

Mother's Influence on the Unveiling of Sexuality

Your early feelings about yourself as a female originate from your mother's feelings about herself as a woman. Whether or not your mother is comfortable with her adult sexuality will profoundly influence your feelings about your own sexuality. You watch and experience your mother relating to your body. You watch your mother relating to her own body. You see how she deals with her lover and with all men. All of these observations profoundly influence your impressions about sexuality at a very early age. Your mother touches you, bathes you, diapers you, dresses you, talks to you. How she relates to you in a physical manner conveys her comfort about her own body and yours. You watch her dress herself. Perhaps you watch her take a bath. You see whether she walks naked in front of you or your father.

As you grow older, your mother either talks with you more about your body and sex or gives you a very clear message in her avoidance of the subject. Either way you learn, through subtle or not so subtle messages, whether or not your mother is comfortable with sex. She may look you over when you come home from a date. She may insist that you account for every second of your time. She may treat you with either trust or suspicion. Directly or indirectly she may say, "You're like me, and sex doesn't mean much," or "Don't you dare get pregnant," or "Girls must always be virgins when they marry," or "It wasn't worth it, was it?" or "I don't see how you can marry someone if you haven't slept with him." She may tell you how wonderful or disgusting sex is. She may be happy or jealous when you fall in love. She may caution you against being impulsive in your eagerness to rid yourself of your virginity. She may help you to make your early sexual experiences as rewarding and rich as possible. You learn from your mother to feel good and excited about sex or guilty about it.

Guilt frequently shrouds sexuality. Sexual values and morals have changed rapidly in this society, making it hard to live by your mother's dictates. Hers were values of another time, another generation, another system of morals. Now you are revising old codes, but not without difficulty. You have internalized your mother's sexual values and disobeying her early messages makes you feel guilty. You feel as if you are being a "bad girl" if you behave in ways that she would not approve of. She always told you to be a virgin when you married, so now you wonder if it really is all right to have sex with your fiance.

On the other hand, your mother may have tried to be a "modern" woman, telling you that sex was something you were free to enjoy. But, underneath this, her behavior may have indicated otherwise. For your mother, in turn, had internalized her mother's messages, which were also communicated to you. So on one level you were told that sex was fine, while on another level you sensed that your mother felt sex was shameful, dirty, and something to feel guilty about. Suppose, for example, you at nine years old are with your mother at a movie in which the word "masturbation" is used. After the movie is over you ask your mother what masturbation means. Though she tries to be comfortable in her explanation, her reddened face and quivering voice belie her attempt at casualness. She is clearly flustered, leaving you confused. On the one hand, she is telling you that masturbation is a natural part of everyone's life, on the other, her nonverbal message is that there is something wrong and embarrassing about the whole topic.

Jane, age 24, is an example of a woman who internalized her mother's attitudes about sexuality. She could not tolerate being touched, hugged, or kissed. Even as a little girl, Jane did not like to sit on anyone's lap. She withdrew from embraces. She felt uncomfortable at even the slightest contact. Jane's mother was also repelled by touching. Her pregnancy with Jane was extremely objectionable to her. She vomited throughout her pregnancy and felt as though there were a strange, foreign thing growing inside of her that made her feel fat, bloated, and ugly. After Jane's birth, her mother was repulsed by the smelly odors and the messiness of it all. She managed to toilet-train Jane by the time Jane was a year old. From a very early age, Jane knew that her mother did not like to touch her. She picked up on her mother's discomfort at diapering, bathing, and clothing her. Their physical contact diminished until it was virtually nonexistent.

Jane's father was a trucker who was often absent from the family on long-distance runs or, when there, tired and preoccupied. Jane was an only child who, except for her difficulties with physical closeness, had a fairly normal childhood. In fact, her difficulties with physical closeness were not apparent to her since they meshed perfectly with those of the other members of her family. It was not until Jane went into high school that she began to realize how different she was from the other girls in her class. While her friends seemed to enjoy combing each others' hair or tickling each others' backs, Jane felt only discomfort with this expression of affection. Her friends liked to hold hands with their boyfriends and delighted in slow-dancing and "making out." These activities were almost repulsive to Jane. She could not tolerate being kissed. She would think of one excuse after another not to be alone with a boy in a car and, eventually, not to go on dates at all. She could not believe that her girlfriends looked forward to the day when they would be able to go to bed with their boyfriends. Jane prided herself on her reputation as a "cold fish" and felt herself superior to all her immature teenage friends.

When Jane went to college, however, she began to see that her difficulties with physical closeness would prove to be a more serious problem for her. Gradually she realized that if she could not allow physical closeness with a man, she would not be able to develop a relationship for future marriage.

Jane's difficulty with allowing any sensual or sexual pleasure stemmed primarily from her internalization of her mother's attitudes and messages. Just as her mother did not like to be touched or to touch, so too it was for Jane. Jane's mother had withdrawn from any physical contact with Jane, and now Jane withdrew from all physical contact. Her mother had taught her well. It is not that her mother had overtly told her to avoid physical contact or bodily pleasure, but rather that she had given Jane indirect messages to that effect. Thus Jane's inability to allow sensual and sexual pleasure was an internalization of her mother's messages.

Father's Influence on the Unveiling of Sexuality

Just as feelings of guilt concerning sexuality might arise as a result of internalizing your mother's sexual messages, so might they arise from your sexual feelings toward your father. As discussed earlier, all of you have experienced a time in your life when you were in love with your daddy; when you wanted all of him and saw your mother as the arch rival. Depending upon how your sexual feelings were handled within the family, you may continue to feel guilty about all sexual feelings because they are reminiscent of the feelings you had toward your father. Thus as a teenager when you experienced the first flush of sexuality, you may have become uncomfortable, guilt-ridden, distressed.

Just as you unconsciously knew what your mother's feelings were toward sex, so you also felt your father's sexual feelings toward you. Suppose, for example, you were used to crawling onto your father's lap, putting your arms around his neck, and burying your head in his shoulder. This was always warm and comfortable and pleasurable for you. As you grew older, however, your father became increasingly unaccepting of your physical affection and began to push you away. You did not understand your father's behavior. You felt rejected and confused. It was, of course, your father's own sexual feelings toward you that were causing him to place this wall between you, but you did not know this. You experienced it only as a rejection, as a past pleasure you would now be denied.

Sometimes it is you who may reject your father. Perhaps he has been abusive or distant to you, your mother, or your siblings. You may then feel angry at him · You may also displace this anger onto other men and, as a result, have difficulty enjoying men sexually. In addition to being a displacement of anger at your father, anger at men may also be a defense against sexual feelings toward your father. Suppose, for example, that you as a young girl felt sexually drawn toward your father and that he was unable to deal with your feelings in a manner which helped you to develop your sexuality without fear. He may have patted you on the rear and suggestively commented on your developing breasts. This would have left you feeling sexually stimulated, but with the growing sense that these feelings were somehow wrong. You did not feel safe in your sexuality. You might attempt to deny your sexual feelings toward your father by replacing them with anger. This anger would then be a defense against your sexual feelings toward your father. You would feel angry rather than sexual because it feels safer. Anger at men can be expressed by a variety of different behaviors, ranging from the extreme of withholding sex to promiscuity or prostitution.

Your father's sexual feelings toward you and his inability to handle them are what cause him either to oversexualize his relationship with you or to abruptly push you away as you enter puberty. You may react to this either by feeling guilty about your sexual feelings toward all men because all men become symbols of your father, or by becoming enraged at all men as a way of avoiding your sexual feelings toward your father.

There are, of course, fathers who are able to deal with their own sexual feelings and to help their teenage daughters deal with theirs. For example, a 13-year-old girl was watching an arousing scene on television and felt herself becoming excited. The sexual sensations were very pleasurable, and she became aware of her desire to express them. She ran into the next room where she gave her father a rush of kisses. Her father was amazed by this sudden show of affection and responded with delight, saying, "Boy, is she gonna be something!" The message to the daughter was clear: "Your sexual feelings are fun and exciting and safe with me." The father was able to appreciate his daughter's feelings and to recognize and reinforce her blossoming sexuality without increasing her sense of danger that those feelings might be acted out between the two of them. This nurtured her acceptance of her developing sexuality and helped her look forward to its expression with other men.

At 28, Diana was not so fortunate. Her difficulties with sexual contact and intercourse were increasing. Sex had never been easy for her, for she had always found herself vacillating between intense excitement and extreme boredom. But recently she could barely muster up the interest to go through with it. In the middle of intercourse, strange ideas and images would pop into her head. She found these images both strangely exciting and very dismaying. She told herself she should not be aroused by these images; they were linked to past memories and were best forgotten. She wanted to wall them off with feelings of anger and sadness, not to respond to them with passion and excitement. Now when she had intercourse she tried to push the arousing thoughts away and felt eager to get the whole thing over with. Then suddenly she would have an orgasm and be overwhelmed with guilt. She wanted to push the man away from her; she did not want him to touch her. She could not look at him. She felt as though she had done something very wrong.

What were these images that Diana tried to wall off from

her awareness and which she still found so exciting? She knew what they were but did not know how to deal with them. She insisted to herself that she remembered all those incidents with anger and loathing, all those times her father's best friend had seduced her. For years it had gone on, from the time she was nine until she started menstruating at 13. Diana would go and visit him, and he would stroke and caress her. Initially he fondled her only with his fingers, kissing her entire body. With time he taught her the pleasure of orgasm, yet she sensed that what she was doing was terribly wrong. She vacillated between visiting him more frequently and steeling herself to avoid him. But when she did not visit him, he sought her out and seduced her back into continuing their sexual contacts.

Diana viewed their sexual acts together with pleasure and guilt. She felt that it was wrong for her to be sexual and that what she was doing was dirty and sinful. Additionally, she felt he was somehow connected to her father for he was, after all, her father's best friend. It seemed as though her father should have protected her from these acts. Thus surrounding her guilt was enormous rage. After all, she was a child and should not have been taken advantage of. Her mother and father should have prevented it. Sometimes she thought that they knew but did not care enough to stop it. She felt different from all other children, because she knew her friends in school were not doing this. Diana felt as though she wore a mark of shame for all to see; everyone must know how different and strange she was.

When Diana began menstruating, her father's friend cut off all sexual contact with her. She then tried to wall off all her feelings about her past sexual experiences with him; she tried to put them away and forget about them. The shame of her childhood need be no more; she was 13 and now a woman. Indeed, Diana had succeeded in putting this all away until she began to be sexual again in her twenties. Then she found that her feelings about sex and men had generalized from the experience with her father's friend to her feelings about all men. She always felt as though there was something wrong with sex, that she was doing something wrong, something dirty, that it was somehow incest, and that, of course, could not be allowed.

In all other areas of her life, Diana was able to function well. She found her job as a teacher specializing in emotionally disturbed children meaningful and satisfying. She had women friends with whom she traveled and shared closeness. However, she had not told anyone about the shameful events of her childhood. It was Diana's increasing guilt about her early experiences, as well as her increasing discomfort during sex, which finally brought her into therapy. With much trepidation and fear she told her therapist about her shameful, embarrassing, humiliating past experiences.

The therapeutic issue for Diana was the resolution of her guilt feelings about her sexual experiences with her father's friend, as well as the resolution of her anger toward both her father's friend and her family for not protecting her. She felt guilty because she had received from this man the affection, warmth, caring, and loving that she did not feel from her rather cold and distancing parents. She felt guilty because she enjoyed the sexual experiences and felt that she was bad and wrong for having done so. She felt guilty because she was involved with her father's best friend, and this felt not only sexual but incestuous as well. It was society's worst taboo. However, once Diana could forgive herself for the sexual pleasure she had experienced and allow herself to express her rage at her father's best friend and her parents, she could free herself from seeing all men as the "bad" men of her childhood and permit herself adult sexual pleasure.

Control Issues in Unveiling Sexuality

Control issues are frequently manifested in sexual behavior. Fear of loss of control means fear of letting go, of relaxing, of being free enough to let your mind wander and get into the sexual feelings in your body. If you do not have difficulties with issues concerning control, you can let go of your inhibitions and restraints and allow yourself simply to feel. You can give yourself over to pleasure and feel rather than think; you can become your body. You can surrender yourself to the moment and to the pleasure of your body.

Problems with fear of losing control can stem from issues concerning omnipotence and vulnerability, fusion, or fear of death. If you are afraid of becoming increasingly vulnerable, of surrendering some of your power to another human being, of giving another person the power to please you, you will obviously have difficulty letting go and feeling sexual with another person. If you are overwhelmed with fearfulness when you turn yourself over to another human being for pleasure, you can obviously not let go sexually. You are afraid that by allowing someone to please you sexually, you give him too much power, which he will then use to control you; he will do with you as he wishes because of your need for the pleasure he can give you.

Control issues in sexuality can also be viewed in terms of a fear of fusion, a fear of losing yourself, a fear of losing your identity and merging with the other person. This may be particularly true if you are already in a fused relationship with your lover and the added closeness of orgasm would make you feel that you would be obliterated. Orgasm then becomes far too frightening, and you keep yourself from losing control by not giving in to orgasm.

Underlying both fear of vulnerability and fear of fusion is a fear of death, a fear of so increasing your vulnerability or so losing yourself in the other person that you will simply no longer exist, you will die. At the moment of climax you are aware of nothing but your physical sensations; they are all that exist. You as a separate person, woman, worker, spouse, parent, all are irrelevant, eradicated, erased from your conscious awareness. The obliteration of your separate identity is the closest experience of nonexistence that you, as a living person, can have. If you already have problems concerning vulnerability or fear of fusion, you cannot allow this close encounter with nonexistence. You must hold onto yourself and inhibit yourself from letting go.

At 35, Hillary was a content, married woman and the mother of one child. She described her life as fairly happy and considered herself fortunate to have survived her traumatic childhood. Hillary's only concern was that after all these years she was still inorgasmic with her husband. She could come when she masturbated, but could never allow herself to let go totally when she was with him. And she knew it was not only with her husband, for she had been inorgasmic with other men earlier in her life. She simply could not let go enough to give in to orgasm when she was with another person. She could feel the pleasure of sexual involvement but remained inorgasmic. On the other hand, she loved to have her husband come. She loved to hear his breathing increase rapidly and then to have him groan and cry out with release and satisfaction. She felt as though his orgasms were enough but realized his hurt and disappointment at her inability to climax.

Hillary had difficulty with control issues in other areas of her life. She was obsessive, given to making long lists and worrying about future events, particularly when they involved other people. For example, when they were going to a dinner party she needed to know exactly who would be there and what to wear or what to bring. She needed to plan her family's social life down to the last detail a month or two in advance. It was important that she always know where her child was and what she was doing at every moment. Although Hillary recognized that her need to have everything in order was too important to her, she also felt that it did not interfere too much in her day to day living. She knew it was neurotic but did not feel that it was disabling.

Hillary understood the origin of her control issues. She had been orphaned at age 3, after which she had spent the rest of her childhood and adolescence being passed around from one foster home to another. She never knew how long she would be with any one particular family. She never knew when her newly developing roots would be disrupted and she would be placed with another family. She never knew if the new family would be kind and loving or hostile and chaotic. How she felt about a particular family was irrelevant in determining her length of stay with them. What she felt, what she wanted, or what she hoped for never mattered. She was entirely at the mercy of the bureaucracy and forces outside of herself. The only stable, loving person in her life was an older brother who had made all these moves with her. He was crucial to her for he was always there. They loved each other a great deal and were able to give each other much support and affection. Additionally, Hillary did find that some of her foster parents were kind and giving, and on one occasion she was even allowed to stay with a particularly loving family for a period of five years. But, here again, she never knew for certain; her future was never her own. She was always at the mercy of other people.

Thus as an adult Hillary was always terrified of losing control. She was afraid to be in any way vulnerable, in any way helpless, for it stimulated her childhood vulnerability. She unconsciously felt that the more she could maintain control and order, the less likely it would be that she would again be a helpless and vulnerable child. As a child she had controlled what little she could, and as an adult she continued this behavior. In her adulthood her sphere of control had expanded, including the sexual arena. Hillary withheld her orgasm in an attempt to feel more powerful. It was not that she consciously chose not to be orgasmic, but rather that giving in to her orgasm made her reexperience her childhood powerlessness.

Each of you has experienced stages of growth which determine your sexual capabilities. As with other issues, messages from your parents are crucial; the internalization of your mother's attitudes and the delicate sexual tensions between you and your father are the backdrop for your sexuality. The resolution of control issues centering around closeness, trust, vulnerability, and death determines your freedom to let go. Allowing sensual pleasure and allowing and owning sexual pleasure are necessary to be free sexually.

Getting Free: Merry

Merry, whom you met at the beginning of the chapter, came into therapy because she was unable to be orgasmic with her lover, Jeff, in spite of the fact that she had been orgasmic with her tricks. Additionally, she was feeling tremendous waves of guilt about her previous life as a prostitute. Merry specifically chose a woman therapist whom she knew had worked with a number of prostitutes. She felt she would be more comfortable sharing her secret life with a woman. Merry was able to be open in the first therapy hour and felt some relief from her oppressive guilt after she told her therapist about her dual life. Because the therapist was able to be non-judgmental and to accept her, Merry was able to begin to accept herself as well.

The first thing that Merry and her therapist looked at were the ways in which her childhood fostered a dual existence both then and now. Her family had always led two lives. They portrayed themselves as upper-class gentility, in spite of the fact that they were poverty stricken. The message that Merry received was that it did not matter what reality actually was so long as it looked palatable. Reality did not dictate what was accepted as real. Merry learned at a very early age to put a veneer over reality. Hence her childhood training made it easy for her to be the perfect coed Monday through Friday and the high-class prostitute on Saturday and Sunday.

Merry also learned from her family a sense of gaming about money. Her father was a gambling addict who had gambled away his inherited fortune, while her mother continually denied that they were poor and put on a façade of aristocracy. Money was there but not there; it was important, revered, but thrown away. Like her father, Merry was able to make it seem as though money came from nowhere. She was continually winning at "the game." And, in that way, she was beating her father for, unlike him, she never lost. Additionally, Merry had surpassed her mother because she was able to enjoy sex. Her mother had always communicated the feeling that sex was something bad and dirty that women suffered through as part of their wifely duties. To Merry's surprise she was able to enjoy sex and at the same time receive money for it. She thought that she had pulled off the greatest trick of all—she was paid for that which she enjoyed most. However, she had learned from her mother too well and had internalized her mother's feeling that sex was dirty and disgusting and not to be enjoyed. And so the guilt came down on Merry.

This guilt was one of the things that prevented Merry

from enjoying sex with Jeff. It seemed as if a trick had been played on her that she had been able to enjoy sex with her clients but not with her lover. She had not really won at all. She and her therapist spent a good deal of time looking at her inability to be orgasmic with Jeff. Merry learned that she had internalized her mother's feeling that sex was bad and that "nice girls" simply do not enjoy it. While Merry was being a "nice girl" with Jeff it was, of course, difficult for her to enjoy sex. Merry discovered that she was enraged at her mother for giving her this message. How dare she make the world seem different from the way it really was. Merry recalled anew the years her mother had painted a glossy veneer over the murkiness of their real situation. She had even tried to move Christmas to fit her façade of pleasantness!

While Merry was feeling her rage at her mother, she was able to get in touch with her rage at her father as well. She was angry at him for his chronic deceit, his never being there, and his unreliability. As a child Merry had idolized her father and now saw him for what he actually was, an irresponsible spendthrift and a liar. In therapy Merry was able to feel all the anger and sadness she had bottled up for years. All the old disappointments felt like fresh wounds.

Although her father did not have much genuine feeling to give, what feeling he did have went first to Merry. And Merry felt guilty that her father had preferred her. Her mother had lost out. Her mother, who had tried so hard to cover up his inadequacies and to make him feel good about himself, had received only the leftovers.

Because Merry felt as though she had won the family romance, her adult sexual involvements were always tinged with incest. It was easy for Merry to unconsciously equate her sexual partners with her father. When she was not close to the man, as had been true with her tricks, she was less likely to feel this uncomfortable, incestuous feeling and thus more able to let go and relax sexually. When, however, she felt as close to a man as she did to Jeff, her past feelings for her father came to the fore. This closeness was the bridge between sexual feelings for her father and her sexual feelings for other men.

Additionally, prostitution had provided an excellent way for Merry to act out her anger at her parents. It was an expression of rage at her mother in that she was being exactly what her mother would not tolerate or approve of. She was expressing her rage at her father by directing it toward all men. As a prostitute she had the power; she was in control. She could sell herself to whomever she wanted; they were on her turf. Thus prostitution was a way for Merry to express her rage at both parents, surpass her father at his own game, and allow her to be sexual without having to deal with her sexual feelings toward her father.

In therapy, Merry also learned that she had many issues to deal with concerning control and vulnerability. These were made manifest in two ways. First, prostitution seemingly put Merry in total control, relegating to her all of the power. The second manifestation was her inability to be orgasmic with Jeff. As a child, Merry had felt totally without control. She had never known what to expect next. One day they would have a windfall from her father's winnings and the next day they would not have enough money for food. Nothing was certain. She felt powerless in the situation that existed for her. Because of this childhood powerlessness, Merry now felt the need always to be in control. She was afraid that if she relinquished any control, she would be thrown back into her helpless childhood state. It was this that made it impossible for Merry to allow Jeff to give her sexual pleasure. That would be terrifying, as if she were giving over to him all of the control and power which she had struggled so hard to achieve and maintain.

Merry is a portrait of a woman who had sexual difficulties stemming from all three sources. She had internalized her mother's negative messages; she had unresolved sexual feelings toward her father; and she was terrified of relinquishing controls. In therapy, Merry needed to look at what she had internalized from both her parents, namely, her father's attitude toward money and gambling and her mother's messages about sex. She also had to look at her anger and sadness in relation to her parents. She was furious at them both for their deceptions and their inability to give to her in a real, genuine manner. She felt sad about all the warmth, love, and security that she had needed and had not received as a child. Lastly, Merry needed to forgive her parents and realize that they were not malicious but had simply done the best they could. She needed to feel and let go of her anger so she would not focus it on all men. She had to recognize her adult strength and power so that she would no longer be terrified of allowing a moment of fusion. Once Merry could accomplish all this, she could be sexually free.

8

Sexuality
ISSUES AND EXPRESSION

Vanessa arrived home and saw the candles on the table, testifying to Rhoda's amorous desires. She knew the stage was set for the beginning of yet another seduction scene. Her stomach knotted. God, how she hated these scenes! Even though she loved Rhoda, she could not bear the thought of what was about to occur. Her anxiety rose. How had this originally passionate relationship turned so cold?

Vanessa, who was now 35, had met Rhoda four years ago in the cafeteria at the hospital where they both were working. Immediately drawn to Rhoda, Vanessa wondered if Rhoda were a lesbian too. She approached her and the two began an intense yet cautious period of exploration. They had to find out how open they could be with each other, and then whether their friendship could blossom into a sexual love.

One night they confessed their sexual attraction for each other and began a wild and passionate love affair. They spent hours making love. Their lovemaking was tender, creative, thrilling, and passionate. They were both very comfortable with their lesbianism and enjoyed exploring each other's body with passion and abandon. They spent hours caressing each other, giving each other body rubs, and taking bubble baths. Slowly they would bring each other to the height of ecstasy, reveling in their bodies' pleasure. Never had either of them experienced such sexual compatibility. Together they felt that their lovemaking was so natural, so complete, that it was inexplicable to them how anyone could view lovemaking between women as strange or unnatural, or as simply cuddly and affectionate.

Now, four years later, Vanessa dreaded any form of sexual contact with Rhoda. She could feel her skin crawl at the mere thought of Rhoda's embrace. She had to steel herself at every encounter. Rhoda was becoming increasingly distraught about their lack of lovemaking. Again and again she had tried to talk with Vanessa about what she perceived as their sexual problems. And again and again Vanessa had drawn back from any discussion, trying to lay the blame on their busy schedules or other external circumstances. Yet Rhoda had continued to complain. Finally Rhoda had sobbed as she told Vanessa that she was not sure she could continue in their otherwise perfect relationship unless Vanessa did something to alleviate this problem. In spite of their great mutual love and the close companionship between them, a relationship without sex did not seem possible. Vanessa finally understood that Rhoda was at the end of her rope and agreed to see a psychotherapist.

Vanessa had grown up in a Jewish middle-class family in Manhattan. Her father, a grocery store owner, was a warm, affectionate, and loving man. He saw Vanessa as his princess. She was everything to him. She could do no wrong. He always gushed in expressing his love for her; she was his eldest, his first, his pride and joy, and the light of his life. Her two siblings never seemed able to live up to Vanessa's achievements. Her sister, the middle child, was closer to her mother and he was less involved in her rearing. The youngest, a boy, was a hyperactive child who proved to be quite a disappointment to Vanessa's father. He was sure his son would never make anything of his life because he never did well in school or applied himself to anything. He simply demanded time, attention, and money.

Vanessa's mother was quite different from her warm and loving husband. She was a very prim and proper woman who had difficulty being affectionate. She was more concerned with appearances. Years later, Vanessa was to think about how similar her mother seemed to the character portrayed by Mary Tyler Moore in the movie *Ordinary People*. It did not matter to her how people felt, only how things looked.

Vanessa's childhood was happy in spite of her feeling that she was missing something in her relationship with her

mother. She felt able to get more than enough from her father so did not dwell on her relationship with her mother. She
did well in school, had lots of friends, and knew at a very early
age that she wanted to be a physician. She nursed all the
wounded animals in the neighborhood, and her father joked,
"My daughter the doctor."

When Vanessa was a junior in high school she developed a
crush on her female math teacher and would hang around
after class to talk with her. Sometimes she would even man-
ufacture a problem to give herself an excuse for her visit.
Initially, the teacher was excited about her precocious and
eager student, but soon she began to find Vanessa annoying
and discouraged her attentions. Vanessa was confused by her
new feelings. She felt different and frightened. She was afraid
that people would find out the kind of fantasies she was having about her teacher. She imagined herself crawling into her
teacher's lap and being rocked and kissed by her. Vanessa
then began dating boys and tried to diminish her feelings
toward her teacher. By dating, she felt that she was doing
what she was supposed to, but she always found the boys
unexciting and immature.

In college Vanessa continued to date men and continued
to find them rather dull. She began having intercourse with
one of her boyfriends and although she found the sexual relationship unsatisfying, she was comforted by the assurance that
she was "normal." At the same time, she continued to feel
attracted to women but tried to keep these feelings at bay.
Then, in her junior year, Vanessa fell madly in love with Joan,
a woman who lived on the same floor of her dormitory. Joan
was a known lesbian who made no attempt to hide her sexual
preference. She preferred women; she loved women. She
rallied around the gay cause. Once Joan realized that Vanessa
was attracted to her and fascinated by her life style, Joan
made herself available to Vanessa, spending hours talking
with her about what it meant to be gay and to be a feminist.
As the relationship deepened and their sexual feelings for
each other grew, they finally decided to make love. At last
Vanessa had found someone who was like her. She had feared
that she would never be able to express these hidden sexual

feelings, but now at last she could. A whole new world opened up to her, the world of sharing her sexuality with freedom and joy. Vanessa did not feel alone any more; there were other people like her in the world.

Vanessa finished college and entered medical school. She and Joan continued their relationship until one day Joan announced that she had fallen in love with someone else and that, in fact, she had been having an affair with this other woman for some time. Vanessa had been totally unaware that Joan's feelings had changed; she was badly shaken and depressed. She felt that this betrayal and abandonment eliminated any possibility for future relationships. She plunged herself into her career, doing exceptionally well in medical school, but continued to feel empty and lost.

When Vanessa was an intern she fell in love again. At this time she told her parents that she was a lesbian. She wanted her parents to know of her life style so that she could share more of her life with them. She wanted to take her lover home and be recognized as a couple. Her father was supportive, as always, telling her that he would stand by any decision she made. All he wanted was her happiness. And then he laughingly said, "All men are shits anyway." Vanessa's mother reacted quite differently. She became hysterical. Concerned that the neighbors and the rest of the family would find out, she insisted that Vanessa promise she would not tell anyone else. She never wanted the subject mentioned again and was going to continue with her life as though she had never heard it. At least her daughter was a doctor, she sighed.

After completing her internship, Vanessa had to leave New York for a public health fellowship. Although she looked forward to actually practicing medicine, she felt distraught about leaving her lover. But she knew that at this point in her life, career opportunities dictated her decisions. She and her lover attempted to maintain a long-distance relationship, but in time it simply withered away. Both of them became involved with other interests and eventually with other women.

After completing her public health obligation, Vanessa began her surgical residency. She was now 29 years old. Toward the end of her residency, she met and fell madly in love with Rhoda, who was a medical social worker. This time Vanessa had been sure that it would be forever. And now, here she was again, threatened with the loss of a relationship, but this time because of her own sexual difficulties. Vanessa could not allow this relationship simply to end. She had to do something about her lack of sexual interest.

Your Body and Your Culture

Being capable of sexual expression is an important aspect of being a fully functioning adult woman. Your attitude toward your body and your womanhood greatly affects your freedom to be sexual, whether the avenue for your expression is masturbation, heterosexuality, or lesbianism.

Beauty is defined by culture. Rubens's seventeenth-century culture dictated that lush was beautiful. The rounded curves of breasts, stomach, thigh, and hip were considered sensual and womanly. In the nineteenth- and early part of the twentieth-century, Western culture reverted to an adoration of the hourglass figure. The tiny waist, offset by big breasts and big hips, was considered beautiful. Women increased the size of their hips by bustles and the size of their breasts by push-up bras. They cinched their waists with corsets to attain the ideal 18-inch waist. In the mid-twentieth century this image changed drastically. Instead of the hourglass, the cylinder, as typified by Twiggy, became the norm. The slender woman, with small breasts and hips, was "in." The motto became "You can't be too thin."

Most of you, regardless of the ideal, feel incapable of living up to it. If you had lived in Rubens's time, you would have felt that you were not curvy enough. If you had lived at the dawn of the twentieth century, you would have felt that your waist was too big or your breasts too small. And now many of you feel that you are too fat or at least too fleshy. Your breasts and hips poke out annoyingly. Thus cultural messages help most of you never to feel beautiful enough, perfect enough. You agonize over your body, spending an inordinate amount of time in front of the mirror, concerned about pimples at one age, bulges at another, and wrinkles at still another. You fuss about your breasts; they are too big or too small, the nipples stick out too much or not enough. You fuss about your thighs, the bulges, the cellulite. You feel nothing is ever good enough. Your body is not perfect enough. It is as though you as a woman must view your body as marketable and are thus responsible for achieving the best product possible. It is as though your life is dependent upon how you look.

Although much of what you feel about your body is dependent upon its congruence with the current cultural norm, some of your feelings about your body also depend upon parental messages. Your parents may subscribe to the cultural norms and, trying desperately to make you into a long, sleek cylinder, be concerned about the extra potato you eat for dinner. Or your parents, particularly if they are from an ethnic background, might subscribe to a different cultural norm and tell you, "Es, es, mein Kind" ("Eat, eat, my child"). Parents additionally may be concerned about your developing sexuality and treat with either pride or dismay your budding breasts. Parents thus inject their own nuances into the culture as they present it to you. And, of course, as in other areas of your life, the messages from your parents regarding sexuality take on an overwhelming importance. Your father's comment about your fatty thighs could prove to be far more devastating than your mirror's reflection. Your mother's commands to eat lest you fade away may influence you more than the opposite message in your *Seventeen* magazine. Thus, as always, your parents affect you significantly. But, regardless of the content of these messages, the reality is that you feel your appearance is paramount. During teenage years, your success in life seems to depend upon it. At times it seems that you will be loved only if you are beautiful, and, of course, you can never be beautiful enough.

Then, with the onset of middle age, your beauty begins to change and you fear the loss of love. If love is dependent on beauty, and beauty is dependent on youth, when your youth goes you fear the whole house of cards may crumble. It is no wonder, then, that so many women find reaching middle age so devastating. The cultural perception is that men become more distinguished as they age, more experienced, more attractive, and more capable of attracting younger, sophisticated, beautiful women. In contrast, the notion of the older woman and younger man still provokes ridicule. Our culture scorns the idea that an older woman could possibly be attractive to any man, let alone a young one. Older women become your mothers, and mothers simply are not sexual.

While the middle age woman mourns her menses, the prepubescent girl either dreads or relishes its onset. Menstruation is the culmination of puberty. Developing nipples and breasts and the pubic down that turns to curly hair are signs of approaching womanhood. Menstruation marks its beginning. It is the definitive event, signaling your ability to produce children. Different cultures, of course, deal with menstruation differently. In one culture, a woman may be considered unclean during her menses while in another, she may be the center of a joyful celebration.

Cultural messages in conjunction with how and what your mother tells you about menstruation significantly shape the way you view it. There are all variations and extremes in our culture. A girl totally unprepared for menstruation may believe that her first menstrual flow is a sign of serious illness. She may hide this "illness" from her parents and worry about whether her life is in danger. Obviously this girl's sexuality has been ignored. Another girl may anticipate her menstrual period eagerly, wondering when that red sign of womanhood will arrive. And then when the day does arrive, she may feel very proud to know that at last she can become pregnant, and that this is an experience she can share with all women.

Age at onset of menstruation can be crucial. For example, if you begin menstruating at age nine, you may feel very uncomfortable and awkward with this new burden of womanhood. Suddenly you are no longer a child; you have been thrust too quickly into womanhood. Your breasts, your pubic hair, your menstrual period, all are signs of the difference between you and your peers. You feel emotionally like a child, but physically you have become a woman. It is too much, too soon. On the other hand, if you do not start menstruating until you are 15, you may be quite worried about whether you are "normal." You may go to doctors to determine whether something is wrong. You may feel dislocated; emotionally and intellectually you are ready to experience the fullness of your teenage years, but physically you remain a child.

The Culture Gone Crazy

Anorexia and bulimia are manifestations of our "thinness" culture gone crazy. In these eating disorders, which have both a cultural and a psychological component, women are literally starving away and/or vomiting up their sexuality. Both are eating difficulties which usually have their onset after the beginning of menstruation. On a cultural level, both the anorexic and the bulimic attempt to attain the present norm by being as thin as a cylinder. The anorexic has an intense fear of being fat and, regardless of how slender she actually is, still feels fat. Other people may see her as emaciated, as looking like a concentration camp victim, and yet she still sees herself as fat. She points to a jutting rib and sees a roll of fat. Anorexics sometimes starve themselves to the brink of death and need to be hospitalized where they undergo painful intravenous feedings in order to reverse the malnutrition. As the body becomes too thin and malnourished, menstruation ceases. The person diagnosed as bulimic manifests a somewhat different pattern. She secretly eats huge amounts of highly caloric food, sneaking off to gorge herself, and then induces vomiting or uses laxatives to rid herself of the food before her body can turn it into fat. Women with bulimia are always aware that their eating pattern is disturbed and try to hide it, whereas women with anorexia feel that people are forcing them to eat in order to control them or make them fat.

Psychologically, both the anorexic and the bulimic are trying to avoid dealing with sexuality. The woman who diets away or vomits up sexuality is attempting to remain childlike, to remain her father's little girl and, at the same time, to avoid winning her father as a sexual partner. Her fear is that if she matures into a sexual woman she might win the Electra complex and win her father as a sexual partner. Then she would have to deal with both the incest with her father and her mother's rage. This rage is particularly frightening since, in such family constellations, the daughter is competitive with her mother. Thus the daughter may be both enraged at her mother and attracted to her father, hoping and fearing that he feels likewise.

Twenty-two-year-old Doris came into therapy because she could not stop her binge eating and self-induced vomiting. Sometimes two and three times a day she would gorge herself on her favorite binge foods—Twinkies, cookies, and ice cream—and then force herself to vomit. She had always known that her eating habits were not normal. She even knew that the condition was called bulimia. But things had gotten so out of hand that for the last week or so she had been vomiting up blood. Afterwards she would become so dizzy that she felt she might faint. She knew she had to stop but was powerless to do so. Eating and vomiting were her secret obsession. From the moment she woke up until she went to bed, her thoughts were preoccupied with what she would eat, when she would eat it, and how she would force the food out of her body so that her body did not get fat.

Doris's bingeing had begun four years earlier when she entered college. She had told herself that it was important for her to be thin, to be attractive, so that the men in her class would notice her and ask her out on dates. Now she was 5 foot 7 and weighed 110 pounds. She was definitely skinny, although she did not view herself in that way. She experienced herself as fairly attractive, although she would have preferred to be a few pounds lighter. At present it was not her appearance that was disturbing her but her eating habits.

Doris was a bright, well-educated young woman. She held a BA in social work and was employed in the welfare office at a job which she enjoyed. Except for the deep, dark secret of her eating behavior, Doris viewed herself as a fairly chic career woman. She dated and slept with a lot of men, enjoying being held and cuddled. These casual sexual encounters provided the sum total of her sensual and sexual experience. Doris enjoyed the sexual encounters, although the sex itself was unimportant to her. Doris was never orgasmic and, in fact, never even masturbated. But she loved to be held and cuddled. Doris kept the relationships casual, never wanting to investigate the person who lived in the warm body next to her for fear that if she allowed closeness, she might get hurt. She feared that if he knew her he might find her not perfect enough, not beautiful enough, or not thin enough, and that he might leave her.

In therapy Doris spent a lot of time talking about her background. Her mother had run away with another man when Doris was three, leaving her husband to care for Doris and her older brother. Her father was enraged at his ex-wife and was never able to forgive her either for abandoning him or for leaving him with the total responsibility for two children. Doris was a good little girl who did exceptionally well in school and seemed popular with her peers. She took care of her father and tried hard to please.

Doris learned how her family tragedies had influenced her present behavior. She unconsciously felt that she had won the Electra triangle. She had her daddy all to herself; she was the woman that he came home to; she was the only woman in his life. This was, of course, both thrilling and terrifying to Doris. As her sexuality grew, her sense of the unspoken possibilities between her and her father also grew. And then, shortly after puberty, she gained weight. Her father made a few comments about her chubbiness and Doris, thrown into agonies of self-reproach, started dieting. She had to get thinner so that her father would adore her again, and so other men would adore her too. When Doris entered college, she found the perfect solution to her weight problem. She discovered that she could eat any amount of forbidden foods and then induce vomiting. This way she would not gain an ounce. She could eat her cake and lose it too.

Doris also learned in therapy that she was enraged at her mother for abandoning her. She recognized her long denied sense of not being lovable enough to keep her mother at home. It was as if her mother had nursed her and then discarded her. Eating was a way for Doris to fill herself up, to nurture herself, to give herself the mother she had lost. The food she ate was symbolically the food her mother gave her. It was as if in her infantile mind she were constantly eating her mother to keep her inside, and then needing to throw her up because of her rage at her.

Vomiting was therefore Doris's way to both release her rage and rid herself of her sexuality so she could remain "daddy's little girl." Her vomit was both her mother's milk and her father's sperm. It was a symbol for all that which was simultaneously good and terrifying to her. In order for Doris to stop bingeing and vomiting she needed to learn to express her anger. She also needed to feel more comfortable about her past sexual feelings toward her father while at the same time separating herself from him. She did not need to be his little girl; she could be a grown woman.

Anorexia and bulimia result from a combination of psychological and cultural factors. As in Doris's case, psychological reasons always underlie binge eating and vomiting. However, the fact that Doris expressed her difficulties in this manner is a reflection of this culture. Food, body size, and thinness are overwhelming concerns today. Many people have one problem or another centered around food. Eating can be a source of either pleasure and companionship or anxiety and concern. Hence the national passion for thinness and youth has facilitated the development of a new, self-destructive way to express unresolved conflicts.

In twentieth-century America, young women are starving themselves almost to death in the midst of affluence and plenty. In a perverse way, twentieth-century America has become analogous to the Victorian era. Women are surrounded by horns of plenty, barraged by advertisements and photographs extolling the pleasures of food and eating. Yet women must not enjoy food too much. Women must stay thin. In the Victorian era, women were not supposed to enjoy sex and as a result had numerous emotional difficulties centering around sexuality. In twentieth-century America, women are not supposed to enjoy food, and the result has been the development of anorexia and bulimia. In both eras the denial of pleasure has bred severe emotional problems.

Pregnancy and Childbirth

Most of you have a biological need to reproduce, a yearning to get pregnant. Often this is expressed in dreams occurring in conjunction with ovulation. These might be dreams of eggs, kittens, babies, or of filling boxes, dreams that reflect your hormonal readiness to be impregnated, your need to be maternal. You need to nurture, to help someone grow and develop, to create and watch the unfolding of life.

When you have a fulfilling, passionate relationship with a man, your yearning to reproduce this love in the form of another human being becomes intense. You may want to see the positive proof of your shared sexuality, your love, your commitment to each other in the existence of another human being. Thus your need for a child may increase with your expression of love for another.

In addition to your biological and emotional need to have a child, our culture stresses that women are best fulfilled in motherhood. You are told that mothering is the essence of your life and the sole avenue toward self-fulfillment; that you are not truly a woman unless you have borne and reared a child. On the other hand, having a child may be more than a cultural expectation for you; it may be a role you always looked forward to with eagerness. Bearing a child as an expression of your womanhood or as an expression of your love for another are both healthy reasons for looking forward to mothering.

Unresolved conflict also can provide the motivating force to bear a child. For example, if you had a miserable childhood, you may want to redo it by being the perfect "fairy godmother" with your child. This does not work because, of course, no one can be a fairy godmother. However, if you are able to redo your childhood by being the "good-enough" mother, and in so doing can heal yourself while giving to your child, you may have found a happy solution to your old dilemma.

You may also want to have a child because you need to have someone dependent upon you. Perhaps you never felt totally loved and feel that a little baby would provide the love that you so desperately want. Or motherhood may be a way for you to hold onto your own childhood. By identifying with your child you may be refusing to move into adulthood. A child may also be experienced primarily as an extension of yourself. You may want to show the world what you created. If you have a child for any of these reasons, you will be disappointed. A child is not capable of redoing your past or of being perfect, or of giving to you without needing a great deal in return.

In the past, many women became mothers because it was impossible to imagine doing anything else. Today you have options. You are free to not bear children. This too can be a healthy choice. To decide that your life is fulfilled without the experience of a child can be a healthy and viable adult alternative.

Madeline was 16 years old when she discovered that she was pregnant. She could not believe it. Even though she had not been reliable about her use of contraceptives, she did not think that it would happen to her. At first she and her boyfriend planned to run away and marry, but then he decided that neither of them was prepared to assume the responsibility of a child. So, feeling that she had no alternative, Madeline told her parents about her pregnancy. She dreaded this, for even before her pregnancy Madeline had felt alienated from and misunderstood by them. She felt as though they did not care about her and were indifferent to her conflicts as a teenager. But she told them of her pregnancy and her boyfriend's insistence that she have an abortion. As she expected, her parents were very angry but concurred with her boyfriend and agreed to help her through the abortion. Life at home, however, became intolerable. Madeline's mother cried a lot, telling Madeline what an awful child she was for the pain and suffering she was inflicting on them. Her father simply gave

Madeline the cold shoulder, seeming to prefer no contact.

As the day of Madeline's abortion approached, she was aware of feeling more and more frightened. Part of her really did not want to lose this baby and, in fact, wanted the baby even though she had not planned it. Now that she was pregnant, she had many fantasies about bearing and rearing her child. She would love her baby as her parents had not been able to love her. She would be the perfect mother; she would undo all their mistakes. She would show her production to the world, and the world would applaud both her baby and her. But her boyfriend and her parents remained adamant about the abortion, and Madeline knew she had no way out. She was terrified. She could not imagine what it would be like to be up on a table, with her legs spread apart, having her insides scraped out. Her nakedness and sexuality would be exposed to the world.

As Madeline had feared, the abortion was humiliating and painful. It was a nightmare come true. She had sat in a room with other women, knowing they would be experiencing the same pain and degradation. She felt as if she were in a factory in which she was a piece of meat—just another slab on a table to be cut up. And it had hurt. She had screamed and cried but no one seemed to care. The nurse's attempt at support was simply not sufficient. Her pain and anguish did not diminish. After the abortion she was alone again. She did not even have that growing baby in her body. Then Madeline became depressed. She felt totally alone and lost; she felt as though she had done something terribly wrong and was being punished for it. She wanted what had been taken from her. Finally, in desperation, Madeline went to talk with a counselor at her school. The counselor helped her to look at the issues and to resolve her feelings of loss and anger.

Madeline was able to see that her pregnancy was partially an expression of anger at her parents, a way of rebelling against them as well as commanding their attention. Having a baby was also her way of redoing her childhood in a more loving, caring manner. Additionally, it was her way of having someone who would love and need her consistently. Not using contraception in a responsible manner was also her way of denying her sexuality. She was not owning her own sexuality. This, along with her psychological need to bear a child, motivated her to flirt with pregnancy. Instead, each time she was sexual she could feel as if it were the first time, as if it were a surprise.

Madeline's inconsistent use of contraceptives stemmed from her own psychological problems with sexuality. Some of you, however, may have conflicts concerning contraceptives which are external to your psychodynamics. In the past, women often had unwanted pregnancies because they lacked education about birth control or because contraceptives were not available. Today, in spite of the availability of information about birth control methods, conflicts around birth control remain. There simply is no perfect, fool-proof contraceptive device, and many contraceptives have serious side effects. To avoid these side effects, many of you have returned to less reliable birth control methods. Thus today a woman who does not want to become pregnant may do so from psychodynamic reasons, but she may also do so from practical, health-related reasons as well.

Lillian is a woman who had the opposite problem: she was unable to conceive. She had a very good relationship with her husband to whom she had been married for eight years. They enjoyed each other, both as friends and as lovers. They shared mutual interests, but also had many individual interests outside the marriage. For four years they had been trying to have a child. Lillian was now 32. She and her husband were saddened and angry about their inability to have a child. They wanted a child as an expression of their love for each other; they wanted to share their lives with a human being who had been created from their act of love. Lillian wanted to nurture the child, show the child some of the joys of her own childhood, and help the child explore the world. When she saw a little baby, her arms ached. During the past four years, Lillian felt she had done everything possible to become pregnant. She had gone to many different doctors; she had had her tubes blown out; she had had her endometrium count checked and her cervix dilated. Her husband's sperm count was at the low end of the normal range. For two years Lillian had been taking her temperature every morning so that she and her husband could make love at a time that would facilitate pregnancy. The temperature chart began dictating their passion and their positions. Lillian and her husband were very distressed about their inability to conceive a child.

Lillian was feeling very sad one evening during a talk with her husband about their inability to conceive. He pointed out that even if they never became parents, they had a full, rich life. They had their love for each other, jobs they enjoyed, friends they cared about, and activities that kept them interested. Certainly a child would be the icing on the cake, but at least they had the cake. This conversation freed Lillian to imagine a life without a child, to realize the positive aspects of not being a mother. She would not have to interrupt her career. She would not have to undergo massive changes in her body and in her relationship with her husband and other people in her life. By consciously accepting the "price" of being a mother, Lillian freed herself to reexamine her options. She now realized that she had a choice and that she could live a fulfilling life no matter which she chose. Reviewing her situation in the light of this realization, Lillian decided that indeed she did want to be a mother, although she did not need to be one. She and her husband threw away the temperature charts, stopped "working" to have a baby, and relaxed into their future.

Five months later Lillian became pregnant. She was thrilled and frightened. She was concerned that her "over thirty" status might put her baby in jeopardy. However, she felt she had made the right decision and was excited about her pregnancy, the changes in her body, and was looking forward to caring for her newborn child. As her pregnancy advanced, her concern and worries about the welfare of her child seemed to diminish. She laughed at herself, realizing how much she fulfilled the stereotype of the contented pregnant woman.

Labor was relatively uneventful. Lillian had wanted to have natural childbirth, but the pain was so great that she requested a local anesthetic; her pain reduced, she could witness her baby's head push out of her vulva. Then the wet, red body was placed on her stomach. She held her new baby, Rene, and felt an overwhelmingly loving, protective gush. She had fallen in love with her baby.

The next days and months were given over to caring for and loving the child. Lillian's husband was also thrilled with Rene, and both of them spent hours staring at Rene as she slept, marveling at the teeny fingers and the creases in her legs. Lillian knew, however, that she was exhausted. She had adapted her sleeping schedule to the baby's, and it seemed that she spent her entire life sleeping and feeding. When her husband wanted to renew their sexual contact, Lillian was, at best, disinterested. She was tired and a piece of her was always listening for Rene's cry. She felt as if her body belonged to Rene and not to her husband. Her breasts were for Rene to suck, not for her husband to fondle. Her arms were to hold Rene, not her husband. Her whole body had changed its purpose. It was now only for her child to use. As Rene grew older, Lillian was able to reclaim her own body. It was hers again, hers to own and hers to enjoy. She was again able to own her sexuality and to allow sexual pleasure. Her sexual interest increased as she redefined her body as that of a woman and not simply a mother.

Ways of Expressing Sexuality

Masturbation. Masturbation is usually the first way you begin to express your sexuality. It is a normal, natural part of growing up and exploring your body. All infants explore their bodies, including their genital areas. You learn that touching your body, your hands and toes and your genitals, gives you pleasure. You enjoy exploring yourself; you enjoy finding out what feels pleasurable and what hurts. In time, most of you learn that touching or playing with your genital area gives you pleasure; it feels good. It is soothing, even if there is no orgasmic release.

Whether or not a child continues to masturbate into adulthood depends a great deal upon parental or cultural messages. If you are caught masturbating and are threatened

236 · GETTING FREE: Women and Psychotherapy

or punished, you may stop this behavior for some period of
time, perhaps even permanently. Or you may continue masturbating but feel terribly guilty, as if you are doing something wrong, something sinful. Resolving this guilt around
masturbation is an important accomplishment, because it
paves the way for you to give yourself sexual pleasure whenever you want. It permits you to own sexual pleasure, to know
that it is all right for you to be sexual and, in fact, to revel in
the joy and pleasure you can give yourself.

Masturbation is simply a different kind of sexual pleasure,
a different way to be sexual. It is something that you can do
throughout your life. You can masturbate when you are involved in an intimate relationship; you can masturbate if you
are divorced or widowed or without a sexual partner. Age is
no barrier to masturbation. From birth until death you are
able to give yourself sexual pleasure. This is something that is
yours.

Masturbation is also a way to teach yourself how to be
sexually responsive, to train yourself to be orgasmic by bringing yourself to orgasm. Having orgasms strengthens your vagi-
nal muscles. Regardless of your psychological conflicts
concerning sex, this physical ability is necessary for orgasm.
Being fearful of swimming offers an analogy. Once your fear
of swimming has been resolved, you do not automatically
know how to swim. You must develop your muscles and learn
the rhythm necessary to propel you across the water. Thus it
is with sex. You must have an "all systems go" psychological
stance plus physiological know-how in order to be orgasmic.

Only recently has masturbation for women come out of
the closet. Previously, most of you masturbated secretly, feeling ashamed and convinced that you were engaged in abnor-
mal behavior. You believed yourself unique and strange
because you felt so much pleasure when you touched yourself
in these secret ways. You also felt as though you were the only
woman who ever reveled in reading sexual stories to further
arouse yourself and heighten your pleasure. Certainly you
were the only person who had ever been stimulated by pictures of people making love or who had ever used a sexual
fantasy while masturbating. You felt as though you had an

excessive sexual drive which you discharged through masturbation. For many of you, masturbation was your secret pleasure, and only recently have you realized that you are not
alone in this pleasure. Most women have been enjoying it in
secret silence for years.

Pornography is another secret kept under wraps by
women. You may have become sexually aroused by reading
Lady Chatterley's Lover, Peyton Place, or *True Confessions*
magazine and wondered if there was something perverted
about you. Did other women get "turned on" by this explicit
sex? Although you may have been repulsed by violent pornography, you may have found it very arousing to look at
pictures of naked men, naked women, or couples making love.
Coming to grips with all these avenues for the expression of
sexuality is the blooming of adult sexuality. These are ways to
learn about your body, explore your sexuality, and give yourself pleasure. It means undoing the cultural expectation that
you as a woman are here to take care of other people but not
to give yourself pleasure. You, as a sexually free woman, can
undo this proscription. You can own your sexuality, you can
use your imaginative powers to enhance your sexuality; you
can give yourself pleasure.

Fantasies. Most of you also have sexual fantasies. These
can be fantasies of passionate, romantic encounters; of sex
with a multitude of men serving your every wish; of violence
or rape or submission; of the perfect "fuck." You may fantasize while making love or while washing dishes or while driving a car. At times your fantasies may seem to come out of
nowhere, not directed by you, simply there. You may be surprised to find yourself fantasizing about making love on the
top of the Eiffel Tower. On the other hand, your sexual fantasies may be brought forth by you to further your sexual
stimulation or entertainment while you are involved in more
mundane activities. Sexual fantasies, like fantasies in general,
are a pleasurable part of everyday life. You need not feel bad
or guilty about what you fantasize, because fantasy is not
reality. You need not be held accountable for what you fantasize, only for what you do.

Twenty-four-year-old Lara felt guilty about having sexual fantasies about another man when she had been married for only a year. Lara had been a virgin when she married and was very much in love with her husband. They had an excellent sexual relationship. She felt very committed to her husband and to the notion of sexual fidelity. Then a new salesman came to work at the company where Lara was employed. He was an exceptionally good-looking man, the stereotype of a tall, dark, handsome stranger. He was like a character in the Gothic novels she so loved to read. And then one night, while she was making love with her husband, she was startled to find herself fantasizing about being with this other man. She felt as though she had been unfaithful to her husband. Lara shook off the fantasy with a tremendous amount of guilt and promised herself never to think such thoughts again. However, on her way to work the other man's face would suddenly loom before her, and she would imagine him sweeping her away to some secluded spot where they would enjoy mutual caresses and lovemaking.

Lara was determined to stop these fantasies. She felt guilty. This kind of thinking was wrong. She felt as though she were committing adultery, and she feared that these fantasies indicated a lack of love for her husband. So she turned off all her sexual fantasies and, in so doing, was unable to feel sexual at all, even with her husband. Her passionate, loving sexual relationship with her husband was gone. Now she felt only numbness, nothingness, and sometimes even disgust.

Lara is a good example of someone unable to differentiate between fantasies and deeds. She felt as if the thought were equal to the deed, that wishing for something was tantamount to acting on it. She could not separate her desires from her actions, and in an effort to stop her desires she had turned herself off completely, thereby eliminating the passion and joy in her life. The irony is that in an effort to be more devoted to her husband, she had rendered herself unresponsive to him.

Heterosexuality. Beginning in adolescence, you started sharing your sexuality with other human beings. For most of you this was a slow process, fraught with difficulty and anxiety. At 11 you were concerned about where to put your nose when you kissed; at 18 you were concerned about where to put your hands when you had intercourse. Most of you chose males as sexual partners. You may have been fascinated by the male organ and how it works. Or you may have been frightened by a penis, concerned about whether it could fit inside you and if it would hurt. Later you may be excited by an erect penis.

Melissa, who was 17, was both frightened and excited by the whole idea of sexual intercourse. She looked forward to the end of each date with her boyfriend when they would kiss each other passionately. When he first touched her breasts, she felt uncomfortable, wondering if she should allow it. But his touch made her tingle in a way that she had never known. She felt tremendous excitement when he put his hand in between her legs, but again wondered if she should let him go "this far." Could she trust him? Would he hurt her? Would he stop respecting her? She was apprehensive about touching him, curious about what she would feel, but also discomfited by the thought of her hand on his erect penis.

As time went on, Melissa knew that it was just a matter of time before she and her boyfriend went "all the way." She had many concerns about intercourse. Melissa worried that it would hurt; or, worse yet, that she would hate sex. Maybe she would even find it disgusting. Then what would she do? How could she live as a happy, fulfilled woman? On the other hand, the whole idea of sex was exciting. She had enormous curiosity about intercourse and read her parents' books on sex, trying to discover what it was really like. Her feelings swayed between eagerness and timidity.

Finally one night she allowed her boyfriend to enter her. Intercourse felt new, strange to her. It was difficult for him to totally penetrate her. She felt that she could not spread her legs wide enough to let him fit in easily. Yet she was pleased that she knew what to do with her hips, knew how to move them rhythmically with her lover. She felt close to him. After he had come and withdrawn, they saw a bit of red blood at the base of his penis. Melissa felt a wave of joy and accomplishment. She felt relieved. Although she knew she had not had an orgasm, she had found sex exciting and was proud of her new achievement. Melissa felt close to her new lover.

Like Melissa, once you have rid yourself of your virginity, you must then decide how to continue the exploration and enjoyment of your newly expressed sexuality. In what type of relationship do you wish to share your body? Do you want to have casual sexual encounters without much intimacy or involvement? Do you want to share your body only with someone you love? Do you prefer to be sexual with only one person at a time? Throughout your life you will be deciding whether to involve yourself in numerous sexual relationships or in a committed, monogamous relationship. Obviously this decision is subject to change, depending upon the circumstances of your life and your feelings at any given time.

Many of you choose a long-term, monogamous relationship with either a husband or live-in partner. This choice is encouraged by society. A committed, monogamous relationship is also something within which you can grow. It is a way of nurturing intimacy and personal growth. The intensity of intimacy adds another dimension to your life, another avenue toward self-actualization. A long-term, intimate relationship also provides a safe, secure base from which to explore the world. You can grow both within the relationship and beyond it.

On the other hand, there are alternatives to such a monogamous relationship. The joy of exploring a new partner, both physically and emotionally, can be intense and exciting. You may enjoy getting to know a variety of men, personalities, and sexual styles. You may choose sexual and psychological variety and experimentation. There is no way to have the intimacy of a long-term, monogamous relationship and at the same time the excitement of a variety of relationships. These are mutually exclusive life styles. Sometimes you may feel you would like to have it all. You would like to have the intimacy and the safety of a long-term, monogamous relationship along with the excitement and intensity of exploring new sexual partners. Perhaps the ultimate in peace and contentment derives from realizing that you cannot have it all and that you must choose the life style that best satisfies your needs.

At the age of 46, Sandra had been married for 23 years. She felt as though she had a good, supportive marriage characterized by compatibility and friendship. The early years had been passionate, intense, and filled with understanding and mutually shared experiences. Their love for one another was tremendous, and they both delighted in the three children they had brought into the world.

In the course of rearing those children, however, something had disappeared from their relationship. Something now was lacking. They no longer had time together. They related as mother and father rather than as man and woman. Lovemaking had been placed on the back burner, while runny noses and driving the children to the dentist had taken precedence. Now all the children were out of the home, and Sandra hoped that she and her husband would be able to recapture some of the intensity of their early relationship. However, it did not happen. They were unable to recapture their past passion, the past intensity. Now they found sex simply boring, unexciting, and mundane. Sandra found herself having a flirtatious relationship with a man at work and considered the possibility of embarking upon a new sexual adventure. She was at the point of choice. Was she going to remain committed to her long-term, monogamous relationship, or would she choose a new alternative?

Sandra felt as though the issue in her relationship with her husband was sexual boredom, but clearly sexuality was not the only issue involved. Boredom is not simply boredom; it is often a symptom, a screen for other feelings and emotions. It may be a cover for anger, depression, or lack of intimacy. The boredom in Sandra's sexual relationship with her husband resulted from their lack of intimacy. It was hard for her to be sexually excited about a man whom she had stopped exploring as a human being. He was "just her husband," the man with whom she had raised three children. When they stopped sharing an excitement about each other as people, they could no longer be sexually excited about each other either.

Lesbianism. Although most of you choose to share your sexual self with men, some of you choose women as sexual partners. All of you are potentially bisexual; that is, you can enjoy your sexuality with either a man or a woman. This culture strongly reinforces heterosexuality, so most of you direct your sexual feelings toward men. Some of you, however, feel strong sexual yearnings toward women.

Given the cultural support of heterosexual as opposed to homosexual relationships, the choice of a lesbian life style results from psychological, sociological, and political considerations. Several psychological patterns within the family romance increase the likelihood of your being a lesbian. Probably the most common of these patterns is a cold, distancing relationship with your mother and an overly stimulating or seductive relationship with your father. On the surface, one would think that a child growing up with a nurturing, loving father and a cold mother would feel closer and more intimate with men. However, the reverse is often true. Those of you who grew up in this type of family may have fled from your sexual feelings toward your father and, at the same time, may have tried to win the unattainable closeness and love from your mother. Thus as an adult you seek to win in the present the love that you did not have in the past, that is, the love of a woman. An example of the above-mentioned family background is Vanessa, who was discussed at the beginning of this chapter. She chose a partner, Rhoda, who was warm and loving, in an attempt to receive from a woman the warmth and love that she had not received from her own mother.

In a family constellation such as this, another factor which fosters the development of lesbianism is that you as a young woman prefer your father to your mother. You want to be more like your father than your mother. You respect your father more. As a result, you identify more with your father and model yourself after him. In so doing you make the same choice he made in a sexual partner; you choose women to relate to sexually. Choosing women protects you from restimulating your past sexual feelings toward your father and at the same time allows you to be like him. In this circumstance, you, like your father before you, may choose cold, distancing women to relate to, still leaving you deprived of the warmth you so desperately want.

Another family constellation which nurtures lesbianism is

one in which the father is particularly abusive physically, sexually, or psychologically. If you grow up in an atmosphere of terror at your father's potential or actual violence, you may love women as a defense against possible future brutality. In addition to the direct fear of your father you may feel, you may also internalize your mother's feelings about her husband and men in general, and fear that all men are dangerous. Thus a negative attitude toward men, in addition to your own fears, might encourage you to look to women for love and intimacy.

Thirty-four-year-old Charity is a lesbian who grew up in a family with a physically abusive father. She was always terrified of her father's return from work. He was often drunk and always explosive. Anything could send him into a fury—an unwashed fork, a spot on her dress, an unwanted giggle. And when his wrath was provoked, he would yell and scream and swing at anyone within his sight. The entire family lived in fear of him. Charity's mother was a martyr, a passive, ineffectual woman who cried and whined and pleaded with her husband to stop his abuse but did nothing to protect either herself or her children. She made a virtue of being long-suffering. At a very young age, Charity knew that she would never risk being involved with a man. She assumed that all men would be abusive like her father; they were animals that charged around, indifferent to the needs or feelings of others. The news media reinforced this belief for Charity; she continually read about men raping and murdering others, especially women. However, neither did Charity want to be like her mother. She did not want to be a martyr. She did not want to suffer any more. She would take charge of her own life; she would be strong and assertive. Lesbianism was her solution.

Although Charity enjoyed the world of women and felt safer than she ever had as a child, she found that her relationships were not fulfilling. They did not involve any physical violence or abuse, but they all seemed to be painful. First she found herself in relationships in which she was victimized and criticized, much as she had been by her father. She could do nothing right. Either she did not look right or she did not act right; her lover always found something to attack. Charity would finally extricate herself from these relationships only to find herself in other destructive relationships, but this time she became the critical one. Now her lovers, regardless of how devoted, warm, and giving they might be, simply could not satisfy Charity. They were either boring, or too fat, or too thin. Charity did not like this behavior in herself. She feared that she could never be satisfied, that she drove away the very people who could love her.

Thus in all her relationships Charity replayed her family script. She was being either her father or her mother. When she was being her mother, the victim, she was abused, attacked, and criticized in the same manner as her mother had been. She was being like the woman she had most contempt for. When not playing the victim, Charity became the victimizer. At these times she was identifying with her father and taking his position of power. Like him, she abused her power. Then she was being like the person she hated the most.

Although it is common to find one of the above family constellations among women who are lesbians, there is no one-to-one correlation between the above dynamics and a preference for women as sexual partners. In addition to psychological dynamics, political and sociocultural factors enter into a woman's choice to be a lesbian. With the upsurgence of the women's movement and the recognition of men's oppression, many of you felt that it was politically more correct to love women. Some of you felt that continuing to relate to men sexually while trying to battle them for power or status would be like cohabiting with the enemy. Therefore you allowed the expression of your sexual attraction toward women and submerged your sexual feelings toward men.

American culture as a whole does not support your becoming a lesbian. It screams out against this turning away from what is seen as woman's primary task to support and nurture man and his children. Lesbians have dealt with their rejection from the "culture at large" by forming their own community. This community can be close and accepting of you as a lesbian and can provide the support that you cannot get from your family or society at large. The lesbian community can create a sense of belonging and provide a family atmosphere for holidays, funerals, and other traditions. Additionally, this community offers you models for how to be a lesbian and supports you in your decision not to be involved with men.

Sometimes what fosters your becoming or owning yourself as a lesbian is this close sense of family and community. You especially need the lesbian community during that period when you are coming to grips with your sexuality and owning your lesbianism. You need to decide whether you are going to identify yourself as a lesbian, and then whether you should "come out" to family members, friends, and colleagues. The lesbian community may help you in making these decisions. Usually you experience a tremendous sense of joy in coming out. At last you have found yourself. At last you have found others who are like you. You are no longer alone. You can share your sexual preference with others who respect and approve of your choice. And again, if members of your heterosexual world reject you because of your lesbianism, the community is there to comfort you and function as a substitute family.

However, there is a price for this support. The community maintains rigid rules regarding acceptable behavior. This rigidity seems to be an inevitable result of lesbians' attempt to define themselves as separate from the "straight" culture. For example, certain attitudes and behaviors are politically correct. To behave otherwise invites negative judgment from the lesbian community. In addition, the smallness of the community makes individual and couple boundaries difficult to maintain. Personal privacy is not respected, and triangles abound, as few women are competing for even fewer resources.

In addition to the difficulties with the community, you as a lesbian face other problems. Some of the rules available to heterosexual women are not available to you. For example, heterosexual women know that women are likely to be friends and men are likely to be lovers. You as a lesbian do not know this. When meeting a new woman you must decide whether this person is going to be a lover or a friend. The standard gender markers which usually help with these decisions do not exist for lesbians. The boundaries defining these relationships are very fluid. Your friend may become your lover, and your lover may become your friend.

As a lesbian you, of course, face many of the same issues

about sexual relationships that heterosexuals face. You still need to decide whether you are going to wait for a primary, monogamous relationship, or whether you are going to explore a variety of partners. Negotiating role behavior for many lesbian couples is, however, somewhat different from what it is for heterosexuals. You and your lover are in uncharted territory regarding rules. You must allocate all duties and responsibilities without even the old-fashioned markers about sexual roles. Each decision is unprecedented. You have to decide whether there will be a primary breadwinner, who will initiate sexual contact, how the household chores will be divided, who will play what role in lovemaking.

Many of you who are part of a lesbian couple react to the larger culture's disapproval by focusing inward and solidifying your coupleness. You may want your partner to meet all of your needs. You may feel as though the whole world must take place in your apartment. You must each be everything to the other. No one else is allowed in. Because friends may become sexual partners, separate friendships outside the dyad are discouraged. Couples relate with other couples, making single friendships difficult to maintain. Hence the lesbian community, because of its smallness, becomes inbred and also inadvertently encourages fusion for the lesbian couple. Thus sociological issues enhance psychological ones and fusion among lesbian couples becomes an overwhelming issue.

Although the culture increases difficulties with regard to fusion, many of you as lesbians enter an intimate relationship with fusion problems of your own. Because you may be searching for the perfect mother to make up for the lack of mothering in your childhood, you may easily surrender yourself totally to another woman, hoping that all your unmet needs and hopes will be realized. You may long for the time when you were an infant, held in your mother's arms, sucking on her breast, protected from the rest of the world. You may look to your relationship to redo this early infantile experience. In addition, it is easier to fuse with someone who looks like you, is shaped like you, and has the same organs as you. It may even be like making love to your mirror image. Additionally, women are reinforced for surrendering themselves to a relationship. Their role is to care for others and consider themselves second. Obviously, when two people are doing this simultaneously the probability of fusion increases dramatically.

Many of you as lesbians share the family constellation of the cold, distancing mother and the seductive father. Many of you as heterosexuals also share a similar family constellation. Any sexual preference has a concomitant psychodynamic basis. Regardless of family history or sexual preference, the primary issue is the attainment of personal freedom and the maintenance of quality relationships.

Getting Free: Vanessa

Vanessa, presented at the beginning of the chapter, began therapy at the insistence of her lover, Rhoda. Rhoda had become increasingly dismayed by their lack of sexual activity and was not sure that she could continue in the relationship if the sexual part did not improve. Since Vanessa felt very committed to Rhoda and wanted to preserve the relationship, she entered therapy after seeking out a female therapist who was comfortable with and respectful of the lesbian choice.

Initially, therapy focused on Vanessa's relationship with Rhoda. Vanessa reported that she and Rhoda had an almost ideal relationship. They loved one another and were committed to spending their lives together. Given the lack of stability in the lesbian community at large, they considered themselves to be very fortunate. They spent all of their time together sharing friends, activities, and even professional interests. They worked in the same hospital and usually ate lunch together. They spent their lives together. When necessity separated them, their reunion was filled with mutual sharing of the details of their time apart. Rhoda loved to hear about Vanessa's operations, and Vanessa was likewise intrigued with Rhoda's family therapy sessions. Vanessa presented this picture to her therapist as proof of how well the relationship was working. She could not understand why, since she loved Rhoda so much, she could no longer be sexual with her.

The therapist began urging Vanessa to look at some of the issues involved in the intense closeness between them. How did it feel to sleep alone when Rhoda was called out on an emergency? How did it feel when Rhoda's family arrived and Vanessa was left to spend an evening alone? Consideration of these questions brought Vanessa the realization that separation from Rhoda was always gut-wrenching. She hated even brief separations. Her stomach knotted; she felt alone and isolated and abandoned. She felt as though she would never see Rhoda again. The intensity of Vanessa's feelings about these separations suggested that the closeness between Vanessa and Rhoda was not really an indication of love but rather a defense against fears of separation. In other words, Vanessa was afraid of being abandoned and clung to Rhoda in an effort to avoid it. Vanessa and Rhoda had a fused relationship. Each had given herself over to the other person; they had no individual boundaries; they were entwined with each other. They were not mutually interdependent and loving but dependent and unable to experience themselves as separate identities.

Vanessa began to understand how her childhood had prepared her for a fused relationship. Although her mother had no doubt been warm and loving during the first six to eight months of Vanessa's life, she had then become aloof, cold, and distant. Having not received the warmth and love that she needed as a child, Vanessa then sought it as an adult. She was trying to recapture the first eight months of her life. Since Vanessa's early relationship with her mother was of necessity fused, it was easy for her to redo the fusion as an adult. She was seeking in the present that which she had once had but lost too early. She unconsciously wanted Rhoda to be the mother she had lost in her very early months. Vanessa began to understand the impossibility of maintaining an adult sexual relationship within the context of an otherwise fused relationship. Since orgasm involves a healthy temporary fusion, for Vanessa it meant expanding the fusion of an already fused relationship. This was unconsciously terrifying. It meant that she might totally lose herself.

After Vanessa began to explore these issues, she reported

an uncomfortable fantasy that she often had while making love with Rhoda. She had been having this fantasy for a while but had been trying to push it out of her mind. However, the last time she had had oral-genital sex with Rhoda, she had become acutely aware of the fantasy. As Vanessa was kissing Rhoda's vagina, she imagined herself becoming very small. She first imagined her head and then her whole body going deeper and deeper into Rhoda's vagina until all of her was swimming inside Rhoda's body and then encapsulated within her uterus. Vanessa knew, of course, that this was not truly happening, but the fantasy was discomfiting to her. When Vanessa and her therapist analyzed this fantasy, Vanessa was able to recognize her fear of fusion. She was afraid of being an infant again, afraid of losing her identity, of being obliterated. Sexual intimacy with Rhoda stimulated these fears.

As therapy continued, Vanessa became angry at Rhoda, at herself, at everyone. As she gained insight into her fusion needs and the turmoil and trauma that these unmet needs were creating in her life, she became aware of anger at her mother. She was angry that her mother had not given her what she needed when she needed it. Why should she have to go through this unremitting agony? Why could she not have a sexual relationship with her lover? How could her mother have done this to her? How could her mother have rejected her? How could she have been so cold and distant for so many years? In time, Vanessa became aware that her childhood could not be redone. What was in the past was finished. She could not remake her mother into a better one. She had to give up her yearning and longing for this infantile closeness and bliss. She could not have her mother and she no longer needed her as she had needed her in the past.

In the midst of dealing with her rage at her mother, Vanessa reported the following dream. Several months before, she had seen the movie *Ordinary People* and had admired the male psychiatrist in the movie. In the dream, Vanessa was an adult, sitting in her childhood home, when there was a knock at the door. She opened the door and standing on the doorstep was the psychiatrist from *Ordinary People*. He told her how beautiful she was and how much he loved her. He then seduced her. In the dream, Vanessa felt intensely sexual. In fact, she had an orgasm in her dream.

Vanessa was surprised that she had felt so sexual in her dream and was quite concerned about its content. Did it mean that she was not "really" a lesbian? How could she have sexual feelings toward a man, even in a dream? Her therapist explained that lesbians often have sexual feelings toward men and that this does not make them heterosexual. Similarly, heterosexual women's sexual feelings toward women do not make them lesbains. Many people often have sexual feelings toward people of both sexes. You can have sexual feelings without acting on them.

Vanessa considered the possibility that her dream also reflected sexual feelings toward her own therapist. Maybe the psychiatrist in *Ordinary People* was a stand-in for Vanessa's therapist. Vanessa admitted that she had some sexual feelings toward her therapist, but that she primarily felt close and warm toward her. Her therapist suggested that perhaps she, the therapist, had become, in part, the mother that Vanessa had never had—the warm, accepting, loving woman who was always there for Vanessa. Then the sexual feelings toward her therapist could be seen as a way for Vanessa to be close to her therapist as a replacement for her mother with whom she really wanted to be close. That is, she transferred the yearnings she had for her mother to her therapist.

Still another interpretation of the dream involved Vanessa's sexual feelings toward her father. The dream took place in her childhood home, suggesting that Vanessa was both an adult and a little girl in the dream. And the psychiatrist, like her father, was someone whom she cared about intensely and who was very devoted to her. This interpretation opened up an entirely new realm of exploration. Vanessa had never thought much about her relationship with her father. He had always been her father, the man who adored her and who was warmer and more loving than her mother. The therapist wondered aloud if there had always been unconscious, unexpressed sexual feelings between the two of them. Her father's support of her lesbian choice may have been his way of eliminating all male competition. Similarly, it was not surprising that Vanessa would have had sexual feelings toward her father. He was so much warmer and more loving than her mother; she could hardly help but be attracted to him. Vanessa concurred. There had always been something flirtatious between them, as he had danced her around the floor or courted her as if she were his princess.

Thus Vanessa's family provided her a perfect background from which to emerge a lesbian. A cold, distancing relationship with her mother created her need for love from women. Her overly sexualized relationship with her father fostered her fear of sexuality with men. These circumstances, then, rendered her susceptible to fusion on the one hand and avoidance of sex on the other. With these insights Vanessa reentered her relationship with Rhoda, determined to defuse it, and together they struggled to increase their separateness. They tried to make friends apart from one another. They tried to spend less time together. They tried to do things separately. But somehow it did not work. Something always threw them together. Either they both happened to be having lunch in the cafeteria at the same time, or they were both invited to the same party. As Vanessa made attempts to move away, Rhoda became more depressed and more clinging. They just could not seem to be separate while being healthily interdependent. Hence Vanessa's difficulty with sex continued. She tried to initiate lovemaking on occasion and to be more responsive when Rhoda initiated it. However, it continued to be an uncomfortable chore for her. Vanessa and Rhoda were at the point of choice. They could continue to remain in their fused, companionable, loving, nonsexual relationship, or they could end the relationship and seek a nonfused, sexual relationship elsewhere. Vanessa was free to make a choice.

9

Autonomy:
MAKING YOUR
OWN WAY

Darlene's fortieth birthday was over. There was nothing to look forward to, nothing except her children leaving home, marrying, and making her a grandmother. Other than that, life would consist only of gray hairs, wrinkles, and increasing aches and pains. She felt empty; she could find nothing exciting or meaningful in her life. Darlene was depressed. She felt as though her life were a prison sentence in which the only parole was death.

Darlene wondered who she was and tried to remember if she had ever been certain of her identity. She was able to remember herself as a confident and capable high school student, attractive and popular with her classmates. Her membership in the student council and her excellent performance in art classes had been both fun and fulfilling. Her high school years had been punctuated by her marriage to the best looking boy in school. As a new bride, Darlene had felt important; she had worked as a secretary while her husband learned the plumbing trade. He had needed her so much then; her wages had been vital to the maintenance of the family and had enhanced her feeling of self-esteem.

When her husband became a journeyman plumber, she helped him in his new business until he was able to earn enough money for her to stay at home. Then they started a family and she cared for their children, the house, and him. The children were now 15 and 17, ready to embark on journeys of their own. Darlene was very proud of them and had enjoyed raising them. But that task was completed now. For the last two decades of her life she had totally dedicated herself to caring for others. She was a mother and a wife; but the cheerful, vivacious, competent young woman seemed to have disappeared. She was hidden beneath the middle-aged Darlene who went to PTA meetings, attended her children's school events, cooked for her husband, and met with her card club. Her enthusiasm and lust for life had been buried under piles of dirty dishes, dusty floors, and a few extra pounds. Her life was a tedium, each day a repetition of the one before. Life had lost its spark, and she had nothing to look forward to.

Shortly after her fortieth birthday, Darlene scheduled her annual gynecological exam. While talking with her physician, Darlene found herself in tears for no apparent reason. Her doctor expressed concern, and Darlene talked about her feelings of emptiness, depression, and despair. The physician suggested that a psychotherapist might be helpful. Darlene was taken aback by this suggestion. She had never thought of herself as the type to need a "shrink," and it certainly had never occurred to her that she had any alternative but to live out her life sentence. However, she agreed to consider seeing a female therapist, for she felt that only a woman could understand her feelings and her sense of imprisonment. After calling the therapist recommended by her doctor, Darlene was surprised to find herself looking forward to talking with someone about herself.

Autonomy

As an autonomous woman you choose how to spend your time in work, love, and play. It is this choice which makes you autonomous. One woman may choose to stay home and rear children. Another woman may choose to be a physician. Both of these women are equally autonomous if they have freely chosen their situation. It is not *what* you choose but rather your freedom to choose that manifests your autonomy.

As an autonomous woman you make choices within the many arenas of your life. You decide what kind of relationship you want to be in and with whom. You decide whether to work and, if so, what kind of work you want to do. Then, even if you choose not to work at any given time, you know that you can work, thus assuring yourself of your ability for self-sufficiency. You decide how to spend your leisure time and what activities excite you, whether they be running, arts and crafts, cooking, or bridge. Clearly, any of the decisions which you make at one point in your life you may remake at another point. At one point you may choose to be single; at another you may choose to marry. Although none of your autonomous choices need be permanent, those choices, at any given time in your life, paint the picture of your identity. Of course, as a free, growing woman, this identity is not written in stone, but rather shifts on the sands of time.

Autonomy and the Culture

At any given time the culture largely defines the prerequisites for autonomy. For example, in twentieth-century America you must be able to read and write in order to be autonomous; you must also be able to operate various types of equipment including automobiles and stoves. This culture does not necessitate that you know how to grow your own food or make your own clothing. Functioning within the culture does, however, require a basic understanding of law and government.

The above are prescribed, generalized norms that every adult American needs to know in order to survive within the culture. In addition, cultural norms dictate behavior for various groups of people, often dividing along class and sex lines. For example, a lower-class man may be expected to be knowledgeable about the repair of an automobile or a washing machine, whereas an upper-class man may be expected to be knowledgeable about finances and economics. Similarly, a woman may be expected to cook and diaper babies, whereas a man is expected to take out the garbage and build bookshelves. Although the culture puts pressure on you to live within these rules, it does not coerce you. Being autonomous does not mean following these prescribed behavior patterns so that you reflect the stereotype of your class, sex, age, or religion. Rather, it means having the freedom to choose whichever life style best suits you. For example, you, as a 35-year-old, middle-class woman, do not have to stay home, clean floors, diaper babies, sew clothes, prepare dinners, and go to PTA meetings. You may, instead, choose to be a literary agent who enjoys traveling and flying planes in your spare time.

The feminist movement has done a great deal to increase your options. Before this movement, not only were you expected to live within rigid roles, but you were also limited in terms of how you could experience and define yourself. Your worth was defined in terms of other people. Were you a wife? Were you a mother? Your husband's job and your children's accomplishments defined you and your value. You were the wife of a factory worker or a dentist. Your children were bright, clean, and well-mannered or dirty, unkempt, and incorrigible. Other people were your reflections. You had no intrinsic worth or value, only the value gleaned from your family. The irony of your situation prior to the feminist movement was that your autonomy was defined by the achievements of others. You were Mrs. Robert Jones and Bobby's mother, not Jeanette Smith Jones. But you cannot be autonomous by giving away your autonomy. You cannot find yourself by giving yourself away.

In addition to living within rigid roles, you were also reared to be financially dependent on a man. You were taught that you would not have to work outside the home or be knowledgeable about financial matters, as this was the man's job. He would make the world financially safe for you. He would care for you financially as your parents had done. Needless to say, as you surrendered your financial security to this man, you potentiated the possibility of disaster. What would happen if your marriage broke up or your husband died? What would happen if he became seriously ill? You would be stranded in an economic sea. Your financial security would come crashing down and there would be nowhere to turn. You would have no skills or experience in navigating the financials waters.

Ironically, though you were dependent on others financially, they were dependent on you emotionally. You were taught to define yourself as the caretaker, as the one who would nurture others and be responsible for relationships. You were taught to devote yourself to others: your husband, your children, or your students. It was your job to make everything all right and everyone happy. You were to set a pretty scene while life went on around you.

As the caretaker, you were programmed to care for everyone else first and consider your own needs afterwards. When something went wrong, when someone was not happy, when you felt angry about your own needs being neglected, you felt guilty. This was your trade-off. You were cared for economically but in exchange had to take care of everyone else's emotional and psychological needs. Then, when you, of necessity, failed in this impossible task, you felt guilty. You felt that you were not a good enough wife and mother, that you were not a good enough woman. You felt like a failure. Thus a woman's burden was wrapped in guilt. Being a female and feeling guilty became almost synonymous. You could not do enough, you could not be enough to make everything all right.

The feminist movement provided a way out of this dilemma. It allowed you, as a woman, the right to your own feelings, your own desires, your own needs. Conceivers of the movement claimed that you were a valuable person in your own right. Alone and separate, without regard to a mate, you were a worthwhile human being. You could fulfill your own dreams and aspirations without feeling guilty. And your aspirations did not have to include making someone else happy. You could be your own person and achieve your own goals. The women's movement allowed you true autonomy. It allowed you to choose from various life styles and from variations within life styles. No longer was there a prescribed way to be a woman.

Hence your life as a woman has been revolutionized. You can now choose whether to have a vocation and what that vocation will be. Your vocational choice can be either a traditionally female role such as that of nurse or a traditionally male role such as that of electrician. You can choose to marry, to live with someone without the legal documents, or to live alone. The movement vehemently denied the traditional dictate that womanhood means being submissive, subordinate, and dependent on a man. Now you can be involved in a relationship forged by both of you. You can choose whether to be a mother and how the parenting will be shared between you and your partner.

A whole new world is open to you. You can choose autonomy rather than dependence, self-definition rather than fusion. Regardless of how you choose to express your adult self, it is your ability to choose which manifests your autonomy. The women's movement, in carving out freedom for women, has inadvertently helped to free society at large. By becoming economically independent you free your male partners from the burden of providing total economic support. This restructuring spreads across class lines, resulting in greater freedom for people of all classes. For example, a woman who learns to operate efficiently in what was once the upper-class man's world of business, the stock market, and the *Wall Street Journal* redefines that role as one open to other than upper-class men. It becomes a role open to people at large, regardless of sex or class. Similarly, a man who achieves competence in parenting and child rearing frees that role from being one considered exclusively female. Thus across class and sex lines people become more free to choose.

There have always been brave women like Jane Addams or Margaret Mead, who insisted on making their own choices regardless of societal pressures. Today, women are sociologically freer to be more autonomous than they were in Jane Addams's day. However, many subtle pressures live on. Most men and women give lip service to the autonomous woman, but really working out and living with the details of equality is much more difficult and at times still greatly resisted.

Singleness

Most of you experience singleness at some time in your life, either as an interlude between relationships or as a permanent life choice. If your singleness is an interlude, you have a right to feel good about yourself during that time, to enjoy the interlude and not to experience it only as a bridge to somewhere and someone else. Similarly, if you choose singleness as a permanent way of life, you have a right to feel fulfilled and happy in that choice.

When you are single, various cultural, psychological, and practical difficulties face you. For example, if your singleness lasts for more than a brief period of time, you are often pressured to marry and are made to feel as though there is something wrong with you. In time you may begin to feel incomplete and marred. You may hate attending a party alone, feeling as though you wear your singleness like a scar for the world to see.

Shelley, 29 years old and a successful interior decorator, is an example of such a woman. Her three-year marriage had ended in divorce. After a period of intense anger and mourning, she settled into her single life. In most respects, she was fulfilled and happy. Her career was skyrocketing; she found herself in great demand and more financially successful than she had ever dreamed possible. She enjoyed redecorating her apartment, which was always beautifully done as an expression of her creative energies, and she had a cadre of friends with whom she spent quality time, enjoying shows, concerts, and skiing. Shelley had made a full, rich life for herself; it looked as if she had it all—career, money, and friends.

Yet her yearning for a man was exposed by the new toothbrush she kept in her medicine chest. Shortly after her divorce, Shelley began frequenting the various bars, often engaging in "one-night stands," hoping that one of them would turn into a permanent, meaningful relationship. Like Cinderella, she hoped that she too would meet her Prince Charming. But it did not happen. Instead, she had sometimes exciting and sometimes awful one-night stands; yet Shelley continued to look for the man of her dreams. She wanted a permanent relationship because she felt incomplete without a man by her side. For Shelley, only a man would complete her picture. In her head she knew that her life was full and that she really had neither the time, the emotional energy, nor the desire to compromise her life style enough to commit herself to a permanent relationship. Despite this, she kept looking for a lifelong mate. Her head could not change what she felt.

Shelley was unable to feel at peace with being single as a temporary but satisfying life style or as a permanent choice. Her singleness made her feel incomplete.

In addition to making you feel incomplete, your singleness may also interfere with your sense of yourself as an adult. Marriage and adulthood in this society are frequently perceived as synonymous, and being single may well result in your being treated as a child by your parents as well as by friends and acquaintances. As a single woman you may still be viewed as your parents' child and not yet the possession of a man. Here is yet another irony for you as a woman; you are not considered an adult, separate person until you are a man's possession. But, of course, if you are owned by a man you cannot possibly be your own person.

Being single also brings with it increased difficulties in satisfying your needs for intimacy, which are most easily fulfilled within the context of a long-term, close, sexual relationship. If you have been involved in a close, trusting relationship for a long period of time, it is easier to share your deepest experiences and feelings. When you are single, you must fulfill your intimacy needs with close friends, be they women, men, or couples. Intimacy in this situation may require greater courage; you must risk opening up and revealing yourself to someone whom you may not know really well. On the other hand, when you are single, fulfillment of your intimacy needs leads you to involvement with more than one person and hence can enrich your life.

There are also practical problems in daily living which prove more difficult to handle alone. How do you get to work when your car breaks down? How do you let someone into your home to repair the telephone while you are working 30 miles away? How do you deal with the mounds of snow that cover your driveway? All these concerns are less easily dealt with in a single household. You have to arrange a ride. You have to arrange with your neighbor to let the phone man in. You have to allow an extra hour in the morning to shovel your drive. Thus singleness can increase life's practical problems, but it can also allow you greater degrees of freedom in organizing and living life your own way. You do not have to contend with a mate's grumpiness in the morning or with socks on the floor. So your life is, on the one hand, more complicated, but, on the other hand, more simple.

Being single has both its joys and its headaches. As an autonomous woman, you must learn to deal with both, so that you can experience the years of your singleness as a time of fulfillment, growth, and fun.

Mothering Again

Choosing whether or not to be a mother is one of the most serious decisions of your life. As discussed in Chapter 8, both cultural and biological pressures push you toward motherhood. These pressures are abating, however, allowing motherhood to be more of a free choice. As a result, you may decide, for any number of reasons, not to be a mother.

If you do decide to give birth and mother a child, you have made one of the most permanent commitments of your life. It is crucial that this commitment be made from a genuine desire to bear and raise a child, and not as a badge of your femininity or proof that you have fulfilled the traditional requirement of your sex role. Once you become a mother, your life is thereafter inextricably interwoven with the life of another human being. There is no way out; there is no backing down; you cannot divorce your child. Unless you sever your parental rights, allowing your child to be adopted by another family, you are bound forever to that child. For the next 18 years you are responsible for the emotional and physical care of another human being. The degree and intensity of this responsibility vary as the child grows. For the first five years your child's needs determine your schedule. Your life is structured around her eating schedule, her sleeping schedule, the babysitting schedule. Later, when your child is able to dress herself, feed herself, and toilet herself, the responsibility lessens. Your freedom has increased. Your responsibility changes again as your child involves herself in life at school; and as she increasingly explores and conquers the world, your responsibility diminishes. However, throughout your life you are her mother. Her life is inextricably bound with yours and the kind of person you are. Your life is inextricably bound with hers and the kind of person she becomes.

The ease with which you and your child are able to establish a close, intimate relationship and then slowly separate while maintaining an appreciation of one another will depend partially on your internalization of your own mother. Of course, this internalization has affected your entire life, but never is it so intense and all-encompassing as when you are a mother yourself. You may find yourself using the very words that your mother said to you. Some you remember with joy, like the rhyme your mother recited when she tucked you in at night: "Good night, sleep tight, see you in the morning light." With love and nostalgia you may repeat these same words to your own daughter. But you can also remember how you felt enraged and demoralized when your mother chided you to "get that hair out of your face." And again, you may be sending the same messages to your own daughter.

The repetition of these kinds of phrases is a concrete example of repeating with your own child the mothering that you experienced as a child. Even if you do not consciously know how your mother felt about you at various times in your life, you unconsciously behave toward your own daughter as your mother behaved toward you. If your mother loved you as a helpless baby and reacted against your growing separation, you may find yourself repeating this same pattern with your own daughter. At first you may be overly smothering and then, when your daughter attempts to move away from you, you may react with hostility. Similarly, if your mother was cold and distancing and unable to cuddle you, you may find yourself behaving in a similar manner toward your daughter.

The above is not meant to imply that there is a one-to-one correlation between your mother's mothering and your mothering. As a child you had a distorted image of your mother and were unconsciously impressed or dismayed by various aspects of her. It is these distortions that your unconscious internalized and that you now tend to replay with your own child. For example, you may have felt that your mother punished you for every little infraction. As a mother yourself, you may react against your upbringing and become permissive, allowing your children to behave in ways which others would not allow. Then, one day in a conversation with your brother, you discover that it was he who was actually punished in many of the incidents you recall. You had experienced all the agony of your brother's life as your own and internalized a biased image of your "witch" mother. She was not really a witch, but you had experienced her as one. You then reacted against this distorted image of your mother by becoming the reverse and attempting to be the fairy godmother to your child. Unfortunately, just as you felt that your mother did not care about you because you felt overly disciplined, your child may also feel uncared about because of your unwillingness to set limits.

How you feel about your own child is not solely a reflection of your relationship with your mother. Other family members are embedded in your unconscious, and your relationship with them is also played out in your mothering. For example, if your daughter represents your older sister to you, you may react to your daughter with the mixture of awe, jealousy, and competition that you felt toward your sister. Or you may see your daughter as your mother and relate to her as you related to your own mother, expecting her to mother you. If you have a son, you may project onto him your images of your spouse, your father, your brother, or your mother's images of men. A male child may also represent the son that your mother never had, and you may feel that you have at last outdone your mother by producing this male person. Or you may react to him with rage if you felt that your mother would have preferred for you to be a boy. Relating to your child as a separate, unique human being is thus made more difficult by the internalizations of your own childhood.

In this culture, childrearing presents the problematic issue of your being an extension of your child or your child being an extension of you. Giving birth suddenly defines you as someone's mother. Your other identities may slip away. In the park you are your child's mother and no longer a unique, separate woman. At school you are Jane's mother, rather than Yvonne Smith. Your other accomplishments may lose their meaning. Your separate personality is lost. You are merged with your child. Clearly, it is difficult to maintain a sense of yourself as an autonomous women if society defines you only in relation to your child. And so the difficult business of maintaining your autonomy while mothering your child is an issue with which you must deal.

For some, what society does not impose upon you, you impose upon yourself. That is, you view your child as an extension of yourself and consider yourself worthwhile only if your child is attractive or accomplished or has whatever characteristics you value. Here again your own identity and accomplishments are surrendered to your child's achievements. In this case, the child is burdened with enormous pressure to be "right" enough for you. She is expected to live out your dream; she must live for you rather than for herself. She has to make you proud of her and, by so doing, make you feel good about yourself and your ability as a mother.

Treating a child as an extension of yourself heaps burdens on both you and the child. For example, your daughter may be reluctant to really talk with you about what is happening in her life for fear of disappointing you. Additionally, separating from you to develop her own identity will be extremely difficult for her if you experience her as your extension. And when she does finally separate, you will be left feeling empty and alone. After all, if she has defined your identity, then her adult leave-taking will only make you feel abandoned and deserted.

Thus viewing your child as a separate human being rather than as an extension of yourself is vital to mothering. First you must remind yourself that your child is, in fact, a human being with her own talents and abilities; that although she came from inside your body, she is now separate from you and must be allowed to live in her own way. You must encourage her to develop her uniqueness, not to replay yours. This is most easily accomplished if you have a fulfilled life apart from your child. Then she is not required to live for you; you are doing it for yourself and can enjoy your daughter's accomplishments and successes for her, not for you. You are both your own person and your daughter's mother; the two are distinct.

Being a mother involves both joys and agonies. As a mother, you have the tremendous task of caring for the needs of another human being. This is a difficult job which inevitably ties you down. You cannot leave your child for any period of time without providing for her supervision. During her infancy and toddler years, your own needs usually are secondary. If she is hungry you feed her before you sit down for your own meal.

In addition to your child's physical dependency, her vulnerability, sadness, anger, and love can all hook into some previously repressed or unexplored areas of your own psyche. You may see your own feelings, your own self, past and present, acted out again before your eyes. You may see again that which you had toiled to leave behind. Thus your child may recall your past for both you and the world to see. This can make you feel terribly vulnerable and exposed. Your child is able to call up both the best and the worst in you. Your intense feelings of love and rage, your problems with the issues surrounding omnipotence and vulnerability, and all of your separation difficulties may need to be reworked during your years of mothering.

It is also easy for you, as a mother, to feel all the responsibility and, hence, all the blame. Society has colluded with you in this self-blame; psychoanalytic theory, popular literature and magazines, and education all point the finger at you, the mother. You are responsible for your child's behavior, her intelligence, her performance, her sexuality, and her psyche. This is an unremitting burden, and at the first sign of a problem, you may feel that you are not fulfilling your responsibilities, that you are not a good enough mother.

Because you are usually the primary parent and seem very powerful to your child, she joins in the collusion and also blames you. You are supposed to be the fairy godmother who insures that life is always perfect for your child. Thus if something goes wrong in your child's life, she may hold you responsible. For example, your three-year-old is playing in the next room with her balloon. She is enjoying kicking the balloon around and tossing it up in the air. Suddenly, it breaks. Your daughter comes to you and asks, "Mommy, why did my balloon break?" She feels that it is your responsibility to prevent these unhappy events and to provide her with a happy childhood. Any deviation from this scenario is your fault.

Living with your children's competition and jealousy toward each other is another difficult task of parenthood. Sibling rivalry can be expressed in a variety of annoying or enraging ways. These can range from mild bickering and name calling to physical confrontation. The close, high-quality family time that you were looking forward to can easily be destroyed by a silly, quarrelsome disagreement. Of course, the children try to involve you in their battles, wanting you to take sides, hoping you will punish their sibling and carry the banner of victory for them. Trying to be fair is like walking a tightrope because they are fighting about an issue that cannot be resolved. Each of them wants all of you and is enraged at the other for his or her very existence. From this perspective, recognizing the inevitability of your children's squabbles can facilitate your tolerance and free you from interpreting their rivalry as indicative of poor mothering.

In addition to the psychological pressures of caring for another human being, there are numerous practical ones. Time, chores, space, and money are all issues which need to be dealt with. You want quality time with yourself, your mate, and your child and may find there are simply not enough hours in the day. You want the house looking neat and the chores accomplished with some sense of equal involvement—an unlikely possibility, particularly if there are young children around. You want some space for yourself but may find it available only behind a locked bathroom door. You may worry about having sufficient money to feed, clothe, and house your child. You may not know how you will get her the glasses she needs or the dancing lessons she wants so badly. All of these issues place additional strains on both you and your relationship with your child.

Many of you will decide that the negative aspects of mothering are far outweighed by the positive joys. Some of these joys are so repetitively portrayed that they have become almost trite. Your baby's first smile, the way her eyes light up with delight when she sees you, her first step, her first tooth, and her first day in school are all events filled with joy and a tinge of sadness at the unavoidable awareness that she has already begun her journey toward separation. But the joy is paramount, the joy in sharing her life, watching her grow and evolve into her own unique person. You delight in the funny ways she uses the language and thrill when her proficiency increases and she invites you into her inner world. Her fears, accomplishments, and joys in the world she is newly discovering are all exciting events for you too. The quiet times that she looks forward to, sitting by the fireplace, playing Monopoly, playing dress-up, being cuddled or sung to, are all cozy, peaceful times for you too.

Watching your daughter mature and become a woman is another joy of mothering. You share her excitement when she dresses for her first date or falls in love for the first time. Each event which you and your daughter have shared, the intimacies of infancy, the discoveries of toddlerhood, and the learning of latency, all add up to a reservoir of history that is unique to the pair of you. This history creates a bond of understanding and knowledge that will be shared by the two of you for life. Thus the joy of parenting lies in watching and nourishing another human being's unfolding while enjoying the shared experiences and mutual understandings.

Tina, a mother for the first time at 22, was afraid that she would never be able to experience these joys of mothering. As she held her newborn daughter Emma in her arms she did not feel the emotional rush that she thought she should. She knew from books, paintings, and even commercials that a "real" mother felt an immediate bond with her infant, an immediate tie. Tina did not feel this. She looked at her red-faced, squirming, crying infant and felt only dismay. My God, she had failed already. How could she possibly care for this infant whom she did not even like?

When Tina came home with her daughter, her mother-in-law was there to help out. Knowing that Tina needed rest, she took over the household tasks so that Tina could enjoy her new baby. Tina had always felt close to her mother-in-law. She was a warm and bubbly woman who took life as it came and who was always generous with her time and affection. Tina's mother-in-law fell in love with Emma, feeling as though she was the perfect baby. Wasn't Tina proud that she had produced such a good child? Why, already she was almost sleeping through the night. She taught Tina how to burp Emma and how to test the milk. She showed her how to pin the diaper carefully on Emma so that if the pin opened it would not scratch the baby's tender skin. Lastly, she taught Tina how to bathe a wet, slippery baby. As Tina became comfortable with these tasks, she also became more comfortable with her baby and, quite to her surprise, Emma began to respond. She snuggled up to Tina when Tina held her, her eyes lighting with joy. Tina could swear that Emma had even smiled at her. Tina actually began to look forward to her mother-in-law's departure so that she could be alone with her baby. At that point, Tina realized that she had accomplished what she had feared would be impossible; she had fallen in love with her baby. Caring for Emma and enjoying her responses had created the bond that Tina had feared would never exist. Tina was now ready to embark on the journey of motherhood, with all its joys and sorrows.

Aloneness

Aloneness is a fact of human existence. You are born alone and die alone. In fact, most of your agonies and joys are felt alone, although sharing them with others can diminish or enhance them. You cannot escape from your existential aloneness. You must be alone at various times in your life, and you can become comfortable with your aloneness and enjoy it. Your basic aloneness arises from the fact that you exist in your own body separated from every other human being. The combination of your brain cells, biochemistry, nerve endings, and physical body marks you as a separate distinct human being apart from all others. Given your unique and separate body, you can never directly know accurately what it is like to see through another person's eyes, to feel what another person feels, to react the way another person reacts. You can certainly empathize with another or imagine what that person is feeling, but you can never know it completely. We are all, in this sense, alone.

Although aloneness is a necessary fact of human life, it can also be a great joy, a time to reflect on yourself, to enjoy your own pursuits and solitude. You may enjoy the relaxation and peace of sitting by yourself in front of a fire, watching it burn quietly. You may enjoy sitting alone and reading or crocheting or writing a letter to an old friend. You feel comfortable enough about yourself to enjoy being alone with yourself.

Some of you cannot tolerate being alone for even a moment. You are terrified of your time alone and find it necessary to temper it with the background noise of a radio or TV. But even this does not help sufficiently. You feel the need to have someone with you at all times. If you are alone for even a moment, you may feel overwhelmingly anxious and fear that catastrophe is about to strike. To avoid this anxiety, you may keep your life overly scheduled and busy, flitting from one person to another, or from one activity to another, always insuring against being alone. This fear of aloneness may stem from the feeling that you do not really exist unless you are experiencing yourself reflected in another person. In this case, it is as though the other person validates your existence and identity. Fear of aloneness may also stem from your feeling of helplessness and vulnerability. You may feel that you need another person with you to protect you from the cruel world. In either instance, you are avoiding a basic fact of life, your existential aloneness.

Aloneness is very different from either loneliness on the one hand or isolation and withdrawal on the other. Loneliness is inflicted upon you; it is not something you deliberately choose for yourself. When you choose to end an unhealthy relationship, you are not choosing loneliness; rather, the loneliness that follows is an inevitable result of your healthy choice. If you are lonely, it is usually because you are alone and would prefer to be with someone but feel as though there is no one with whom you can share yourself at that time.

Since you want to be interacting with someone and cannot, you feel sad, empty, and despondent. Loneliness has become an increasing problem in this society. More and more often, more of you feel lonely, set apart, and alienated. You crave closeness, warmth, and intimacy and despair because you cannot have them. When you are lonely, you may feel as though you matter to no one, that no one cares. You need not be alone, of course, to experience loneliness. You may feel lonely in a crowd or lonely in a relationship. It is a feeling of insufficient intimacy, a feeling of wanting more meaningful human interaction.

Voluntary isolation or withdrawal is different from aloneness and occurs usually as a defense against either rejection or fusion. If you have been hurt in an important relationship, you may feel too vulnerable, too "gun-shy" to open yourself up to the risk of future rejection. Hence you may withdraw, keeping yourself at a safe distance from intimacy and its potential to hurt you.

Similarly, you may be terrified of getting too close to another human being for fear of being swallowed up or losing your identity in that relationship. As a defense against such fusion, you may isolate yourself, maintaining a great distance from others and keeping yourself totally separate. In this stance you may feel intensely lonely, but your loneliness is less terrifying than your fear of fusion which is stimulated when you become close to another person. A desperate need for love and affection also may motivate you to isolate yourself as a defense against your fear of not ever getting enough. Rather than risking an insufficient amount of love, you may choose none at all. Self-isolation is always hurtful because you deprive yourself of that which you want most. Neither self-isolation nor loneliness are synonymous with aloneness. Loneliness may be inevitable at certain times in your life. Aloneness is an existential fact. It is inevitable, and as such can only be accepted and, at best, enjoyed.

At 63, Daisy had now been a widow for one year. She had had a good relationship with her husband and had been terribly sad and hurt when he died suddenly of a heart attack just prior to retiring. Daisy was angry about his death, feeling that it was totally unfair. They had planned to travel, garden, golf, and spend time enjoying each other. Suddenly he was dead and Daisy was alone for the first time in her life.

Daisy spent a year mourning his death and learning to cope with being single. At first she was so lonely that she thought she would not survive. She felt that no other human being could understand her pain. She missed the closeness and interaction with her husband. She craved his physical warmth. Her loneliness was always with her. She was sad, angry, and at times desperate. There was so much she had never learned to do. She could not even balance a checkbook, and suddenly she was burdened with the entire financial responsibility for running both her home and her life. She had to sell the home, decide where to live, and manage the move. She had to cope with friends who were sometimes overly solicitous and sometimes rejecting. She had to help her children cope with their reactions to their father's death and her new widowhood. She had to learn meaningful ways of filling her time. She had to decide which friendships to nurture and which ones to let go. In other words, at the age of 63 she had to carve out an entirely new life for herself.

Now, one year later, Daisy was pleased with herself. She had learned to handle her finances. She had moved. She had made new friends and lost some old ones. She was still sad about her husband's death and felt cheated about the lost plans for their retirement years. On the other hand, Daisy felt more like a person in her own right than at any other time in her life. She was accountable to no one except herself. She was no one's possession or appendage. She was Daisy, an autonomous woman. She supported herself, valued herself, and thrived on the knowledge that she could "go it alone." By coming to grips with her basic aloneness, she learned to enjoy her separateness and appreciate herself.

Success

Success is greatly esteemed in this society. The successful person becomes a model, a leader, someone to be emulated.

The modern-day Horatio Alger is esteemed and valued as a model for success. Some of you may hope to become movie stars, others strive for the Nobel Prize, and yet others seek fame as writers or artists. One of you may see herself as a famous surgeon, saving lives and making important discoveries. For another of you, success is maintaining a farm in the Midwest and raising a family. Success is subjectively defined by each of you. What one of you considers successful, another may abhor.

It is within the context of your own personal definition of success that success issues arise. Whether you define success in terms of money, fame, or happiness, it remains elusive to many of you. Achieving success is not dependent solely on talent but also on your motivation, perseverance, and psychological traits. Success can be elusive because of both realistic societal barriers and your own psychological barriers. For example, you may unconsciously sabotage and undermine the very success that you so desperately want. In this instance, success remains unattainable not because of any physical or intellectual lack, but rather because of your unconscious motivation which hampers your freedom to achieve success. Sabotaging success can result from very different personality dynamics or needs. You may, without realizing it, be so afraid of success that you guarantee its opposite by sabotaging your efforts. Or you may be so afraid of failure that you are immobilized and thus unable to risk any action necessary for successful ventures.

Fear of Success

If you are afraid of succeeding, you may consistently undermine your attempts to succeed. For example, you may never quite be able to complete your Ph.D. thesis, although you so desperately want to teach on the college level. Or, you may find that just before your career goal is in sight, you become bored and switch, first to a different goal and then to another, never allowing yourself to successfully complete the requirements necessary for any single goal. Or you may finally land the job of your dreams and then find that you are consistently late or absent. This is your unconscious undermining of the success that you consciously desire. You may have always wanted to own a home, but after its purchase you manage to lose your job, so that you cannot possibly afford the house payments. You may need a scholarship for graduate school but insure inadequate grades by falling alseep in classes. Thus, despite what you say and feel you want, if you always behave in a way that sabotages your success you are unconsciously afraid to succeed. This fear is not conscious; for so long as you are preventing yourself from succeeding, you avoid the necessity of dealing with your underlying issues. In other words, so long as you act out your fear of success by avoiding success, you can also avoid your underlying feelings. These fears can originate from a variety of sources, including fear of going beyond your family, fear of succeeding and still not being loved, fear of being in competition with one or the other of your parents, or fear of not being able to be both a sexual and a successful woman.

Fear of Going Beyond Your Family

Twenty-five-year-old Lana wanted to be an attorney. She had done very well in law school but now, for the second time, arrived one day late for her bar exam. She could not believe she had done it again. She had been looking forward to becoming a full-fledged attorney, joining a law firm, and practicing in the court room with a case of her own. And now she had again confused the correct date of the exam. She was shocked and panicked. She knew that she was hurting herself but did not know why. Feeling out of control, and wanting to stop this destructive behavior, she decided to go into therapy.

Lana was the oldest of seven children in a poor Puerto Rican family. Much to everyone's surprise, she always did very well in school, enjoying reading and learning about new and different things. Her brothers and sisters teased her about her interest in school, but Lana did not care. Her friends ostracized her, but still she did not care. Lana found solace in her books, identifying with the heroine and famous characters. Her teachers encouraged her and some of them even devoted extra time to her. In high school she became the favorite of one of her English teachers who supported her involvement in the debate team, which Lana enjoyed tremendously. She loved being on a stage confronting the world and winning. At last she could prove that she was right; she could argue and win in the presence of an admiring audience.

The world at home receded. The world of six noisy, bratty children, greasy forks and spoons, and ugly cockroaches faded from view. Lana did not want it and would not allow it to be part of her any more. When she was on that stage debating, nothing else mattered. She was a different person, separate and apart from her past and her family.

Lana won a scholarship to college where she continued in debate and decided to become an attorney. She performed brilliantly in school and had little difficulty in winning another scholarship to law school. Again, she did very well. She developed many new friends and interests and at last felt accepted into the world of the middle-class professional.

However, along with her academic success came the realization that she was entirely different from her family. She had nothing to talk to them about and so disliked spending time with them. Actually, she did not even like them. And she did not like herself for not liking them. She knew intellectually that they were not bad or inferior people. But in her "guts" she was enraged at them. She was enraged at the lack of a stable father in her life and the continual poverty and despair of her childhood.

Lana graduated from law school and set about preparing for the bar exam. She had little involvement with her family and did not feel supported by them in her success. She looked forward to passing the bar exam, which she considered the final union card. And now, for the second time, she had undermined herself. Again, she had not allowed herself to succeed and, in an attempt to stop this painful behavior, Lana went into therapy.

During the course of her therapy, Lana learned that she was afraid of surpassing her family's position in the world. She was afraid that if she actually became an attorney she would be out there all alone, totally different, forever abandoned and isolated. No one would be there for her. She would suffer loneliness, alienation, and despair. She would again feel like a helpless, vulnerable infant. As her awareness of these issues grew, so did her anger at her family. On the one hand, it was her anger that spurred her to leave her family and strive toward a successful professional life which was totally different from her background. On the other hand, her anger was very frightening, for it emphasized the chasm between them. It also intensified Lana's fear of her family's rage at her for leaving and being different. She feared that they would experience her success as a rejection of their life style and of themselves and would, in turn, reject her. She feared that they would be as angry at her as she was at them. It was this fear of both her own rage and her family's which stimulated her terror of the final success. This in turn caused her to undermine herself at the last hurdle.

Lana clearly demonstrates the fear of succeeding too far beyond one's family. Such success brings with it the terror of being without loving connections, the terror of being totally alone and abandoned. Hence being less successful is chosen as the better option. Lana had gone far beyond her roots and had used her anger to propel herself out of the family, but also was so terrified of the aloneness she feared would accompany her success that she unconsciously stopped short of her final goal.

Fear of Not Being Loved

Fear of success can also result from fear of not getting the love that you hope will come with success, that is, fear of succeeding yet still not being loved. For example, suppose you grow up in a family in which high achievement is expected; it is the norm. Somehow you never feel that you measure up to everyone else's accomplishments. You even wonder if you really belong in this family. You look about and see that achievement seems to be rewarded with love. It appears that your sister is loved and valued when she makes the varsity basketball team and when she receives straight A's on her report card. You, however, are not a straight-A student. You tell yourself that if you were, you too would receive this bountiful love. Part of you, of course, is afraid to test this out. What if you do perform great athletic feats and achieve straight A's but still do not receive the love that you so desperately want? Then you will have to confront the terrible possibility that there is something wrong with you or that you are not lovable. So long as you do not succeed, you can maintain the illusion that surely you would be loved if you just worked harder.

How can you resolve this dilemma? You need to see your parents' conditional love as their own inability to love freely and not as a comment on your unlovability. Additionally, you need to realize that your success will not bring you the love that you want. Regardless of your success or prominence, you will not feel your parents' love in the way that you always wanted to feel it. Your success is irrelevant to being loved by your parents. They are incapable of giving you the love you needed as a child and as an adult you no longer need it. Once you have given up the hope of succeeding for the sake of your parents' love, you are free to decide whether you want to succeed for yourself.

Fear of Competition

Fear of competing with one of your parents is another reason you may be fearful of success. For example, suppose you are from a middle-class, white-collar family in which your parents have had only a moderate degree of success. Suppose, too, that your relationship with your mother has always been highly competitive, either overtly or covertly. Your mother always encourages you to play the piano, but while you are practicing she screams at you for not having cleaned your room. Similarly, although your mother preens herself before the mirror, she may adamantly oppose your wearing makeup or dating boys until well after all your peers have started doing so. You feel your mother's anger. You feel her disapproval. You feel her wanting to prevent you from becoming a successful, adult woman.

If there is sufficient rage and competition between you and your mother, you may grow up being afraid of succeeding for fear that she will retaliate against you for your success. At the very least, the message that you hear is that your mother does not want you to be a better woman than she. At the very worst, you may feel the threat of infanticide—the threat that your mother will kill you if you surpass her. This is illustrated in the fairy tale *Snow White*, where the wicked stepmother attempts to kill her daughter when the mirror on the wall indicates that her daughter is becoming more beautiful than she. The stepmother cannot tolerate the competition and wants her dead. This fairy tale elucidates the most extreme form of competition between a parent and a child. Your experience may not be this extreme. You may simply feel your parents' disapproval or hostility and may thus curb your success for fear of being attacked or criticized. Fear of going beyond your roots, fear of not being loved, and fear of competition are psychic barriers to success.

Fear of Being Asexual

Fear of becoming asexual is this culture's contribution to your fear of success. Within this culture, the successful woman is portrayed, at best, as the hard-driving aggressive woman and, at worst, as the "castrating bitch." In a less extreme version, you may fear that if you are successful, men will not be interested in you. They will see you as beyond their reach or, more likely, will be threatened by your success, since part of the cultural norm is that men are less adequate if they are not more successful than women. You may fear that if you are too successful you will drastically diminish the number of men available to you. These cultural realities may be particularly difficult for you if you are raised in a family in which success is discouraged for women. If your mother portrays womanliness as passivity, softness, lack of assertion, and dependency upon a man, you may feel that you are not a woman if you are independent and able to care for yourself. Extricating yourself from this situation involves psychological separation from your family and sufficient courage to violate the cultural prescription. Thus fear of success can originate from a variety of sources, all of which can be equally incapacitating to you in your struggle to attain the terrifying goal of success.

Fear of Failure

Most of you have experienced feelings that you can identify as fear of failure. You may be afraid to make a mistake, become a laughing stock, and be humiliated by your error. You may be fearful that your image as a competent person will be shattered, either for the moment or permanently.

Fear of failure can arise from several sources. As an example, suppose you are in the third grade and are reading in front of your class. You mispronounce a word and the class bursts into laughter. You are absolutely mortified; you feel as though you are two inches tall. Your esteem is shattered. The next time you are called upon to read in front of the class, you feel exceedingly anxious. What if it happens again? What if you mispronounce or stumble over a word and everyone laughs at you? This is the precursor of stage fright, which many of you experience throughout your lives. It is also an example of being so terrified of making a mistake that your anxiety precludes your attempts at success and so necessitates your failure. It becomes a self-fulfilling prophecy; that which you most fear occurs because of your anxiety.

The pressure to succeed in this society exacerbates fears of failure, since your value as a person is often equated with your accomplishments. As the women's movement continues to foster the development of success-oriented and career-oriented women, you are beginning to buy into success standards similar to those of men. For years, men have felt that their esteem and value were dependent upon the money they accrued and the goals they accomplished, and now you too are accepting a similar norm.

Shame and Belittlement

Cultural aspects of the success issue are made particularly difficult if you are brought up in a family in which you are repeatedly shamed or belittled for any mistake you make or any expectation you do not meet. Perhaps if you do not receive an A on a spelling test you are called stupid. Perhaps if you do not know the name or date of a particular event your father chastises you, telling you that you will never amount to anything. Perhaps if you hand your mother the wrong kitchen utensil she laughs at you, saying that you will never learn to cook. Given these experiences, you grow up terrified of making a mistake, terrified of being laughed at and embarrassed, and losing your self-respect. This upbringing may nurture a tendency toward perfectionism in you, causing you always to strive to do everything perfectly and never to make a mistake in order to avoid the risk of mortification.

Georgia is an example of a woman who was terrified of being belittled and who, as a result, experienced a tremendous amount of anxiety about failure. Georgia had grown up in a wealthy and successful family. Her father was a prosperous businessman in their community; her mother was an accomplished musician. Both her brothers were M.D.'s, and her elder brother also held a Ph.D. in physiology. The pressure was on Georgia to succeed.

Now, at age 20, Georgia was attending one of the top universities in the country. She knew that she had to succeed on the level of everyone else in her family. She also knew what would happen if she did not succeed. All her life, her father had responded to Georgia's minor mistakes by calling her silly or stupid and laughing at her. From as early as she could remember, he had engaged her in intellectual discussions, quizzing her and waiting for her "brilliant" reply. And each time, Georgia's anxiety rose. She became terrified, clutching for a response. What if she did not know the right answer, or if her answer were not thorough enough? And, of course, both her anxiety and her father's unreachable standards resulted in her giving less than adequate responses. Then he laughed at her, telling her that she would never succeed and live up to the rest of the family. Georgia grew up feeling ashamed of her inadequate intellect. She also felt belittled for being a woman. Her father denigrated women for the importance they placed on emotions, intuition, and relationships. On the one hand, he criticized Georgia for being emotional or irrational in an argument while, on the other hand, he chastised her for not being a more traditional woman, for not being pretty enough, stylish enough, and domestic enough. Occasionally, Georgia was able to produce the "right" answer for her father. At such times he gave her morsels of approval, which amounted to either a slight nod or a gentle tap on the arm. At these times Georgia felt elated at having finally won her father's approval. Georgia knew she must never fall short; she had to succeed all the time or undergo the humiliation and shame of her father's disapproval. She was terrified of any failure, for failure would bring with it feelings of insignificance and mortification.

Thus in college Georgia found herself in the untenable position of feeling as though she had to be the perfect student, "acing" every exam and answering every question in class without error. This created an overwhelming amount of anxiety which immobilized her. For example, Georgia could not take an exam unless she felt certain, beyond the shadow of a doubt, that she was guaranteed an A. However, given her sense of inadequacy, Georgia rarely really believed that she could score perfectly on a test. Hence she often did not take her exams, which resulted in many incompletes. These incompletes only potentiated her anxiety, her sense of failure, and her feeling of devastation and insignificance. Because her anxiety had immobilized her to the extent of being unable to take a risk, her failure was guaranteed. Here was a prophecy fulfilled; her anxiety ensured the failure that she feared most.

Conditional Love

Unlike Georgia, you may not grow up in a home where you are shamed for mistakes but rather where love is contingent upon success. You may feel that your parents will love and esteem you only if you receive A's in school or are a successful athlete. As a result, you may grow up fearing that you are not good enough, not successful enough. You constantly strive for yet one more accomplishment so that you can receive the love which seems contingent upon success. It may be clear to you that success is the most important thing to your parents. You may remember your mother once saying to you that she is not sure whether she could love you if you were of only average intelligence. Your parents may attend all of your class plays but may turn away angrily if you come home crying about doing less than perfectly on a math exam. It is always expected that you will succeed, that you will make significant contributions to society. Nothing less is acceptable. Now you always strive to be good enough, always feeling anxious that you will fail and not receive the love you so desperately want. Of course, what you do not know is that the love you so desperately seek is not really love. Love for a Ph.D., a well-set table, a well-run race, is not love for you as a person. When your mother tells you that her love is contingent upon your intellectual ability, "I don't know if I could love you if you weren't 'smart'," she is really saying that she loves you only as an extension of herself. She loves her own ability to produce an intelligent child. She is not loving you as the separate, unique individual that you are. Thus, because of her own upbringing, the only feeling she is able to have for you is a narcissistic self-love rather than an adult, mature love for you as the human being that you are. Obviously, this mother does not love herself in a real sense or she would be able to love you in a less conditional manner.

Rebellion Against Achievement Prophecies

Rebellion against your family may be expressed by either success or failure. In either case, the great dictator is the expectation that has been devised for you. Your parents may indicate their desire for you to follow the family pattern and become a doctor. You are told that you are bright, capable, and scientific and are pressured toward medical school. On the other hand, your parents may communicate their feeling that you are not going to achieve anything, that you will be an incompetent or a slovenly barmaid, or just a bum all your life.

These are two very different prophecies for your future. You, as a growing child, listen to these scripts and unconsciously decide whether you are going to fill or rebel against the offered part. You may decide, without considering other careers, that you want to be a doctor. You never consider another career, never explore other talents. This obviously is not rebellion but rather capitulation to your family. Or you may decide that you absolutely do not want to be a doctor. It seems a terrible way to live and as your parents push you in this direction, you become enraged. You always wanted to be a rock singer. You never open a biology book or a chemistry book to discover whether you might enjoy this field. It is the strength of your opposition to becoming a doctor which indicates the rebellious nature of your decision. It is the passion with which you refuse this script which confirms it as a rebellious act rather than a free choice.

On the other hand, you may look at the projection of your future as a slovenly barmaid and be enraged that your parents expect so little of you. Unconsciously you think, "I'll show them what I can do!" You keep yourself extraordinarily neat and tidy, dress fashionably, and spend extra hours studying at night rather than sleeping. You are determined to be successful; you are going to become a doctor! You are going to show them how far you can go! You are so determined that you cannot slow down to enjoy life at all. Your goals for success dictate your every hour. Again, it is your passion and intensity that expose the rebellious element of your choice. Rebellion is no more a free choice than is capitulation. If you are driven to be a rock star or a doctor solely because of your angry need not to fulfill your parents' expectations for you, then you remain as tightly tied to them as if you had followed the specific content of their script.

The Workaholic

Plunging yourself into 12- and 14-hour days of working yourself to exhaustion, and returning home only to worry about whether you performed the job adequately, tells the story of a workaholic. Expending most of your energy on work leaves little for the enjoyment of life. Both love and play are sacrificed if your whole being is given over to your work. You are consumed by your vocation. If you are a workaholic, it is possible that you fear failure and are avoiding that fear by total immersion in work. You are always driving yourself, striving to be good enough, to go up one more rung on the ladder of success to receive the "goodies" offered by either society or your family. You may be driven to succeed either to avoid the shame and belittlement that you lived with as a child or to receive the love that success promises to bring. That love can never be attained because you cannot "achieve" love through accomplishments. But not knowing this, you strive harder and harder to jump through the next hoop which becomes higher and higher, making success and love seem more elusive, and your efforts more necessary.

You may also be a workaholic to prove either to yourself or to your family that you are, in fact, successful. If you grow up on the wrong side of the tracks or are programmed to fail, you may need to strive continually toward greater heights in an attempt to negate the prophecy and prove that you can be successful. But your personal history makes it difficult for you ever to feel like a successful person. Since you have undergone so much programming to the contrary, you need to prove to yourself constantly that you are indeed successful and different from what was expected.

Working through your success issues is a prerequisite to the freedom and joy of a satisfying career. It is one of the most crucial issues in autonomy and one of the most significant factors in your happiness. This is particularly true as increasing numbers of you join the work force each year in an attempt to actualize that aspect of life traditionally denied to you. Men have always been aware of the importance of their careers. Now, too, you as a woman must resolve your success issues and actualize your career potential.

Autonomy in Everyday Life

All of you have autonomy issues which arise as you move through life. As you venture into new arenas and take new risks, your anxiety increases. You are concerned about your ability to execute new tasks adequately. As you perform them competently, you redefine your self-concept, and the completion of each new task brings with it an added sense of your own strength.

Taking a Trip Alone

Suppose you are taking a trip alone for the first time. You are anxious about boarding the plane on time and about whether you will find your hotel. You wonder if you will feel comfortable dining alone in a restaurant. You are concerned about how you will spend your evening. Will you sit alone in your hotel room feeling isolated and alienated? Or will you enjoy your time alone? Will you feel comfortable approaching a stranger and initiating a conversation? If this is a new experience for you, some anxiety and trepidation will accompany it. And, of course, some difficulties are guaranteed to occur. Perhaps the limousine takes you to the wrong hotel, or you discover that eating alone in a restaurant is even more desolate than you had imagined. But you also realize the intense enjoyment of being able to read without interruption in your hotel room.

You may decide that your first trip alone was not only successful but that you look forward to traveling alone again at some future time. Maybe you will fly off to Acapulco and spend the week sunbathing on the beach by yourself. Or, you may decide that although you are able to travel alone when necessary, you do not really enjoy it and would prefer not to take a vacation alone. You may find, on the other hand, that throughout the trip your anxiety never abates and the trip leaves you feeling devastated. In this case, other psychological issues must be operating for you. Perhaps you are having difficulty separating from someone at home. Possibly being on a trip by yourself has restimulated your terror of abandonment or your difficulties concerning vulnerability. If so, an exploration and reworking of these issues is in order to assure the autonomy necessary for you to travel alone if necessary.

Graduating from School

When you complete your student training and graduate into the working world, it is likely that you will experience anxiety about this major change in your life. It is a step toward adulthood and autonomy. It may be the first time in your life that you are viewed as an independent, adult woman who must now care for yourself. You must find a job. You must find an apartment. You must decide how you are going to spend your time and with whom. Your parents and professors will no longer dictate the rules to you. You are now a separate, adult person. Your life is ready to begin; all of the foregoing was just the preparation. Now the real action begins. Assuming responsibility for your own life can be an awesome experience, and it is likely that you will have some difficulties dealing with your newly found independence. Perhaps you will not find the apartment you want. Perhaps you will not find the ideal job. But as you negotiate the world, you carve out your niche in it. As you become more capable, more competent, and more autonomous, your sense of yourself strengthens.

Enjoying Separate Activities

Engaging in activities separate from your lover also involves issues of autonomy. Suppose your husband enjoys watching Monday Night Football but you hate football, despite all of your attempts to appreciate it. Being married to a football fan does not sentence you to suffer through the game. You can decide to do something on your own. You can enroll in a karate class, a glass-blowing class, or pursue whatever interests you.

Some of you may have problems with fusion which make it difficult to pursue separate interests. You may feel as though leaving your husband for an evening is akin to abandonment. It may be a gut-wrenching and desolate experience to go to a movie without him. You may choose to sit next to him on the couch because being close to him is more important than doing anything for yourself. If you are so tied to your husband that you cannot separate from him to pursue your own interests, then you have difficulties centered around fusion. The same is true if all his interests become your interests. If your problem is one of autonomy rather than fusion, your anxiety originates from reluctance to venture out to a new place or activity. Autonomy issues involve concern about doing something new and being successful at it, whereas fusion issues involve difficulties with separation and abandonment.

Managing Your Money

Managing your money is another big autonomy issue which most of you have to confront at some point in your life. Women generally have not been socialized to believe that they will need financial knowledge because they are not considered to be independent, self-sufficient self-providers. Particularly in the past, women were taught that they should "catch" a man who would be a "good provider." Today, however, many of you manage your own finances. This involves the struggle to manage your money efficiently while maximizing your enjoyment of life. You need to know that leaving large sums of money in a passbook savings account does not combat inflation. You need to learn not to invest in the stock market beyond your means, putting yourself in a state of anxiety about losing your assets. You need to know that credit cards really do bring with them a bill and do not simply satisfy your dreams free of charge.

As you have more access to money, you also have more responsibility about it. You have to become financially knowledgeable if not astute, unless you are willing to pay the unhealthy price of being taken care of by someone else. Even if you do have a husband or lover who takes care of the financial arrangements, you need to understand your family's finances so that you are not totally lost or helpless in the event of his death or departure. You, after all, are a responsible adult woman who needs to feel power in your autonomy.

Buying a House

Buying a house mobilizes autonomy issues for most everyone. You are making a heavy commitment. You cannot so easily pack up and move. You are bound to your house, at least for a given period of time. Additionally, once you sign the mortage agreement, you have committed yourself to mortgage payments every month, and this is a tremendous responsibility. You must conduct your life in such a way as to ensure a regular source of income which will enable you to make the monthly payments. Additionally, you must be responsible for the maintenance of the house. Roofs are known to leak; pipes are known to freeze. When something goes wrong with the house, you must either repair it yourself or have it repaired and assume the cost. Owning a home also means paying taxes. A house is a never-ending source of responsibility and chores. It is a profound statement about your autonomous functioning as an adult woman.

Overextending Yourself

Many of you are fully functioning, autonomous women. You may even feel that you are too autonomous, that you are doing too much. You may feel almost as if you have succeeded too well in too many areas. You may have an exciting career, a husband, children, a house, and a dog. With such a full life, every moment is at a premium. At times, you may feel overextended. You seem to be always in a rush, whether it is to get the children off to school or yourself off to work. You enjoy your work, feel proud of your accomplishments, and enjoy the time spent with your colleagues. Your career is blossoming more than you ever imagined. At home you enjoy talking with your lover about his job and with your children about their day in school. Then there is the concert to attend or the party to plan. Although each involvement is enjoyable, you feel as though every single minute of your life is planned and already accounted for. You have made your life too busy, leaving no time for yourself, and no time to feel unpressured.

There are at least two very different reasons to account for such overextension of yourself. You may need to prove to both yourself and the world that you are a capable, accomplished person. Your successful achievements as a worker and mother are proof of your competence and belie your hidden sense of insecurity and inadequacy. Conversely, you may overextend yourself as a result of both necessity and your enthusiasm about life. In this case, your excessive busyness may erode your feeling of autonomy and fulfillment. You may feel that you never really have enough time to devote to your children, your lover, your career, or yourself. Although you are secure in the knowledge of your success, you do not have a sense of calm and peace about your accomplishments. You may feel that you could experience everything just a bit more fully and perhaps do an even better job if you only had more time. You feel scattered, spread too thin, and hence not quite adequate.

All of you can probably conjure up dozens of autonomy hurdles that arise every day in your life—new tasks which, once achieved, increase your sense of competence. Taking the risk of attempting new ventures and executing the necessities of everyday life will enhance your feeling of self-esteem and personal strength. These accomplishments snowball, building upon each other as your repertoire of skills and capabilities increases. For example, once you have purchased a car, it becomes easier to purchase a house, and having purchased a house, you find it easier to make another investment. Each of these skills builds upon the other, in turn increasing your confidence to try still new adventures.

Getting Free—Darlene

Darlene, presented at the beginning of this chapter, came into therapy shortly after her fortieth birthday on the recommendation of her gynecologist. Darlene was depressed and discouraged about her life and felt that she had nothing to look forward to. She had been a wife and a mother. She had done just what she was supposed to do with her life, and now that her children were ready to embark on their own lives she felt as though there were nothing left for her to do.

Much to her surprise, Darlene felt both excited and relieved after her first therapy session. Her therapist had listened eagerly to Darlene for an entire hour. She had clearly felt that Darlene was important, that her feelings were legitimate, and that she deserved to be heard. Her therapist had also assured Darlene that she was not going "crazy," but rather that she was a victim of her socialization. She had been socialized to believe that her life's fulfillment would be not in taking care of herself but rather in caring for others, such as her husband and children. Now the therapist was telling Darlene that she had a right to her own life, her own feelings, her own happiness; that she was a vital, important human being who could be a person in her own right.

One of the first issues that Darlene and her therapist dealt with was Darlene's anger about her plight. Needless to say, Darlene had not even been aware of her anger. What she had felt was simply numbness, alternating with depression. She felt her life was over, that nothing was left. But her therapist helped Darlene to explore her underlying anger about spending her entire life taking care of others. During these explorations, her depression gave way to her anger. And her anger, though painful, was mobilizing and freeing. Darlene felt alive again, and enthusiastic about living. As her burden of depression lifted, her relief was immense.

Another underlying issue for Darlene was her concern about her children's departure from home. It was not simply that she experienced their separation as depriving her of a definition for her life, but also that their leaving restimulated some of her own feelings about separating from her parents. It had been difficult for Darlene to leave her parents' home. She had felt close to them and safe with them. Even though she wanted to marry her husband, it was very frightening for her to leave the security of her warm, loving family. In fact, Darlene still remained closely tied to her family of origin. Her parents' approval was important to her, and she frequently sought their advice and comfort. She was also concerned about their increasing age and the possibility of their imminent deaths. Thus Darlene was in the position of having to work through not a severance but a healthy separation from her family, which involved developing a sense of herself as an autonomous, separate adult. Darlene had to separate from her aging parents by maintaining love and closeness while preparing herself for their death. Simultaneously, she had to support her own children's separation from her, again maintaining healthy closeness and love, but diminishing their mutual dependency. These shifts in midlife from parenting children to caring for parents require personal growth and flexibility. The prerequisite to all of these separations was the development of Darlene as an independent, self-fulfilled, autonomous woman.

Darlene wasted no time working through her issues of anger and separation, thus readying herself for the big issue: autonomy. It was true that she was 40 years old and that her life was half over. But this also meant that half her life was still ahead. Darlene realized that having completed her "expected" tasks, she could now venture forth to discover her own self and her own dreams. At times she felt overwhelmed by this. She had ignored herself for so long that she did not know who she was. She had surrendered her real self to the accoutrements of motherhood and wifehood. But slowly Darlene was able to remember some of her girlhood joys. She recalled her delight at being elected to the student council and how much she had enjoyed being a member of the decision-making body. She recalled her enjoyment of art classes and the thrill of learning to draw a human eye and hand.

Her therapist encouraged Darlene to reexperience these past activities and, with much trepidation, Darlene began to do so. She began crocheting, at first kits, then patterns from a needlework magazine, and finally creating some of her own afghans. Then she began making miniature needlework items and, before long, she purchased a miniature saw and began making miniature reproductions of antique furniture. Darlene found great satisfaction in creating a miniature house with a room that looked as if some small person had actually lived in it. Darlene had found an outlet for her creativity. The more she delved into the world of miniatures, the more creative she became. Before she knew it, she was making bedrooms for unicorns and living rooms for centaurs. Her friends and family expressed support for her efforts, describing her creations as beautiful, exotic, and fascinating. But Darlene knew that they found her behavior rather strange. Here was a grown woman playing with dollhouses and fairy tales. However, Darlene continued daring to be different and enjoying it.

Darlene's creation of a world of miniatures nurtured her perspective of her own role in the larger world. Being a Gulliver among Lilliputians in her creations symbolically helped her take a new look at her importance in the world at

large. She began to feel more sure of herself, of her importance, and of her uniqueness. She began to know that she
mattered.

As Darlene felt more secure within herself, she was able to
expose that self to the world. Just as she had risked showing
the world her fantasies, now she could risk showing the world
her feelings. In her card group she began talking about what
she had been feeling about her life. She shared her sadness
and her anger; she shared the difficulties she had had separating from her children and coming to grips with the fact
that her parents would soon die. She was pleased at her
card group's receptivity. They were not only open but even
thrilled. They liked the new Darlene, and they too welcomed
the opportunity to talk about their feelings. Each in her own
way opened up about joys and sorrows, happinesses and un-
happinesses. Darlene was giving to them in some of the same
ways that her therapist had given to her. She was listening to
them, helping them to talk about their feelings and validating
those feelings.

From her experience within her card group, Darlene realized that there were many women with similar problems and
concerns. In fact, there was probably a whole generation of
such women, and Darlene gradually became interested in
communicating with them in an effort to help them. She began attending various community groups, organizing support
groups for middle-aged women to talk about their feelings
and their lives. She had become a woman-identified woman.
At times she could hardly believe where her journey had
taken her; at most other times she just knew that she had
found herself.

As Darlene felt better, her husband felt worse. He became
depressed. When she pressed him, he admitted to feeling ignored by Darlene. It seemed to him that she was committed
only to her women friends and cared nothing about him.
He chafed at his male friends' teasing about his wife, the
"women's libber," yet he could see how much happier Darlene was. He was pleased with her new accomplishments but
could not help feeling that she had chosen these accomplishments over him. He experienced her spending less time with
him as a rejection. Darlene was able to understand her hus-

band's feelings, and they decided to try some new activities together that they might both enjoy.

After a few false starts, they discovered that they both loved fishing. They loved sitting in the boat together, enjoying the peacefulness and the quiet talk, without interruption from the children, his busy plumbing business, or her new women friends. And, of course, there was always the thrill of catching a good-sized fish. They began to explore the outdoors more and soon were going on camping trips together. However, not all was blissful. Although they were having more fun together, they were also arguing more. Darlene's husband continued to resent her organizing activities and could not understand her need for such involvement. Darlene argued back, stood up for herself, and defended both herself and her activities against her husband's criticism. Despite the stress, Darlene was happier and felt that her marriage was more alive.

Darlene's increased activities and improved self-concept had profound effects on her children. Like her husband, her 17-year-old son was confused, if not somewhat angry, at his mother's new "face." It was a startling turnabout after so many years. Besides, his shirts did not get starched as well as they had in the past. Her 15-year-old daughter was even more profoundly affected by Darlene's change. Darlene was showing her an alternative life style, a new way of being a woman. Her mother was finding herself as a woman just as her daughter was beginning to explore herself as a woman. She now had a new model—that of an autonomous woman. She and her mother could be united in discovering themselves and the world.

Darlene knew that her life was vastly improved. She had found herself and, in so doing, had discovered a whole new world, perhaps even changing it a bit for the better. She knew that her life was not perfect, that there were still the inevitable stresses and strains with her husband and children. Yet she was certain of her ability not just to cope but to live life fully with flexibility and a sense of adventure. Darlene was free.

10

Beyond Therapy

Three Women Revisited

Irene sat gazing out at the sea. The salty water nudged her toes as she bent to pick up a bright piece of glass. Turning it around, Irene marveled at the smoothness of the discarded glass that had been polished by the sand. "Such a simple thing to get pleasure from," she thought. Six months ago Irene had not thought that she would ever feel pleasure or peace again. She had thought that the tornado which killed her son had shattered her capability for fulfillment forever. She gazed off into the distance, beyond the expanse of white beach to where the sea met the sky. She remembered her son as a little boy playing on the sand; how he would spend hours building walled cities and decorating them with colorful stones. Thoughts of her son caused her eyes to fill with tears and she felt the familiar wave of sadness. She recalled the agony of his sudden death. Remembering the happy, shared times that were gone forever created a peculiar mixture of sadness and wistfulness.

Irene recalled her husband's attempts to take her on a vacation to Mexico shortly after their son's death, and how adamantly she had refused. The idea of leaving home and boarding an airplane, to be deposited into a strange, foreign land, was overwhelming to her. It generated only anxiety and terror. After all, she could hardly leave her home to go to work; how could she possibly go off to a strange country? Now here she was in Mexico, basking in the sun, while the rest of her world lay sleeping under a blanket of snow. She was enjoying the sun's warmth on her body. She was relishing memories of dancing, talking, and making love with her husband and looked forward to her future. After the sorrow and agony of her son's death she was back in the world of the living and enjoying her life once again.

It was now six months since Irene had terminated therapy, and two years since she had first walked into her therapist's office. She had learned a great deal in her year and a half of therapy. The problems that originally took her into therapy— her nightmares and fearfulness of leaving home—were gone. In the process of ridding herself of these terrors, Irene had discovered a lot about herself. She understood now that her nightmares were a message from her unconscious, letting her know in a dramatic way the depth of her distress, turmoil, and conflict about her son's death. Spending her dreamlife struggling to find his body parts and bring them back together was her attempt to undo his death and gain omnipotence in a situation where she felt overwhelmingly helpless. His death had restimulated her sense of infantile powerlessness, of being at the mercy of mindless forces. As a result, she had attempted through her dreams to regain power where she had none. Irene had generalized her feelings of vulnerability and helplessness regarding her son's death to all of her life. She felt powerless, totally out of control, and terrified of the disasters that might befall her. This led to her increasing terror of leaving her home, making that home her only hope of safety and security.

Irene's therapist helped her to reclaim some of her power and control. She helped Irene to feel that, while she did not have any power to prevent her son's death, she did have personal strength and could control sufficient aspects of her own life. She could not prevent the sky from falling in, but she could be an active participant in shaping her life. Even though she was not omnipotent, and hence could not have prevented her son's death, she was not as vulnerable as the helpless infant she once was. Of course, Irene had not been consciously aware of feeling so vulnerable and, in fact, had used her anxiety to screen her feelings of vulnerability. This was manifested most dramatically whenever Irene attempted to leave her house. She would feel terrified. She would perspire, her heart would pound, but she did not know why. She was chronically anxious, and this anxiety covered her feelings of vulnerability and helplessness.

Anxiety was not the only screen Irene was using to avoid her feelings. When she was not feeling anxious, she felt depressed; she felt as though she were carrying around a huge weight. She felt weighed down, lost and empty. She felt as though there was nothing to look forward to. The only time she did not feel this heaviness was when she was able to feel her sadness, when she was mourning the loss of her son and cried as waves of sadness and grief washed over her. Irene's depression and anxiety screened her anger. She had not allowed herself to be angry, for whom could she be angry at? There was no one to blame; or was there? Sometimes Irene blamed herself. Why hadn't she asked her son to come home that weekend? Why had she let him go off to college in the first place? Certainly there must have been something she could have done to prevent his death. Over waves of sheer panic and guilt, Irene remembered that she had even been glad when her son went off to college. She had been excited about his venturing into the world and had looked forward to more time for herself. Then this terrible catastrophe had struck. She felt as though she were being punished for her selfishness.

Thus at times Irene felt guilty for all the things she had and had not done; guilty for all the things she had and had not felt. Of course, by blaming herself, Irene was also unconsciously attempting to diminish her sense of vulnerability by increasing her sense of omnipotence. In other words, by feeling as though she could have done something to prevent her son's death, she was giving herself a power she really did not have. Hence Irene's guilt enabled her to feel less vulnerable than she otherwise would have, but acted to her detriment by not allowing her to be angry at anyone but herself. She felt guilty rather than feeling angry. She felt sad, guilty, and depressed, but not angry. When Irene was able to feel and to know that she was not totally helpless and vulnerable in all aspects of her life, she was gradually able to own her vulnerability and lack of control regarding her son's death. She was able to feel and to know that not having total control of all forces impinging on her life did not mean that she was without any control whatsover. She was then able to stop blaming herself, to feel less guilty, and to be comfortable with the knowledge that her son's death was one of those forces over which she had no control.

Resolution of her omnipotence/vulnerability issues allowed Irene to get in touch with her anger, and she certainly was angry. She was angry at her son's death. She was angry at the unfairness of it all! It was not fair that a tornado had snuffed out the life of a 22-year-old man! Irene's therapist suggested that she might also be angry at her son for being at that particular store at that particular time; angry at him for having decided to go to college in that particular town; angry at him for not being able to protect himself from the falling wall. Irene reverberated to her therapist's words. At first she became angry at her therapist for making what seemed to be such bizarre suggestions. How could she possibly be angry at her beloved son who was now dead? Gradually, however, while arguing with her therapist, Irene felt a welling up of anger at her son. She *was* angry at him; she was angry at him for dying. She was angry at him for leaving her; she was angry at him for causing her this pain. Irene's therapist understood and supported her feelings, helping to validate Irene's anger. She learned that it was all right to be angry at her son and at the uncontrollable forces which had killed him. As Irene became more aware of her anger, her depression lifted. She no longer carried that tremendous sense of heaviness. Since her depression was screening her anger, getting in touch with her anger allowed her to let go of her depression.

Irene was now feeling better about herself and her life. Her nightmares had stopped; she was feeling less vulnerable and more in touch with all her feelings, including anger and joy. She continued, however, to have some difficulties at home, particularly in relation to her younger daughter. She felt anxious about her daughter going very far from home. She felt anxious about her going out on dates, especially with boys who had cars. She felt anxious if her daughter were not home exactly on time. She worried about her friends and about her sports activities. Irene needed to be absolutely certain that her daughter was safe. This was her only child now, and Irene could not bear the thought of anything going wrong. The feelings that Irene had previously had about herself she now had about her daughter; if only she could keep her daughter close to home, everything would be all right. Of course, her daughter chafed under her mother's overprotectiveness. She was a senior in high school and certainly did not want to be home from dates by 10 P.M. Nor did she want her mother keeping tabs on her every move. She would be leaving home soon and demanded more freedom.

Irene's therapist helped her to realize that she could not protect her daughter from all that might occur. Again, she was not omnipotent, nor was her daughter totally vulnerable. It was true that a catastrophe might befall her daughter, but the odds were against it, and, in any event, Irene could not prevent it. This was a difficult issue for Irene to resolve. It meant she had to explore her feelings about omnipotence and vulnerability further and come to recognize that, although she could not protect her daughter from the world, she could love her. Equally important, she had to recognize that she herself would survive if any disaster befell her daughter. Again, on the continuum between omnipotence and vulnerability, Irene, like everyone else, was somewhere in the middle.

After a year of therapy, Irene and her therapist began talking about termination. Irene felt very sad about the possibility of not seeing her therapist again. It meant losing a warm, supportive, and caring person who had been very helpful to her. It meant losing another significant person from her life. Thus Irene's feelings about termination involved both her feelings about her therapist per se and her feelings about her son which she had transferred to her therapist. Irene's therapist assured her that the termination need not be abrupt but could be a gradual process over which Irene would have control. She could decide when and how to end the therapy. Her therapist said that Irene would not totally lose her, any more than she had totally lost her son. Irene had all the years of treasured memories. She had known her son and carried his spirit within her. So too would she have the therapist. Irene now had a "therapist" voice within her, a voice that was more and more becoming the reflection of her own wisdom. This wisdom, learned in therapy, would go with her beyond therapy and help her through troubled times. After terminating therapy, Irene would recall the helpful ways her therapist had assisted her in working through issues. These were the tools of therapy that Irene would take with her. Irene would also remember some of her therapist's exact words. As time went on, Irene would refine her tools, building on what she had learned from her therapist, so that eventually she would develop her own therapeutic methods. These would always be with her, to be used when necessary.

Her therapist underlined Irene's progress, reminding her of the many changes she had made. She reassured her that her door would always be open if Irene felt the need to return. Irene had experienced a great tragedy which irreversibly altered her life. It would be with her forever, but it need not immobilize her or negate her ability to continue with her own life and to do so with joy.

Now here was Irene, lying on the beach in Mexico, six months after her last therapy session. She was able to enjoy her present vacation surroundings and her everyday life at home, understanding at the same time that life would not always be this peaceful and serene. She knew the price that her son's death had exacted; it had indelibly altered her and her perception of life. However, Irene also knew she would not build her sadness as a monument to her love for her son but rather build her life as a monument to her own strength for survival.

Gail snuggled up against Robert's warm body, grateful for this feeling of togetherness and love. She experienced the few moments of cuddling in the morning as the special times that fortified them for their day. His arms were around her, as her head nestled on his shoulder. Gail felt safe, secure, and loved. Her mind wandered. She had been married for a year, and the peace and fulfillment of this marriage represented a dream that she never had thought would become her reality. She felt that at last a man loved her for herself. At last she was able to maintain her sense of herself and to be herself within a loving relationship. Robert loved her but did not need to own her, and she trusted that only death would separate them.

Gail had traveled a long distance from the streets. She had always had a fighting spirit which remained undaunted by life's adversities. She was amused to remember her life as the glamorous, fast, drug-using street hustler. It was in sharp contrast to her life now—college-educated, married, and the mother of a teenage daughter. She recalled herself as a young, cute, bright, black street urchin, fighting her way through the ghetto, and she remembered her mother's dismay. She reminisced about herself as that young girl and looked with pride at her accomplishments as the woman she had become.

Three women had helped her along this journey: her mother, her aunt, and her therapist. All three helped Gail use her anger to propel herself upward toward success. Her mother's dreams for her and her belief in Gail's potential had provided a goal to strive toward. Her aunt, in offering her a home, had provided the physical alternative to the ghetto. She had offered Gail a place to go when Gail decided to leave the streets. Gail realized that her relationship with her mother and her aunt had provided an unusual counterpoint in her life. Her mother had formulated a dream, had pointed her to a star—a star which she had thrown into the gutter. She had cast her mother's dreams aside, rebelling against both her mother's life and the goals she had for Gail. Gail was absolutely determined not to be like her mother; she was not going to be the mother of a flock of children, with only ADC to support them. She would be gorgeous, glamorous, and different. The death of her best friend brought Gail to the frightening realization that street life not only lacked glamour but was dangerous as well; it could even kill! The shock of this death mobilized Gail's anxiety enough for her to reevaluate her mother's words. She realized that what she did not want was to be found dead in the streets. Further, she was surprised to realize that what she wanted for herself and her daughter was some of what her mother had always wanted for Gail. Her aunt then provided Gail with the concrete option of a new place to live, a geographical location more suitable for her to actualize a new life. In living with her aunt in a different city, she was able to shed the trappings of her old life and to try on the new costume of a "straight" college girl, altering it until she achieved a good fit.

Gail knew how much her therapist had helped her, although she had not realized her full impact while she was still in therapy. At that time, Gail had been living with a man, uncertain as to whether she would commit herself to him. She had entered therapy in search of this answer and had found a lot of answers, but not that one.

Just as her mother and her aunt had shown Gail new ways of managing her physical world, so her therapist had shown her new ways of both experiencing herself and relating to men. First, her therapist helped her to understand how her street life was a rebellion against her mother's life. Gail began to understand how in the past she had acted out her feelings of anger rather than feeling them. Her street life was an expression of anger at her mother's impoverished life; it was Gail's way of thumbing her nose. She was angry at her mother for the meager subsistence she had provided for Gail. She was angry at her mother for not creating more stability by keeping her father in the home. In sum, Gail was angry at her mother for not making everything in her childhood right. Gail was not conscious of this anger at her mother, of course, for rather than feeling it she expressed it in her behavior, the streets becoming the stage for her rebellion.

Gail also learned in therapy that she was continually repeating her relationship with her father. Her father had abandoned her at birth and Gail continued to choose men who repeated the abandonment at some point in their relationship. Over and over again she involved herself with men who abandoned her, just as her father had. Thus Gail repeated her relationship with her father in a vain attempt to win his love, the love that she had never received as a child. At the same time, she was rebelling against her mother and acting out her rage. This was Gail's way of dealing with her Electra position in the family romance. Since her father was absent from the home, there was no direct competition with her mother for her father. But Gail was symbolically competing with her mother by choosing unavailable men, in the vain hope that she would win what her mother had been unable to win. If Gail were able to conquer the unattainable, unreliable, street-wise man, it would prove that she was a better woman than her mother.

Gail confirmed her experience that all men were like her father by choosing sexual partners from the street. She had generalized from her knowledge of her father to all men and behaved as if what had been true of him was true of all males. This, of course, was a distortion, because all men do not aban-don their families. But it was an understandable distortion for Gail, because in childhood, the only reality she knew was the reality of her family. She then acted on the basis of this dis-torted reality and chose men who, like her father, were inca-pable of permanent commitment. So they too abandoned her and this proved to Gail again and again that her distortion was reality. Gail's distortion became a self-fulfilling prophecy.

In addition to feeling that all men were bastards who would at some time leave her, Gail anticipated their abandon-ment because of her own doubts about her lovability. After all, her father had left the family shortly after her birth. She felt that she must have been a horrible baby. She must not have been lovable enough to keep him home; there must be something wrong with her. So Gail grew up feeling that she was not lovable. Thus, throughout her life, Gail lived with a terrible feeling of not being good enough, not being lovable enough, not being special enough. Fortunately for Gail, she received different messages from her mother—messages to the effect that Gail was intelligent, beautiful, and lovable. Her mother felt she could be a winner. Thus Gail had two images of herself—one in which she was capable and special, and the other in which she was unlovable and worthless. All her life she had vacillated between these two images, sometimes play-ing one role, sometimes the other. And, since her feelings of unlovability originated in her relationship with her father, it was easy for her to play out this image in her relationships with men.

Gail had several hurdles to leap before she could establish an intimate relationship with a man. First she had to realize that not all men were like her father. She had to rid herself of this distortion and stop behaving in ways which fulfilled that prophecy. The final resolution of this first issue was Gail's becoming secure in the knowledge that there were men who could give to her in a warm, loving, caring way. Second, she had to let go of her father. She had to realize and accept that she had not had his love in the past and could not have it in the present or future. She had to accept that as a child she did not have him and to know that as an adult she did not need him. Third, Gail needed to realize that she was worthy of a man's love. She needed to experience her own lovability. Until Gail worked out these issues she could not have an intimate relationship, for even if she became involved with a man who would not abandon her, she would be incapable of allowing closeness with him. For example, in the relationship that brought her into therapy, Gail had found a man who said that he loved her, acted as though he loved her, and did not abandon her. However, as Gail worked on her intimacy fears in therapy and increased her ability to be intimate, she found that his capacity for intimacy was quite limited. It was not that he did not care about her, but rather that he was actually not capable of real closeness. This had not shown itself until Gail learned to be intimate. Then she found that he would allow only a limited amount of closeness. He had seemed to be very open only when Gail's limits on intimacy were extreme. As Gail grew, she realized that the amount of intimacy he was comfortable with was not enough for her. His limits left her feeling shut out. Thus Gail again felt abandoned by a man, even though this one did not physically leave her. But he could not meet her intimacy needs, and she again felt alone.

It was Gail's increasing sense of security and lovability which allowed her to need intimacy and led her to the realization that her lover could not allow intimacy. This realization left her feeling confused. Much as she talked about this rela- . tionship in therapy, she could not find an answer. She did not want to leave this man, although she knew that he would never be what she wanted; he would never be able to give her genuine intimacy, but at least he was there. Thus she was still repeating the relationship with her father, but in a less complete and thereby less destructive manner. She was trying to get intimacy from a man who had a limited capacity for it. However, Gail could not yet totally let go. She continued her struggle for her father/lover.

Although unable to resolve her relationship with this man, Gail felt that she was growing and learning a great deal in therapy. Her autonomy issues felt resolved. When Gail began therapy, she had recently made a major change in her living situation and had surrendered her street life to become a college student. At that time she had needed support for her new endeavors and had also sought strength to avoid losing her newly found autonomy to another man who might prove untrustworthy. She had also wanted to be a good mother and to provide the best possible life for her daughter. Gail had resolved these issues, and she felt good about her growth. Her difficulties with men, however, lingered. She understood her previous distortion; she loved herself and knew that she was lovable. But she could not totally separate from her father, and therefore could not leave the lover that had originally brought her into therapy. Realizing that she was at an impasse with her lover, Gail felt that therapy was no longer productive. She was not ready to leave this man, even though she thought that she should. She decided to terminate therapy, in spite of her therapist's feeling that Gail's final issue remained unresolved. Of course, her therapist respected Gail's decision, emphasizing the growth that had transpired and assuring Gail that if she ever decided to return she would be welcome. Gail, in fact, had come a long way, and her journey was a testimony to her strength and courage.

It was now six years since Gail had ended therapy, and one year into her marriage to Robert. She had met Robert while still involved with her previous lover and had felt a spark which kindled easily into a passionate, mature bond. She had ended her previous relationship at the first indication that Robert could fulfill her hopes for intimacy and closeness. Now, lying in bed, she thought about Robert. The warmth of his arms around her echoed the warmth in her heart. She was so glad to have him. She knew that he not only loved her but also cared about her well-being. She was secure about the permanence of this relationship. Then, with a start, she realized that she had again managed to repeat aspects of her relationship with her father. Robert was about her father's age; he was 22 years older than she. The chances were great that he would die before Gail, and his death would be another abandonment. She chuckled at herself, realizing that, by marrying an older man, she had married someone who represented the good, loving daddy that she had never had. She thought that she had totally resolved her "father substitute" relationships with men, but realized that she had repeated some of her pattern again. Perhaps these residual elements of her relationship with her father added a dimension of intensity with Robert that was all right. Maybe Gail's issues with men had not been completely worked through, but she had learned to live with the remaining elements in a way that was fulfilling and not destructive. And she felt fortunate as she anticipated the years ahead with Robert. She knew that his death would bring her tremendous pain, but she was willing to pay that price for the joy and fulfillment now.

Mary Ann came into therapy because of her sexual difficulties with Tom, her lover. She was unable to be orgasmic although she enjoyed the warmth and cuddling of sex. These would have been enough for her, but Tom wanted more. And because she loved him and realized his feeling of inadequacy and concern about their future, she agreed to seek therapy. Although Mary Ann had initially been hesitant about therapy, she found the exploration of her past and the journey into her unconscious a stimulating and exciting adventure. There was so much to learn, so many new things to feel. Things were not as she had imagined them. A whole new perspective from which to view her world opened to her.

The major issue with which Mary Ann had to deal centered around her mother who had cuddled her, loved her, and tried to keep her too close. Her mother had lost a leg to cancer shortly after Mary Ann's birth and then, in effect, had substituted Mary Ann for her leg. Mary Ann had become an extension of her mother and was there to be her errand girl. Therein lay the seeds for the growth of Mary Ann's fusion difficulties, and Mary Ann surely had them. She grew up feeling as if she were a part of her mother, never even suspecting such a thing as a sense of separateness existed. She felt her mother's pain, her mother's joy. At times she even felt that she could read her mother's mind or that her mother could read hers. On the one hand, Mary Ann enjoyed this closeness with her mother; it made her feel safe and secure. Her mother was the only person in her family from whom Mary Ann received much warmth and affection. On the other hand, it made her feel as though her mother demanded too much of her; she seemed to demand all of her. Sometimes she felt as though she wanted to keep a part of herself separate from her mother, and at these times Mary Ann resented her mother's intrusiveness. But whenever Mary Ann felt these resentments, she surrendered to guilt, feeling as if she were a bad daughter. After all, her mother loved her, and her mother was an invalid who had suffered a great deal. How could Mary Ann be angry at a crippled, loving mother, particularly since there were times when she wondered whether her mother's leg was the price she had paid for Mary Ann's birth? So whenever Mary Ann felt angry she translated it into guilt and tried even harder to be the good daughter. Thus her anger at her mother intensified her fusion in that she attempted to keep her anger underground to convince herself all the more that she totally adored her mother. Mary Ann's anger indicated her lack of separateness, and the denial of her anger further cemented her to her mother

Because Mary Ann was so fused with her mother, she unconsciously tried to become like her. There were, of course, positive ways in which Mary Ann resembled her mother. Like her mother, she was warm and friendly toward people. Like her mother, she was a good cook. Like her mother, she had an optimistic outlook toward life, despite difficulties and infirmities. Thus she had internalized many of the good qualities of her mother. Unfortunately, Mary Ann had also internalized her mother's asexuality. Mary Ann had always known that her mother slept alone and discouraged her husband's advances. Mary Ann, too, found it difficult to be open sexually; it was not part of her image of a "good" woman. In therapy, Mary Ann realized how she had internalized this aspect of her mother. Again, it was not that Mary Ann had consciously decided to become asexual like her mother, but rather that in becoming so much like her, she had internalized not only her mother's good qualities but also her less functional qualities.

In addition to internalizing destructive aspects of her mother, Mary Ann repeated the fusion of her relationship with her mother in her present relationship with Tom. Just as Mary Ann had been fused with her mother, wanting to stay close to her and feeling anxious when separating from her, so too she felt this with Tom. She did not like being apart from him and felt panicked at each separation, even when it was brief. She would feel butterflies in her stomach and become concerned that some disaster would befall him. She wanted to be with him at all times, wanted to spend all of their leisure time together and to share the same friends and interests. Having learned from her mother that closeness and love meant fusion, Mary Ann fused with Tom.

In therapy, Mary Ann explored her clinging behavior with Tom. She reexperienced particularly some of her childhood feelings, her feelings of being intruded upon by her mother when she wanted some space. This enabled her to understand Tom's need for his own personal space. She began to believe in the need for a healthy distance between them, a healthy interdependence, rather than complete fusion. Mary Ann's therapist also explained that it is difficult, if not impossible, to allow the necessary and healthy fusion during orgasm if your relationship is already fused. The increased fusion necessary for orgasm is too terrifying, too much like a loss of self. Although Mary Ann could not always feel what her therapist was saying, she did understand her and tried to allow Tom some of the space she knew was healthy. She did not act on the panic she felt in relation to separations from Tom, although she often continued to feel it quietly. She acted in a healthy manner in spite of her anxiety.

While Mary Ann was exploring new ways of relating to Tom she was also becoming more aware of her anger at her mother for her intrusiveness, demandingness, and neediness. She was not responsible for her mother's leg amputation. It was not Mary Ann's fault, and she should not have been made to suffer for it. There was no connection between Mary Ann's birth and her mother's cancer; Mary Ann therefore had nothing to feel guilty about. Mary Ann was angry at her mother for being different from other mothers and for the daily difficulties and inconveniences that her infirmity created. The entire family had to adjust itself and always consider her mother's physical condition. Additionally, Mary Ann was angry at how her mother related to her. She had used her illness to tie Mary Ann ever more closely to her. Mary Ann was her solace; she was her leg replacement, both psychologically and physically. She made Mary Ann her comfort and her companion throughout life. Mary Ann was angry at her mother for keeping her so close, for making it so difficult for Mary Ann to be a separate, unique person. Mary Ann felt the full thrust of her anger and, because she allowed herself to feel the validity of this anger, her guilt dissipated. In other words, as Mary Ann felt more angry, she felt less guilty. And since her guilt and repressed anger tightened the original fusion between her and her mother, the diminishing of both allowed a loosening of the fusion.

Getting in touch with her anger at her mother allowed Mary Ann to break the fusion and relinquish some of her internalizations. She was better able to choose which aspects of her mother she wanted to model. Yes, she liked being a good cook; she liked being warm and friendly; she felt comforted by her optimistic view of life. However, she did not want to be asexual like her mother. This was an aspect of her internalization that she wanted to give up. As Mary Ann resolved her anger and guilt, she was able to surrender her asexuality. Thus, as she separated from her mother, she gradually became orgasmic with her lover. And with orgasms, sex took on a new dimension for Mary Ann. She still enjoyed the cuddling and closeness but reveled in her newly discovered sexual passion. She was proud of this accomplishment and felt herself to be a more fully functioning and fulfilled woman than she had ever imagined possible.

Mary Ann was aware of some residual anger at her mother. She sometimes had difficulty getting along with her or bristled when she talked with her on the phone. Mary Ann was not able at this point to let go completely of her anger, to forgive her mother for the difficulties she had created in her life. Instead, she dove into the passions and fulfillments of her adulthood, trying to banish and forget the angers of her childhood.

After three years of seeing her therapist twice a week, Mary Ann ended her therapy. She felt content and happy with her life. She and Tom had been married for a year and were enjoying their life together, their mutual interdependence, and their separate careers.

Three years after termination of her therapy, Mary Ann, at age 36, gave birth to a beautiful little son. She enjoyed breastfeeding, cuddling, and nurturing her baby. She totally gave herself over to the task and enjoyed the experience of motherhood. However, six months after his birth her old sexual problem presented itself again. Mary Ann understood herself well enough to know that the birth of her son had restimulated her own issues with her mother and thereby her sexual difficulty. In becoming a mother, she had temporarily become her mother again.

Mary Ann reentered therapy with her previous therapist to look at the conflicts restimulated by the birth of her son. This therapy was brief, for Mary Ann had resolved most of these issues in her previous therapy. She and her therapist confirmed that, indeed, the birth of her son had restimulated the old internalization of her mother's asexuality. Additionally, Mary Ann still harbored some anger at her mother and, in so doing, was avoiding the final separation. This anger was her tie to her mother. Thus, in not resolving the last remnants of her anger, Mary Ann maintained aspects of the old, fused relationship. Now it was her anger that tied her to her mother, whereas her guilt and neediness had bound her years ago. Mary Ann had to let go of her anger in order to let go of her mother.

In the process of surrendering this anger, Mary Ann experienced, for the first time, her underlying sadness. She was sad about not having had the relationship that she had wanted with her mother. She was also sad about her mother's painful life and the burden she had to bear. When Mary Ann was able to mourn her relationship with her mother, she was able to appreciate its positive aspects. Finally, Mary Ann resolved her final anger and forgave her mother. She was then able to be orgasmic with her husband again. She was free.

Ten years later, at 46, Mary Ann was a reasonably happy woman. She enjoyed her career, was proud of her son, and was enjoying her relationship with her husband. Their sexual relationship continued to be satisfying even though they did not make love as frequently as they had. Some of the old intensity was gone, but Mary Ann's orgasms had improved through time as she became more easily and more frequently orgasmic. Then her mother died. Mary Ann was forced into the final separation from her mother. Never again would she be able to share anything with her mother; all of their shared joys sorrows were over. Never would her mother be able to give her any of those things Mary Ann had wished for but not received. All possibilities died; it was over, and now Mary Ann was alone and without her mother for the first time.

Mary Ann experienced many feelings—sadness, anger, loss, fear, and some guilt. To her dismay, she was again inorgasmic. At first Mary Ann thought it was her preoccupation with her mother's death that disallowed her total involvement in the world of the living. But as her lack of sexual responsiveness continued, she acknowledged it as a problem. This time, however, she decided to resolve it without professional help. Mary Ann began to explore her guilt and soon realized that she felt somewhat relieved about her mother's death. No longer would she have to worry about an intrusive telephone call; no longer would she have the burden of anxiety about her mother's health, about her mother's capabilities, about having to care for her. Mary Ann experienced a sense of freedom that was totally new to her. It was this sense of freedom and relief about her mother's death that she covered with a blanket of guilt. Her guilt, then, hooked her into the old fusion with her mother, causing her sexual difficulty to resurface. Mary Ann was again using her guilt to hold onto her mother. As Mary Ann arrived at these insights, they, in turn, allowed the realization that it was human to be in some ways relieved by the death of a parent. She was slowly able to accept the humanness of her response. This did not mean that Mary Ann was glad about her mother's death but rather that, along with all the sad and lonely feelings, there was also some relief. Mary Ann also realized that, in addition to holding onto her mother by feeling guilty, she could also hold onto her by not letting go of the sadness about her death. Now that her mother was dead she could hold onto her by being asexual like her, or by feeling guilty, or by not getting beyond the sadness about her death. Or Mary Ann could hold onto her in a more healthy manner by being herself while having her happy memories of her mother and continuing to model her more positive aspects.

These insights again freed Mary Ann to be orgasmic. She continued being like her mother in those ways which had been beneficial to her but not in those ways which had created pain. Mary Ann reminded herself again of her mother's optimism, her friendliness, and her reputation as a gourmet cook. These were some of the positive ways of being that her mother had given her and that she would carry on. The destructive ways of her mother, like her asexuality, Mary Ann could relinquish. She was free again.

These three women, like all of you, are multidetermined, multidimensional human beings. You, like them, have struggled with universal issues during the course of your life and have experienced their interweaving through time. They appear, get resolved, and then may reappear throughout your life. It is not that you, like Irene, Gail, or Mary Ann, have only one issue with which to deal but rather a multitude of them. Each of these women was also in sufficient pain to seek psychotherapy as an avenue to greater fulfillment. Therapy helped each of them in different ways to gain insights, to feel old and new feelings, to embark on new behaviors. It allowed each of them to explore new aspects of her being and gain new understandings of her history. But therapy was not an end point. No one stays in therapy forever. Therefore, therapy must teach you how to be your own therapist. It must teach you the tools for living and for resolving problems that arise after therapy. Thus your therapeutic tools are originally those of your therapist, but then they are altered and improved upon by you to fit your personality. They are then with you, to be called upon whenever necessary. You can never be finally free of all trauma. You can only become freer as you progress through life and become more secure in the knowledge that you will survive future crises. Therapy can provide you with the tools necessary to resolve future difficulties, but it cannot perform the miracle of eliminating all trauma.

What Cannot Be Changed: The Wisdom To Accept

Life is a mixture of pain and pleasure. No amount of therapy, no amount of analysis, no amount of planning can eliminate pain from your life. Tragedies, agonies, sorrows, and hassles are inevitable parts of human life. There can be no absolute happiness. As Alice James has remarked, "It isn't in the sorrows and pains, but the inexorable inadequacy for happiness that the tragedy lies." Life is a mixture of pain and happiness, and it is best lived with recognition and acceptance of this fact. In order to lead a full life, you must be able to accept your feelings of sorrow, sadness, and anger, as well as to allow yourself to enjoy your accomplishments, your relationships, and your pleasures. At best, your life will be a balance between the two extremes of pain and pleasure, but there is no fairy godmother guaranteeing a happy ending or erasing all past sorrows.

The past cannot be redone. Therapy is not a panacea with which you can erase old scars or undo traumas from your childhood, graphing them over as if they had never occurred.

They did occur; they did happen; that is your personal history. That is your reality. The scars from these old pains are there, and they may be ripped open at various times in your life. Therapy cannot heal all your scars. It can, however, provide the tools with which to heal yourself when the wounds are reopened. Therapy can free you from the immobilizing aspects of your past psychological difficulties and help you live with what cannot be worked through. Mary Ann is an example of a woman who bore the scars of her childhood throughout her life. Even though she worked through much of her fusion difficulties and her internalization of her mother, she still had a tendency to become inorgasmic as a result of certain types of stresses. Therapy had not eradicated her difficulties, but it had provided her with the tools necessary to work through her pain when it occurred. Irene, on the other hand, had to live with the traumatic pain of her son's death. Nothing could take away her pain about losing him so prematurely, but she was able to be comfortable with herself and enjoy her life once again. You cannot live your life without both traumatic pains and psychological scars. These cannot be avoided, nor can they be obliterated once they occur. But they need not destroy you nor sentence you to a life of psychological hell.

In addition to being unable to alter the past or erase the pains, therapy cannot change your basic behavioral style, your basic manner of relating to the world and arranging your life. Behavioral style includes such things as being a homebody rather than an adventurer, an extrovert rather than an introvert, an optimist rather than a pessimist, a preplanner rather than a person who "plays it as it lays." Similarly, your functional defensive style—whether you tend to become anxious rather than depressed, or angry rather than sad—will also remain unchanged. These ways of being are parts of you which remain consistent after therapy has "undone" the destructive or undesirable behavior patterns.

For example, if you are a person who enjoys the safety and security of your home and of the status quo, you will have a very different approach to life than if you are an adventurer, someone who is eager to explore new worlds and reach new heights. Suppose you win a two-week trip to the jungles of Brazil to live with the Jivaro Indians. What is your immediate reaction to this offer? Do you shriek, aghast at the idea of having to leave your cozy home to swat mosquitoes, avoid poisonous snakes, and fend off headhunters? Or are you elated about this exciting adventure during which you will see exotic animals, strange plants, and learn about a different culture? Or is your reaction somewhere in the middle?

If you are a homebody, you may relish the routine in your life and glory in the fact that you know every person and building in your neighborhood. The life you live may be very similar to the life you dreamed of as a child, the role that you planned for yourself, one with all the trappings of similarity, safety, and security. Or you may be a person who has always relished excitement and novelty in your life. You may love buying new clothes and trying exotic foods. You may love redecorating your apartment, moving from one apartment to another, or from one city to another. Life may be an adventure for you in which you react to any new undertaking with enthusiasm. For you, newness may be a goal in and of itself. One of these behavioral styles is uniquely yours. The degree to which you follow it may alter at different times in your life, but the basic pattern remains. For example, you may be an adventurer until you become involved with raising a family. Then the adventurer in you will be tempered. The degree to which you pursue adventure during that period of child rearing will diminish. But your adventurous spirit continues to be an integral aspect of your behavioral style.

Just as your behavioral style is a basic aspect of your uniqueness, so too is your defensive style. For example, suppose you are robbed. What is your reaction to this violation? There are many ways in which to react to the feelings stimulated by a robbery. You may become obsessive and immediately take action, replacing your lost credit cards and executing all of the tasks necessary to rectify the situation. In this instance, you are actively attempting to regain the control you lost when you were robbed and thus personally violated. On the other hand, you may deny the significance of the robbery, shrug it off as though it was irrelevant. After all it is only money, or only credit cards, and can easily be replaced. Or you may become depressed; you may feel a heavy weight of gloom around you. You may feel desolate, empty, violated. You may become immobilized and unable to do anything to remedy the situation. You cannot even imagine how to organize yourself, to contact your bank, the credit card companies, and the Bureau of Motor Vehicles for your driver's license. You are overwhelmed and depressed. This is your defensive style.

You may also intellectualize your feelings, telling yourself that the robber must have come from a poor ghetto family and obviously needed the money more than you, or that the robbery was irrelevant, considering the greater existential meaning of life. In this instance you are using your intellect to cover over your feelings; you are hiding your feelings behind this cognitive defensive posture. Still another style is to reverse your feelings and pretend that you feel good about what happened. After all, you may decide, you wanted to buy a new purse anyway. You had not liked your purse for a long time, and this gives you an excuse to buy a new one. And besides, this is a new adventure. You had never been robbed before. These are just some of the defensive styles you might use to protect yourself from the full impact of your feelings about the robbery. It is the intensity of your feelings, or denial of feelings, which confirms the defensiveness of your stance. You must have feelings about the robbery, and burying them or translating them into easier feelings is a defense posture.

Of course, rather than reverting to one of these defensive styles, you might be able to own your feelings. In any case, all of you will experience situations that call up a defensive style that is part of your unique personality. Therapy may ameliorate your need to be defensive, but it will not change the way in which that style manifests itself when it is called into play.

What Can Be Changed: The Courage To Be

Unfortunately, therapy cannot make your world perfect. It cannot banish all pains, totally heal all old wounds, or change your basic personality structure. However, in therapy you can achieve a great deal. You can gain increased self-awareness and a more positive self-image and reduce, if not stop, self-defeating behavior patterns.

Increasing self-awareness. As illustrated in the preceding chapters, the first step in therapy is self-understanding. Your therapist aids you with cognitive insights, with knowledge about yourself and your behavior. She offers interpretations about links between your feelings and your behavior, both past and present. All these links open up pathways to your unconscious through which you learn to know the whys and wherefores of your behaviors and feelings. This journey into your unconscious allows you to understand the forces that impinged on your development, which in turn allows you to appreciate yourself and engage in behaviors that bring greater fulfillment.

In this therapeutic process of becoming acquainted with your unconscious, you can allow yourself to feel your past and present more sharply and more fully. Self-awareness is thus not only a cognitive awareness but also a receptivity to your feelings as well. You expand your ability to feel your feelings as they occur in the here and now. You are able to feel more of your feelings without defending yourself against them and thus experience your world more richly. You have more options in terms of how to deal with any given feeling. You no longer need to dampen down your feelings; you are no longer afraid that they will overwhelm you or destroy you. You learn that feelings are part of you, and you become comfortable with even the painful ones. You know that you will not be undone by pain, which is inevitable but will not destroy you. No longer are you buffeted around by your feelings; you know that they will not control you. You accept your feelings and you control your behaviors.

Self-image. Therapy also nurtures an improved image of yourself, one in which you have more appreciation of your competence and courage. As you journey through your unconscious you learn to accept yourself in new ways, to forgive yourself, to understand yourself in ways that you had not before imagined possible. Through this journey you also learn new solutions to your old problems. You learn that you do not have to continue applying childhood solutions to old dilemmas, but that you as an adult can behave in different, more functional ways. And as you experiment with new behaviors you develop a sense of your strength and learn to appreciate your courage. Thus these achievements in and of themelves enhance your self-esteem. You feel pleased with yourself. Your increased self-esteem, in turn, enables you to try still newer solutions and reach for still greater heights.

Your therapist assists you through this journey, holding up a mirror for you to better see yourself and your accomplishments. She also allows you to see yourself as she sees you. She may be the first to show you your greater potential. Thus the reflection of yourself that she offers shows you not only the person that you are today, but the person that you may become. As you explore your new potential, you are free to actualize yourself fully, to try new avenues of creativity and to allow yourself to take greater risks.

Self-defeating behavior patterns. Self-defeating behavior patterns involve the repetition of old solutions to old childhood conflicts. As a child, you adopted various behaviors which worked for you at that time. They functioned to prevent you from being overwhelmed by your feelings and threatened by your environment. Because they worked for you as a child, it is easy for you to bring these old patterns into adulthood and to continue replaying them regardless of their ineffectiveness or self-destructive outcome. As a child you had no alternative but these behaviors. As an adult you theoretically have more options available to you, but your unconscious fears or anxieties may prevent you from exploring them. Therapy provides you with a way of understanding the origin of your self-defeating behavior patterns and points you toward exploring new solutions to old dilemmas.

There are nearly as many self-defeating behavior patterns as there are human beings. Human creativity is prodigious, and never are people more ingenious in using it than in designing ways to hurt themselves. You may drink yourself to death, smoke yourself to death, shoot heroin into your veins, or take speed until your brain is permanently damaged. You may trade your anger for headaches. You may repeatedly fall in love with abusive or alcoholic men. You may undermine your success just as it seems within your grasp. You may surrender your feelings to ulcers. You may refuse to let go of your rage at your father and never go beyond that relationship. Therapy is able to help change these patterns if you are willing to take the risk—the risk of allowing the changes that therapy stimulates. Therapy is not an "easy answer." It is time-consuming, costly, and emotionally draining. It is, at certain points in the therapeutic process, downright terrifying. It can disrupt your life for a while, because during the working through of your most traumatic issues you may feel so much pain that you are temporarily less functional than when you began treatment. In short, it is possible that you will get worse before you get better with therapy. The degree of trauma and disruption in your life depends, of course, on how many issues you have to resolve and how much pain and anger you have repressed over the years. If you have repressed a huge amount of feeling for many years, you may have a great deal of potentially disruptive feelings to reexperience. For some of you, being unwilling to take the risk of therapy is in and of itself self-defeating. If your behavior patterns are so self-defeating as to allow little joy and fulfillment, then not taking the risk of therapy is just another self-defeat. If you tenaciously continue in your time-worn destructive style, fearful of embarking on any uncharted territory including therapy because it is frightening, you unnecessarily preclude your own fulfillment and further defeat yourself.

A relationship with another human being is fertile ground for playing out self-defeating behavior patterns. In this arena there is potential for two or more self-defeating behavior patterns to occur simultaneously, complementing, reinforcing, and intensifying one another. Whether you internalize your parent, rebel against your parent, or repeat the relationship with your parent, you are perpetuating only unsatisfying relationships as an adult. Whether you are redoing or acting out your fused relationship with your mother, or trying to win the family romance, you are assuring yourself the same sadnesses as an adult that you felt as a child. Of course, unhooking these old patterns is replete with difficulties. To say that they are hard to give up is an understatement. It is extremely difficult to accept that you cannot win with your parents in the way that you want to win. It is tremendously difficult to move beyond their sphere.

In addition to changing feeling responses to old stimuli, therapy is most effective in helping you to let go of old behavior patterns and to discover more satisfying ones. You and your therapist together can figure out new solutions to these old dilemmas. Just as childhood may be a rehearsal for adulthood, so is your relationship with your therapist a rehearsal for more fulfilling relationships with people outside of the therapeutic situation. You learn new interpersonal skills in the safety of the therapeutic relationship and then expand them to your outside world. You learn new ways of relating to people as you learn to relate differently to your therapist, and then you add this to your repertoire of interpersonal skills.

Letting go is difficult. It means abandoning familiar behavior patterns and feelings, some of which tie you to your parents, creating a false sense of security. Hence discontinuing these old, dysfunctional behaviors means giving up the hope of having your parents as the protecting fairy godmother and knight in shining armor. Letting go requires the courage to be free and the will to be happy. It is your desire, your yearning for freedom and your need for a complete, full life which propel you to shed your old chains. Therapy, though not a panacea, can help you to be free, to risk enjoying life enough to be happy.

Being Free

The great mystery of the human psyche is not its pathology but its strength, its will to survive, to overcome, to enhance life, and to create. The traumas that you have overcome and survived are remarkable. You may point to famous people who have overcome extraordinary obstacles, people like Loretta Lynn, Helen Keller, Anne Frank, Maya Angelou, Harriet Tubman, Eleanor Roosevelt. But you forget the obstacles and hurdles which you have overcome. You have survived the pains of your childhood and, as a woman, you have survived the discrimination of this society. These have placed great burdens on your spirit; yet you have survived. So, too, your mothers and grandmothers before you survived, perhaps toiling under enormous economic, practical, and emotional burdens. Perhaps they were immigrants from Russia or slaves from Africa. But they had the will to survive and the strength to create and nurture you. You are a living testimony to the greatness of humanity; you are a living testimony to the strength and love of the millions of women before you.

This great miracle of survival, in spite of all practical and psychological adversity, is one of the mysteries of the human psyche, one of the great testaments to human resourcefulness, creativity, and strength. Why one person can use trauma to strengthen herself while another person cannot endure the same trauma but folds under it is an inexplicable mystery. You wonder why you have responded to your traumas in a particular way while someone else has responded so differently. Why have you crumbled under adversity while another person has risen above it? Or, conversely, why have you used your trauma to strengthen yourself and spur yourself onward while another person has become immobilized and demoralized? These are the questions of life, the mysteries that remain unanswered. This is the age-old question of what allows health, what allows freedom, and what allows courage. This question gives birth to the various forms of yet another age-old question: "Why me?" "Why has this befallen me?" "Why has this happened to me?" "Why was I not luckier?" Or, "Why am I as lucky as I am?" This too is unanswerable.

The question, "Why me?" brings you face to face again with your uniqueness, your strengths, your personal genetic, historical, emotional, and cultural history. All these sometimes-chance and sometimes-planned elements combine in some inexplicable way to create the human being that you are—the human being that will never again, in all of time, be repeated in exactly the same way. Like a snowflake, you can never be duplicated; you are multifaceted and special. Your uniqueness becomes part of the stream of humanity, and in your unique strengths and creativity lies humankind's greatest power, the power which has formed civilization with all its beauteous and, sadly, dangerous aspects. Art, music, literature, architecture, compassion, love, and sensitivity are all testimonies to your strengths and to humankind's tremendous capabilities and potentialities. You, as the best person that you can be, are free to explore and develop your life. You are free to love, play, and work. You are free to become yourself as a woman. You are you—you are a woman!